3ord

Y0-BRN-492

COLUMBIA UNIVERSITY STUDIES IN ENGLISH
AND COMPARATIVE LITERATURE

FOOLS AND FOLLY

FOOLS AND FOLLY

DURING THE
MIDDLE AGES AND THE RENAISSANCE

BY

BARBARA SWAIN

NEW YORK
COLUMBIA UNIVERSITY PRESS
1 9 3 2

PRINTED IN THE UNITED STATES OF AMERICA
GEORGE BANTA PUBLISHING COMPANY, MENASHA, WISCONSIN

FOREWORD

Much of the source material presented in this book is in French and Latin, and much of its effectiveness and charm lies in the wording or in the verse-form of the originals. The original passages have therefore been kept untranslated in the text of the book and free paraphrases provided in the notes. Since, too, this discussion of the fool is concerned rather with the interpretation of accessible material than with the collection of new material, no separate bibliography has been appended. Complete references to every work consulted are given in the notes.

Grateful acknowledgment is made to Professor Jefferson B. Fletcher of Columbia University for his kindness and patience in reading and rereading the chapters of this study as it developed, and for his unfailing illumination of many kinds of question. I am indebted, too, to Professor H. M. Ayres and to Mr. Henry Wells for reading and criticism of the manuscript. Special thanks are due also to Miss Helen D. Lockwood of Vassar College for her constant interest and active criticism.

B. S.

VASSAR COLLEGE
January, 1932

CONTENTS

Chapter I

INTRODUCTION

Stultorum numerus infinitus est.

The fool, in life and in literature, is a perennial figure. He appears in many forms and under many names. He may be called clown, rustic, zany, boor, or plain fool. He may wear the white circus mask, the comedian's black-face or the cockscomb and bells of the jester of literary history, and he may be distinguished by physical agility or awkwardness, by shrewdness or stupidity, malice, wisdom, garrulousness, or monosyllabic bluntness. But whatever his special attributes, the creature behind the mask and the name when he is genuinely one species of the great genus fool has one inevitable characteristic: he appears from some point of view erring and irresponsible. He transgresses or ignores the code of reasoned self-restraint under which society attempts to exist, is unmeasured in his hilarity or in his melancholy, disregards the logic of cause and effect and conducts himself in ways which seem rash and shocking to normal mortals. But he is a fool because his extravagancies are supposed to be due not to intention but to some deficiency in his education, experience or innate capacity for understanding. He is not to blame for them, and society, amused at his freedom from the bonds of its conventions, laughs at him while it condemns him. Within any society these undisciplined irresponsible individuals are found. They are its "fools," and their reflection is sure to be found in the literature of the group.

During the fifteenth and sixteenth centuries this erring, irresponsible, extra-social, comical creature was popularly, though not exclusively, known in French and English literature by the simple name of "fool" or "fol." Moreover this fool himself became a temporary symbol of man's weakness and strength, and "folly" served for a time as an explicit term for the characterization of human nature. Literary tradition and the visible social order both contributed to this development. Popular proverbs and maxims furnished a precedent for calling all erring human beings fools and for condemning them as such. But fools, in another sense, were the daily or seasonal companions of most fifteenth century citizens. The mentally defective were not then isolated in institutions but supported as harmless dependents in villages, courts and country houses. The toleration and freedom which their defects assured them inspired some of the sane to assume their outer guise and to seek the support of available patrons by amusing them with comical stupidities and impudent witticisms. Comedians, too, entertained the public in the costume of fools, making use of the fool's freedom to push their own ribaldry or satire to the borders of rashness. The unconscious wisdom occasionally brought forth by the unreasonable mind of the "innocent" and the belief in his association with the powers of nature added a portion of respect to the patronizing amusement with which the fool was regarded. The domestic jester thus added a visible personality to be built into the literary figure of the fool.

Late medieval literature made use of and extended the inherited European tradition of calling sinners against law and reason "fools." Brant's *Ship of Fools* described all society as he saw it in terms of its culpable folly. Other pieces of writing blended in various ways the description of erring conduct with the attitudes of tolerance, amusement and respect for weakness with which the living fool was regarded. Erasmus' *Praise of Folly* pictured society as a kingdom of fools, but by shifting from one attitude toward folly to another transformed the fool from a figure cynically denoting man's depravity to an ironic symbol of his composite weakness and strength. The name of "folly" itself thus became with him one of those elastic terms binding together a number of specific meanings, all different, yet all similar in their reference to a common basic image. An expert in the reconciliation of paradoxes had only to draw these specific meanings all back into a composite picture of "folly," and his ironic symbol, the fool, was ready for him. The chapters of this study describe some of these fifteenth and sixteenth century expressions of the various concepts of folly in France and England.[1] They also try to show the manner in which these concepts were extended and limited in Brant's invective and in Erasmus' ironic formulation of his opinion of mankind.

Some enumeration of the meanings suggested today by the idea of folly will show the elements compounded into the late medieval figure of the fool. The basic image associated since earliest times with the words "fool" and "folly" in English and with their equivalents in French is that of the half-wit or simpleton.[2] Whether "fool" refers to the village tattle-tale, to a privileged royal jester or to a particularly unworldly spirit who bears his worldly burdens with gentle amiability, its implication is that somehow the man is defective in nature or education. One's attitude toward these simpletons may vary from serious condemnation to genial tolerance according to one's temperamental bias or what comes perhaps to the same thing, one's conception of the conduct suitable to the fully-developed individual. But whatever form folly appears in, and whatever emotions attend the sight of it, it retains one constant factor: the behavior of the fool or "fonde" man seems to some one, from some point of view, "demens," "exensis," "ignarus," "lunaticus," "ineptus," "insensis," as well as "stultus," "fatuus," "stolidus."[3] These words which are among those given as synonyms for "fonde" in a Latin-English dictionary of the late fifteenth century cannot be translated at their exact fifteenth century value today, but what distils from them is certainly the impression of a man "that lacketh naturall knowledge, an ideote,"[4] or more jocosely an "asse, goose, calfe, dotterell, woodcocke, noddie, cokes, goosecap, coxcombe . . . ninnie, naturall."[5] Folly is basically a condition of witlessness or ignorance or both.

But when the word appears near its frequent companion and antithesis, "wisdom," it suggests something more general than plain half-wittedness, some common type of human behavior, some way of action hindering man's achievement of his desire, some particular aberration of an individual from group standards. This fool is characteristically *incircumspectus*,[6] "withoute any wysedome," "one that dooeth a thing unadvisedly or without discrecion."[7] To the vigorous disciplinarian these failures in achievement, these individual aberrations, are positively sinful. Such a fool as this is either, according again to the fifteenth century word-book, "insipiens qui non attendit pericula futura," or, more grave for himself, "stultus qui, si attendit, non cavet,"[8] a veritable sinner. The literature of proverbs and sententious maxims points out hundreds of ways in which fools of this sort may err, rebuking as folly conduct of all degrees of offensiveness and harping on the antithesis of the wise man to the fool.

On the other hand, folly may be a source not of disaster and sin but of amusement and recreation. "J'aime la joie parce qu'elle est folle," cries Suzanne to the irrepressible Figaro. "The Follies" may appear scandalous or even wicked to some, but to others they provide a refreshment after which business may be resumed with new zest. The fool may be simply the entertainer, "jocularis, qui Principi est a jocationibus."[9] In this capacity the mock-fool appeals to something more naïve than reason for his effect. His performances may freely express the wantonness of the half-wit and may profit by the convention which holds the simpleton blameless for his most rash remarks. In the medieval celebrations in which the folk-fool took part, that wantonness was the very virtue by which the fool was related to the god. No group of people contradicted the authority of the Valois kings more deftly and impertinently than the "fools" of the Joyous Societies who presented plays in France during the fifteenth and sixteenth centuries—and no critic of our national situation today is more alert or more cutting than our seasoned arch-fool, Will Rogers.

Or again, the fool may be the innocent, unworldly, spiritual man whose simplicity, candor and honesty perhaps lay him open to the scornful patronage of his neighbors and whose happiness seems to lie in some experience outside the common objectives of the group around him. These are the people who perhaps account for the presence of the words "purus," "sincerus," "simplex" among the fifteenth century synonyms for "fonde."[10] When actual life in a society or a portion of society becomes too different from a still cherished ideal of life, those who live in the ideal rather than the real appear to be this kind of fool. Although they always exist, they are more visible in times of crisis. The early fathers of the church were acutely aware of the virtue of unworldly folly during the first conflict of pagan and Christian; so too were the reformers of the sixteenth century who within the church itself fought a new paganism in the name of a renewed Christianity.

All these various kinds of fool and many others are familiar to us today and the enumeration of them is the repetition of commonplaces. The history of these same types in their late medieval incarnations has the added interest of picturesqueness. There were fools who were so dubbed because they failed to conform to the prescriptions of a popular manual of conduct, fools who failed to attain prosperity under the system of feudal obligations, unworldly fools, fools who were menials, butts of merriment and mockers in the courts of kings and noblemen, actors who gamboled as fools or used the fool's costume for protection in driving home the moral of their satirical plays. Passed in review they give a lively and varied picture of a society different from our own in its expression but much like ours in its impulses. The fifteenth century itself saw most of them exhibited as the cargo of the famous *Ship of Fools*.

The ironic significance of this parade of fools becomes apparent only when one considers that the comments of the observer on one group of fools connote condemnation of, on the other, tolerance for man's witlessness and ignorance. The word "fool" with its shifting meaning and accompanying shift from approbation to disapprobation in emotional connotation, is like a price-tag attached always to the same article but indicating different values according to the day and the trend of fashion—according to whether witlessness and ignorance or the disciplined reason is, at the moment and to the person concerned, the part of man's nature which seems desirable. This oscillation in the value of folly furnished Erasmus with a symbol for a range of judgments on human nature which suited his purpose of at once criticizing and vindicating that nature.

Disapprobation of folly is expressed each time the fool is mentioned in such a way as to imply that the wise, prudent or virtuous man is his direct antithesis. It is usually assumed that these fools know or ought to know the proper course of action to lead them to success in whatever they have undertaken. Some change in actual situation may, to be sure, reveal that what seemed foolish was actually wise, that judgment had erred in estimating the efficacy of a given action in promoting a desired end. But though "wise" and "foolish" in this sense are terms susceptible of sudden inversion through the uncontrollable progress of events, they both declare the reason to be the one true arbiter of human conduct, the best guide to any desired end. The fool is one whose reason is at fault. The literature describing folly of this sort is usually equally concerned with the corresponding wisdom and is full of statements of how people have acted to defeat or to accomplished what are or are thought to be their own rational purposes.

The reason, however, is not always the guide that brings man satisfaction. When bewildered by experience it may cease to function as purveyor of significances and rationaliser of ends. A man may then turn with the approbation of his conscience to a principle of unreason, illogical, careless of consequences, to replenish his vitality and to restore that zest in experience which is as valuable as the interpretation of experience. He may lift up his heart in faith, repudiating reason for revealed certainty; or, satisfying a less exalted need, he may go in fact to the Follies; he may turn on the radio to hear a bit of badinage. If he lived in the sixteenth century, he might have stopped in the great hall to banter with the domestic fool or paused in the market place to watch the *Enfants sans Souci* perform acrobatics interspersed with covert witticisms at the expense of the government. Folly of this kind is irresponsible, ecstatic or simply gay, the desirable refuge of weary minds and the protection of imprudent critics.

Or, from still another point of view, folly may be both desirable and undesirable. Pure, noble, unworldly spirits both are and are not the objects of the community's admiration. Their objective is too unlike that of the community in which they move. Those who "become fools for Christ's sake" are witnesses to something real but not wholly accepted. The literature of humble devout personal religious feeling, or attempts to justify innocence and integrity in a world of rapacity provide examples of fools of this kind.

The chapters of this study present some of the different groups of fools whose pictures, whether preserved in formal literary composition or in the records of actual life, may be discovered in the writings of Erasmus' age. They try to state the attitude toward man's nature which accompanied the descriptions of these fools and to show the relationship between them which, partially exploited by authors other than Erasmus, was conveniently utilized by him in the Lucianic sermon which he put into the mouth of Folly herself. They do not pretend to be an investigation of the sources of the *Praise of Folly,* but to use contemporary material to show the unique effectiveness and interest of that ironic composition among the many others presenting fools.

Man is a fool throughout his life, in his best and in his worst manifestations, says Erasmus. Part of his folly is highly to be disapproved of, part to be applauded and encouraged. And the gods looking down upon man see him as their jester *par excellence.* In youth and age man is a veritable simpleton, helpless and babbling. In manhood who but the fools carry on the business of society, the men who fight, litigate, buy and sell, marry and raise families, while the sages perfect themselves in virtue? At this point the procession of fools from the literature of proverbs and sentences passes through Erasmus' pages. Yet the sages themselves are fools too, for they seek a kind of life which is incompatible with the existence we must lead, and the proverb states that he is a fool who seeks the impossible. But of course our life itself is the product of the superlative folly of love; these sober sages themselves spring from the incurable wantonness of man. Folly is the true goddess of man's life; she is responsible for the greatest abuses, for the kings, priests, shepherds of the people who deceive and rob their flock, and for the true leaders of mankind who follow the example of Christ in seeking to live in simplicity, innocence and humility. Man's evil and his excellence alike are due to folly.

Erasmus' synthesis of the various kinds of fool and of the attitudes toward them into a full-length portrait of Man the Fool is unique. Unlike Brant, who assumes that man's folly is ridiculous indeed but sinful too, and absolved only through divine grace, Erasmus takes man's situation with gaiety and assumes that he has sufficient vitality himself to digest all his experience eventually into some usable form. But Erasmus' version of human nature did not become common property in the Europe to which he addressed it. His ironic synthesis proved highly unstable. The benefits of unreason ceased to interest a generation

educated in the schools of Colet and Mulcaster or under the tutor-
ship of Ascham. The separate kinds of fool continued to be exploited in literature. Court fools remained the fashion throughout the sixteenth century, and stories of fools filled the popular
demand for facetious narrative. Folk-games persisted in degraded
forms, proverbs and maxims continued to rebuke the unsuccessful and unsocial fool, and the wilfully ignorant man was both
fool and sinner to the Protestant as well as to the Catholic. There
was only one Erasmus to gather together the different motifs that
pass equally for "folly" and to find a significance in their juxta-
position. In fact, the intellectual climate of the times that succeeded the publication of the *Praise of Folly* was inhospitable
in many ways to the ideas back of Erasmus' creation. The new
Stoicism of the time rebuked the fool in the mood of the sententious maxims, but preferred to concentrate upon the development of the wise man. The new Epicureans applauded the natural
man, to be sure, but not under the half-apologetic title of fool.
The later adherents of both Catholic and Protestant parties
found their opponents defective in understanding as well as ignorant, and called them "fool" meaning to say "hopeless sinner."
The Folly of Eramus was alone in offering a joint condemnation
and defense of man the fool. Her mock panegyric is the most
subtle statement contributed by the fifteenth and sixteenth centuries to their chapter in literature's continuous comment upon
error and unreason.

CHAPTER II

THE FOOL IN DISGRACE—FAILURE AND SINNER

Immortal gods! how much does one man excel another!
What a difference there is between a wise person and a fool!
                                                    —Terence

The fool in the late Middle Ages was probably most often
mentioned to be condemned. A voluminous literature of moral
and religious instruction both in Latin and in the vernaculars
was generally familiar all over Europe. Moral writings inherited
from time past were copied in manuscripts, used as text-books
in schools and as material for sermons, and in the last quarter of
the fifteenth century were copiously printed by the newly invented presses. Such compositions for the most part taught con-
formity to an established social or moral code. They described
action suitable or unsuitable to the reputable citizen and orthodox believer. And, sometimes casually, sometimes consistently,
they called offenders against the code "fool." During the fifteenth
century the use of the term "fool" as a synonym for "erring man"
seems to have become more frequent than in earlier times. The
fool of the moralists was thus not at all a symbol of man's double
nature; instead, he represented one side of one of the many antitheses between the desirable and the undesirable in matters of
conduct—like the "good and the bad," the "virtuous and the
vicious"—which are constantly being discriminated by the reason. The wise man was his complement. The presence of the wise
man in fact made the fool visible. For the wise expressed in their
actions the positive goods and virtues recognized by society, in
most of which the fools were deficient. The man who acted in a

way which prevented him from getting what he wanted or ought
to want was a failure, and a fool. The most complete failure of all,
to a Catholic society, was failure to seek the true end of man,
knowledge of God. Since erring and irresponsible fools were deficient in the qualities which should have enabled them to seek
God, they were not only fools but sinners. The condemnation of
the fool could hardly go farther than to assign him to eternal damnation.

Descriptions of the antithetical behaviors of the good, prudent
or wise man and of the bad rash fool appeared in many proverbs
and maxims, along with other contrasting characterizations of
human conduct. Sometimes both wise man and fool were mentioned in the same proverb, sometimes they were etched separately. The isolated proverbs and maxims were built up, too, into longer moral compositions furnishing pictures of a whole society and its code of conduct. Some of these implied, like the
famous *Cato*, that all men were able to struggle toward excellence when properly instructed. Others, characteristic products
of the fifteenth century, inverted the direct precepts of the *Cato*
into the negative form—"He is a fool who does *not*" do thus
and so—and, presenting society as a pageant of fools, suggested
indirectly but vividly that mankind was made up chiefly of the
hopelessly weak and ignorant. The Biblical Book of Proverbs
provided the most complete pictures both of the wise man and of
the fool, pictures which brought out the full extent to which
folly betrayed man, and which included images of success and
failure both in material and in spiritual well-being. From the
commentaries upon the book we learn the most serious result of
folly: in addition to rendering a man unfit for life in the social
group, witlessness and ignorance made him fail to understand
his spiritual destiny, made him a sinner whose failure was the
most terrible of all, failure to save his own soul.

The Latin poem *Doctrina magistri Petri Abaelardi* preached
man's heavenly salvation as well as his earthly prosperity and

introduced the opposition of the wise man to the fool effectively among the usual moral commonplaces:

> Major discendi tibi sit quam cura docendi . . .
> Copia verborum est ubi non est copia sensus . . .
> Instabilis lunae stultus mutatur ad instar,
>   Sicut sol sapiens permanet ipse sibi.
> Nunc huc nunc illuc stulti mens caeca vagatur,
>   Provida mens stabilem figit ubique gradum . . .
> Agnoscat culpas, accuset, corrigat illas,
>   Nec se corde bonum censeat, ore malum.[1]

In many separate Latin maxims too this pair of adjectives served for contrasting prudence with imprudence, success with failure. Even when the fool alone is mentioned, the wise man's shadow hovers behind him:

> Animo imperabit sapiens, stultus serviet.
> Virtus est vitium fugere et sapientia prima stultitia
>   caruisse. (Horace)
>
> Contemni sapienti gravius est, quam stulto percuti.
> Non potest non sapere, qui se stultum intellegit.
> Est enim proprium stultitiae aliorum vitia cernere,
>   oblivisci suorum. (Cicero)
>
> Aliis prodesse et sibi nocere stultitia est, non
>   caritas.
> Stulti timent fortunas, sapientes ferunt.
> Demulcet multum dulcis promissio stultum.
> Stultitia est ei te esse tristem, cujus potestas plus
>   potest. (Plautus)
>
> Si stulti mercantur, mercatores faciunt lucrum.
> Sibi non cavere et aliis consilium dare stultum est.
> Factum stultus agnoscit.[2]

Other "sentences" taught, in the same practical vein, that it was foolish to wish to be revenged upon one's neighbor by fire, to plan to undertake things impossible of fulfillment, or to kill the father in the course of one's revenge and leave the children alive![3]

These isolated proverbs and sentences used the fool only as

a casual symbol of error, to contrast to the wise man. When they occurred separately they did not pretend to build up a full-length picture of society and to qualify its habitual conduct by any general term. Poems like the *Doctrina magistri Petri Abaelardi*, however, did combine moral maxims into a long composition that served as a "mirror" of actions and attitudes suitable and unsuitable to man. Such compositions were popular up to the time of Erasmus himself. The two entitled *Facetus*, the *Urbanus*, the *Moretus* and especially the *Cato* were printed many times at the end of the fifteenth century and were all constructed out of similar sententious material. Some of these works taught table-manners and practical household etiquette, others emphasized more general principles of behavior. Æsop's *Fables*, eternally popular, reviewed man's conduct by means of stories condensed finally to a maxim. The idea of folly as undesirable, unwise action continued to turn up incidentally in most of these tracts. In the *Facetus*, for instance, one reads on one page near the instructions for the young man's deportment in the presence of his overlord:

> Haec tria subvertunt sensus: affectio rerum, multus thesaurus, stultus amor mulierum.[4]

On another page the fool is ridiculed:

> Tres sunt stultitiae, quibus insipiens perhibetur:
> qui tantum loquitur, quod nulla fides adhibetur;
> qui tantum terret, quod nil terrendo veretur;
> qui tantum tribuit, quod mendicare videtur.[5]

Æsop's tale of the fox and the crow points the moral:

> Haec reticere monet stultum, ne forte loquendo secretum prodat quod reticendo tenet.[6]

But the fool here still represented only the defective citizen.

Proverbial saws in the vernaculars, especially in French, described the conduct of the fool with more variety and gusto[7] and were also combined into longer compositions, some of which were devoted exclusively to listing the "follies" of men. These proverbial sayings, through the sheer cumulative effect of quantity, create the image of a society of misguided people all of whom do the wrong thing, jeopardize themselves, their wives, their children, their lands, their social positions, and appear generally unfit for life. They seem to say that the best of men is simple and stupid in regard to some phase of life, and that folly is perhaps the common heritage of man.

The Wise themselves, the admittedly sage or holy, called their fellowmen fools under certain conditions:

> Virgiles dit:
>> Qui le bien voit et le mal prent
>> Il se foloie a escient;
>> L'on doit por fol tenir
>> Celui qui pourchace son ennui.[8]

> *Hic incipiunt proverbia Marie Magdalene*
>> Sachet que sovent mustre le viere
>> Si li home est fol ou debonere.
>> Fol semblant suvent indite
>> La folie que in quer habite,
>> E sovent se repoet celer
>> Par faint semblant de ben overer;
>> Mès meuz vaut aperte folie
>> Ke trop coverte felonie.
>> Trop tost et trop tart se decovere
>> Ke le mal ceile de que le muiere.
>> Fol semblant fet fol reduter
>> E bel semblant prodoume amer.[9]

Some of the isolated vernacular proverbs are direct translations from the Latin. Some of them are more picturesque than any Latin maxim. The total picture they convey is dreary. Fools are stupid and indiscreet in the management of their worldly affairs, cannot keep their property together, cannot turn a disadvantageous happening to their own account, give up what they already have to go seeking some remote improvement of their condition, and seem completely ignorant of what is really best for themselves. They are presumptuous, they give advice uncalled-for and themselves take no one's counsel; they talk too much, they embroil themselves with their superiors. They rashly put themselves in the power of those who are stronger than they, or they go to law when legal procedure is avoidable. They are, in the words of the *Catholicon*, "presumptuosus," "temerarius," "indiscretus," "garrulus."[10]

The contrast between the wise man and the fool, which made the fool's ignominious worthlessness most obvious, provided the skeleton of the *Proverbes du Vilain*. But though constant reference is made to the benefits of wisdom, the poem is practically a survey of human behavior in terms of its witlessness and ignorance. The conventional recommendations to action are summarized in each verse in a popular proverb, and in almost every verse the burden of error is thrown upon the back of the fool; he is a great fool who undertakes two things and finishes neither; he is a fool who loses his property through oversight, who preserves the goods of other people and not his own, and so on. The total poem appears to declare that at least one half the world has not the wit to mind its own best interest.[11]

But it was possible to go still farther and to suggest that mankind is wholly composed of fools. Four lists of follies exist, dating from the late fourteenth and early fifteenth centuries when the popularity of the idea of the fool seems to have emerged. They present a whole series of maxims concerned with human error, without any accompanying reference to its wisdom. Two of them contain a list of thirty-two follies, practically the same throughout.[12] A third is known as the *Enseignements de Robert de Ho, dits Enseignements Trebor*,[13] and is thus sponsored by a local French Solomon. The fourth and longest retails sixty follies, of which fourteen are nearly obliterated by an injury to the manuscript.[14] Those that remain almost duplicate in negative form the commands for living the upright life given in the famous collection of maxims attributed to Cato. A comparison of the two shows how completely the fool could be described as the exact antithesis of the upright man.

Cato was the elementary mirror of conduct *par excellence*, and served many generations as their guide to virtue. Its popularity was universal and enduring. It was known in Latin and in translation throughout Europe.[15] It was printed by Caxton in a version containing illustrative stories,[16] and was edited or commentated by Sebastian Brant, Erasmus, Melanchthon, Luis Vives, Etienne Dolet and J.-C. Scaliger.[17] Erasmus expressed his sense of the value of the treatise in his explanation of its name:

> Catonis ob id tantum arbitror dici quod habeat
> sententias Catone dignas.[18]

It was translated into English verse and printed along with the *Sayings of the Seven Wise Men* as late as 1553.[19] Those who lived according to its direction ran no risk of serious "maladjustment," they were destined to be successful and to enjoy that full free development of the personality which psychologists tell us accompanies success and cannot take place without it! The *Minor Cato* stated in briefest form what the four books of the *Major Cato* expanded into distichs. The *Minor Cato* is a handbook of conduct reduced to lowest terms:

> Ici comence Catun. Cum animadverterem quam plurimos homines graviter errare in via morum, succurrendum opinioni eorum et consulendum fore existimavi, maxime ut gloriose viverent et honorem contingerent . . .
> Nunc te, fili karissime, docebo quo pacto mores tui animi componas . . .
> Igitur mea precepta ita legito ut intelligas; legere enim et non intelligere est nigligere. . . .
> Itaque Deo supplica. Parentes ama. . . .
> Datum serva. Foro te para. . . .
> Mutuum da. Cum bonis ambula. Cui des videto. Antequam voceris ad cunsilium ne accesseris. . . .
> Conviva rara. Mundus esto. Quod satis est dormi.
> Saluta libenter. . . .

Conjugem ama. Majori cede. . . .
Magistrum metue. Vino tempera. Verecundiam serva. . . .
Libros lege, quod legeris memento. Rem tuam custodi . . .
Liberos erudi. Diligenciam adhibe. Blandus esto.
Jusjurandum serva. . . .
Familiam cura. Irasci abs re noli. Neminem irriseris.
Meretricem fuge. . . .
In judicium adesto; ad pretorium stato. . . .
Literas disce. Consultus esto. . . .
Bonis benefacito. Virtute utere. Tute consule. Male-
dictus ne esto. . . .
Troco lude; aleas fuge. . . .
Existimacionem retine. . . .
Patere legem quam ipse tuleris. Equum judice. Nil
mentire. . . .
Beneficii accepti memor esto. Pauca in convivio loquere.
Minime judica. . . .
Illud stude agere quod justum est. Pugna pro patria . . .
Alienum noli concupiscere. Parentes patienter vince . . .
Minorem ne contempseris. Noli nimium confidere in tua
virtute sive fortitudine. . . .
Nil arbitrio virium tuarum feceris. Libenter amorem
ferto.[20]

There is no mention of folly in the *Minor Cato* and only inci-
dental uses of the word in the *Major Cato,* its vernacular translations and the poems which imitate it.[21] These documents seem
to assume that they are addressed to sober people who mean to
do the right things and who are able and eager to take responsibility for their wives, their sons, their servants, their lands and
their duties in peace and war. To such good citizens in the making, the weakness and stupidity of the fool, his running hither and
thither, make him a simple object of opprobrium.

The poem *De stulticiis* is practically a negative *Cato,* sug-
gesting not the power of education and discipline as the Latin
maxims do, but the complete failure of law and order to control
unreasonable man:

De stulticiis
Cynkante e diz folies sont

Ki conversantz sont en le mond,
Mes de totes choses qe sont mals
Ces sont des principals:
Ky Dieu n'ayme ne a li creit,
Ki en morteil peché se tient,
Ki nul bien ne volt aprendre,
K'ad promptée e ne volt rendre,
Ki tut doigne e nient receit,
Ki mult promet e nient doignet,
Ki parle e nul ly escut,
Ki manace e nul ly dut,
Ki tant jure que nul ly creit,
Ki demande qanq'il veit,
Ki a touz son conseil counte,
Ki soi mesmes mette a hounte,
Ki rien ad e tut bargayne,
Ki riot (rejot?) qanq'il gayne,
Ki de ces amys soi loigne,
Ki delaie son bosoigne,
Ki tient son proeme en despit,
Ki creit qanqe homme li dit,
Ki despit piere ou miere,
Ki ne tient s'aspouse chiere,
Ki autre amil haunte,
Ki par mensoigne soi vaunte,
Ki autre chose a tort cleyme,
Ki tant faist que nul sayme,
Ki ne honore saynte Eglise,
Ki sa foy fraynt ou brise,
Ki soi joiist de son malfest,
Ki soi repent de son bienfest,
Ki de bien faire n'ad desire,
Ki de prison ne volt issire,
Ki prodhome despersone,
Ki blasme chose q'est bone,
Ki bien ne fait tant com il poet,
Ki fait envitz que faire li estuet,
Ki ove fole combat ou tense,
Ki juge autri conscience,
Ki hete peese e ayme guere,

Ki hete sa demeigne terre,
Ki trop soi fait hauteigne e fere,
Ki fait ou dist vileigniere. . . .
          (fourteen lines omitted)
Ki de gree ove fals soi joute,
Ki nul esclaundre ne doute,
Ki puteigne treit ou diz querte,
Ne murra ja santz poverte;
Ki bien tient ceste lesson
Il avera de Dieu la benysson.[22]

The tone of this moral poem condemns the fools unreservedly,
They are all going to die in poverty as one feels that they should.
But the fashion of listing errors as follies did sometimes serve a
satiric and a humorous purpose as well as an ominously didactic
one. It was used to advantage in a political poem reflecting upon
the murder of the Duke of Flanders by the Dauphin of France
in 1419. The fool in this case was presumably the Duke, for he
made an alliance with his natural enemy against Henry V of
England and suffered in consequence. He is reproached for having
trusted his enemies, hated good counsel, bought more than he
could pay for, boasted beyond measure, threatened more largely
than he conquered, begun a war without money, made an enemy
of his neighbor for a stranger's sake, and so on through the standard list of mistakes.[23] The poem on the *Sis Manieres de Fols*,
again, chose six particular fools and described them in a tone of
comical warning. "Or, vous tesiez un pou," sings the minstrel,
"and I will tell you of the Six Follies." The first fool is the natural
fool; he is unambitious and does not even care to try to win for
himself a kingdom. If he has enough to eat he is satisfied and
becomes indifferent—"tout met en nonchaloir." The second fool
is the melancholy fool, in whose presence it is advisable to keep
silent. He has large possessions but still he is sad. The proud fool,
third in the list, is overweening and envious; he beats the wealthy
knights at games of chance, but when his turn comes to pay his
debts he has not enough to meet them. The fourth fool deserves

to be despised by all honest men, for by negligence he allows his property to dwindle away, and he prefers to spend his time in sleep. The fifth fool is neither sleepy nor indifferent but expects things to come to him with no effort on his part. He will not work, and the minstrel opines that for his part he cannot be sorry for such a man, even though he be hungry and miserable. Last of all comes the fool who seduces his seigneur's lady during his lord's absence, and the poem ends with a lively story of what happened to one such fool.[24]

Herford has commented upon the late medieval fashion of dubbing all error "folly":

That the world is a kingdom of Fools is a conviction easily detected beneath the fine urbanities of Renan, the glittering irony of Pope. Uttered with more downright and brutal emphasis it is the commonplace in which the decaying Middle Age invested its whole capital of intellectual and moral scorn.[25]

The proverbial and sententious literature of the time is a treasure house of expressions of that scorn. But scorn was not all that the "decaying Middle Ages" visited upon the fool. In another mood, though by the same name, they condemned him heartily and unequivocally for a sinner. The scriptural Book of Proverbs contains most of the exhortations and rebukes, most of the specific descriptions of conduct broadcasted more popularly in the *Catos* and *Urbanuses* and included in the lists of follies—is in fact the familiar source for these commonplaces today. Commentaries upon it, dating from the centuries when the church was first formulating its doctrines and from the later days when the reformers were annotating scripture, stated clearly when and why the fool was a sinner, and discovered neither humor nor irony in the fact.

The Book of Proverbs itself, like the *Cato*, provided practical sober counsel for the conduct of this life. It preached prudence on earth, although a higher prudence—true wisdom—was the result it aimed at.[26] The wise shall inherit glory, and shame shall be the promotion of fools, *perhaps* in a life beyond death, but the primary concern of the proverbs was, as Saint Augustine pointed out, "ad mores pios informandos."[27] It is not surprising, therefore, that the picture of the wise man which stands out from the proverbs is strikingly like that presented by the maxims of *Cato*. The wise man is restrained and neighborly, slow to anger, loyal in friendship; he does not indulge in vain promises, he cherishes his wife, rules his servants justly, educates his children in the paths of virtue, refrains from flattery, and is not easily credulous.[28] On the other hand, the sluggard, the busybody, the sharp dealer, those who go surety unwisely, those who disinherit the fatherless, those who become uselessly involved in lawsuits are all fools. The items of the familiar canon of errors—credulity, faithlessness to promises, detraction, meddling, babbling, boasting, offering unwanted advice, garrulousness and the rest—all appear, and are pointed to show how the fool fails to achieve the end desired by man either on earth or hereafter.[29]

The talkativeness of the fool, his lack of reticence and caution, his mischievousness, impatience and ready anger are among those of his qualities which can be derived easily from mental deficiency or ignorance, and might be excused as such. But other errors he makes are more serious. Fools make a mock at sin; they plan to do evil—their will is in error; the meditation of their hearts is sin, and he who plans to do evil shall be called fool.[30] Such fools as these are certainly not innocently defective and dull. The 1540 edition of the Book of Proverbs points the moral in summarizing the contents of chapters ten to thirty-one: they show, it says, "what profet commeth of wysdome, and wat hynderaunce procedeth of folyshnesse."[31] This hindrance stands between the fool and his advance down the road to man's true goal, and makes the fool-as-sinner a tragic figure.

A condonable "folly" is differentiated from a sin by the importance of the objective which the act "hinders," and the fulfilment of the desires and powers of the spirit has always been considered more important than the fulfilment of the desires of the obviously perishable body. The fulfilment of the life of the spirit is the one true "end" of man admitted by Catholic teaching. The goal of life is beatitude, consuming love for and knowledge of God. This beatitude man must win, through following the discipline of reason and the eternal law, and with the assistance of God's grace. Sins are acts which, by transgressing these laws, cut man off, in greater or less degree, from his attainment of his end. But since man would pursue his end without mistakes, if he were not weak and ignorant, it is necessary to the understanding of sin to admit the basic inadequacy of the human race:

> Without the acknowledgment that the present moral state of man is not that in which God created him, that his powers are weakened; that he has a supernatural end to attain, which is impossible of attainment by his own unaided efforts, without grace there being no proportion between the end and the means; that the world, the flesh and the devil are in reality active agents fighting against him and leading him to serve them instead of God, sin cannot be understood.[32]

Sin is thus apparently due to the weakness and ignorance, or to the inherent "folly" of man. It is the intolerable impediment between man and his desire, or what should be his desire.

This weakness and ignorance are of course part of man's broken nature, damaged in the incurring of original sin; his real nature is of a dignity suited to the supernatural destiny that awaits him. If there is irony in calling him fool, it is tragic irony. For man is in reality made in the image of God, that is: intellectuale et arbitrio liberum, et per se potestativum.[33] All actions that may appropriately be called "human" therefore proceed from a definite will, and that will should be directed toward man's ultimate end:

> Unde illae solae actiones vocantur proprie humanae, quarum homo est dominus. . . . Objectum autem voluntatis est finis et bonum. Unde oportet quod omnes actiones humanae propter finem sint.[34]

Man may be weak, then, but in so far as he may properly be called man, he wills to act in a definite direction. A sin is always an act, and always a voluntary act.[35] It follows that ignorance may excuse sin, if the sinner when enlightened would have willed to act in a different way.[36] A defective power of apprehension, not subject to the will and constituting "invincible ignorance," excuses acts committed under its direction.[37] If the brute animals acting according to an imperfect reason-possessing "voluntarium secundum imperfectam rationem"[38]—receive neither praise nor blame and are not held responsible for their acts, it would seem that such a human being as one thinks of at the word "half-wit" should be excused also. But the fool, half-wit or not, is after all a human being in form and as such cannot be excused for not knowing what man is held to know—ought to know. Nor may the reason be excused, when it does not know what man as man should know.[39] The virgins in the mystery play let their lamps go out; they were only "insipientes" or "fatuae," fools more innocent than "stultus," yet they were carried off by demons while the "prudentes" greeted the bride-groom.[40] The line of responsibility is indeed delicate to draw. In any case, folly represents a lack of some sort, and in so far it partakes of the nature of evil in being a "privation of form or order or due measure."[41] The fool looks like man, yet is not wholly man. Lacking the ability to seek God intellectually through wisdom, and to guide his earthly steps by prudence and right judgment, the fool is cut off from the possibility of living well on earth or of reaching heaven. He is a guilty fool.

The interpretation of "stultus," fool, as sinner is the meaning which it bears to the real disciplinarian, and has been preached by the Puritan spirit in many manifestations. Saint Augustine in annotating the word in his analysis of the Book of Job calls the fool "impious":

Stultos nunc impios accipiendum, ut e contrario sapientia hominis pietas sit, sicut in consequentibus dicitur.[42]

Fifty years later Salonius, "gente Gallus" and possibly bishop of Vienne, wrote a commentary or exposition in the form of a dialogue upon the proverbs of Solomon. Veranus questions Salonius upon the meaning of the proverbs, and Salonius replies with the ethical meaning behind the metaphor and with the ecclesiastical application to be made of it. The exposition of Proverbs is followed by a similar treatise on Ecclesiastes, for the two books, with the Song of Solomon, were looked upon as making a continuous study in which the preacher passed from practical instructions for this world to a survey of the futility of all human activity, ending his lesson with the glorification of the divine redeemer, union with whom is the consummation of all being.[43] The fool is shown to be a sinner who is not headed for the proper goal:

Veranus. Dic mihi, quaeso, quomodo *in facie prudentis lucet sapientia,* sicut ait Salomon: *Oculi autem stultorum sunt in finibus terrae?*

Salonius. Prudens homo saepe in ipsa vultus claritate faciei suae solet praemonstrare gravitatem sui sensus, et claritatem intellectus. Stulti vero ad hanc imitandam et sectandam, videlicet gravitatem, oculos mentis non possunt attollere, sed tota admiratione perquirunt, qualiter ad finem (hoc est, ad impletionem carnalium voluptatum) pertingere valeant.[44]

The same idea is developed in answer to Veranus' question as to why the fools mentioned in Ecclesiastes do not have their eyes in their heads. Salonius replies that Christians do have their eyes in their heads, that is directed toward Christ, but that the fool's vision is obscured by the love of this world:

Odit enim coelestia, et ideo non potest, sicut vir sapiens, ad coelum oculos suos erigere, quia non cogitat ea quae Dei sunt, sed quae hujus saeculi.[45]

Although both the fool and the wise man die, yet their lot is different, for the fool is damned:

Tamen non erit similis memoria in futuro nec aequalem percipient remunerationem, quoniam sapiens in die judicii ad regni coelestis elevabitur gloriam, stultus vero demergetur in aeterna damnationis tormenta.[46]

This downright condemnation of the fool was still the official interpretation of his lot at the time of Hugo of Saint Victor. "Stultus" is the man who "sibi nescit providere in posterum," but he is also—"omnis peccator qui terrenis actibus deditus, futurum nihil praevidet: is disciplinam irridet, dum derogat divinas correctioni."[47] It is a sin for a man not to know his true objective and take proper pains to get there.

More than four hundred years after the death of Hugo of Saint Victor appeared an anonymous English commentary on "that woorthie worke called; The Proverbs of Salomon," in which the fool is yet again rated as impious and a sinner.

The wise shall inherite glorie, but fooles dishonor. (i. shame and contempt, and that before God and man).[48]

A fool is "a very wicked person."[49] "Simple" and "foolish" mean the same thing, and "foolishness" is "wickedness and sinne."[50] Whenever the importance of an "end" is really believed in, the "stultus" who sees his danger of missing that end but pays no attention to it is on the spot convicted of criminal negligence. In this sense folly is the father of sin.

During the fifteenth century translation of the scriptures into the vernacular was at a standstill, and commentaries upon the Book of Proverbs—the "locus classicus" for expressions of the idea that the fool is a sinner—are lacking.[51] Yet examples of casual usage show the currency of the idea that folly leads to sin and does not excuse sin. When Covetise, in the *Castle of Perseverance*, calls upon his fellow Sins to try their wiles on Mankind, he addresses them in these words:

> Mankynde is now com to myn hall,
>   with me to dwell, by downys dry;
> Þerfore ȝe must, what so be-ffall,
>   Feffyn hym with ȝoure foly,
>   & ellis ȝe don hym wronge.
> For whanne Mankynde is kendly koveytous,
> he is proud, wrathful, & Envyous;

> Glotons, slaw, & lecherous,
> Þei arn oþer whyle amonge.
>
> Þus Every synne tyllyth in oþer,
> & makyth Mankynde to ben a foole.[52]

Since the point of the play is to teach man to shun vices and seek virtues, we know in advance that to succumb to the wiles of the Sins is to forfeit man's eternal reward. If Mankynde yields to their seductions, he will be a fool, damned for his irresponsibility. In the play of *Mankind*, the hero is also besought by Mercy not to forfeit blessedness by irresponsibility:

> Be not unkynde to Gode, I prey yow! be hys servante!
> Be stedefast in condycyon! se ȝe be not varyant!
> lose not thorow foly, þat ys sowte se dere.[53]

And Saint Paul himself, in the play of his *Conversion*, condemns witless and ignorant irresponsibility, not as an unfortunate defect in man's equipment for life, but as a sin which can be avoided, taking its origin in pride:

> Pride, that of bytternes all bale begynnes,
> With-holdyng all fayth, yt fedyth and foysonnes,
> As holy scryptur beryth playn wyttnesse,—
> Inicium omnium peccatorum superbya est,—
> That often dystroyeth both most and lest.
>
> Of all vyces and foly pride ys the Roote. . . .[54]

According to the sober fifteenth-century moralist, then, witlessness and ignorance, the qualities that distinguished the half-wit and the dunce, made their possessor a social nuisance and in addition created in him an irresponsible disregard for that "end" of man which no creature in human form might be permitted to disregard. Any lapse from accepted codes of conduct and belief might be considered a hindrance to man on his appropriate progress toward his end, and any man so transgressing the code might be called fool, a bitter fool, for his carelessness. Folly was a pitfall to be avoided, and the fool himself was ruined on earth and damned in the after-world.

Chapter III

THE FOOL TRIUMPHS OVER THE WISE MAN

Tant sage qu'il vouldra, mais enfin c'est un homme; qu'est il plus caducque, plus miserable, et plus de neant? la sagesse ne force pas nos conditions naturelles.

—*Montaigne*

To the conventional medieval moralist and theologian the fool was an object of scorn. His deficiencies doomed him to make mistakes in his earthly affairs and his irresponsibility did not free him from the destiny of those who failed to pursue the true object of man's life. But conventional moralists and theologians were not the only writers to present the fool. Storytellers and dramatists and poets as well as mystics and sceptics made use of him. In their accounts of his nature, his deficiencies often proved sources of power, and he was as often applauded as scorned.

The fool's latent power to succeed depended upon the fact that the wise were after all sometimes wrong. A fool, according to the proverbs, was a poor citizen both of the city of man and of the city of God. Seen against the background of an accepted code or dogma, he was a social burden, a sinner, or both. But codes or dogmas might conflict or be overthrown. Wisdom—decorum, reason, purposefulness—might be proved inadequate to the demands made upon it and defeated by some newer reason and purpose; it might be repudiated altogether as a less direct way to satisfaction than folly—indecorum, unreason, apparent purposelessness. Or the wisdom of one group of people might be condemned as folly by another; the World and the Saint can never agree to call the same conduct wise.

Death destroyed both the wise man and the fool. From the
Christian point of view it ushered both into an eternity of existence, but dislocated some of the relative values of wisdom and
folly as estimated on earth. Moreover, to keep the eye fixed
steadily upon a distant end, earthly or heavenly, was possible
only to the really rational or saintly nature. Man's true nature
might be, as Aquinas had said, "intellectuale, et arbitrio liberum,
et in se potestativum," but among the run of mankind that nature was glimpsed only at moments. Average human beings
needed to be free now and then from the burden of conscious
choice. Human nature in its battered earthly form was something frail and foolish, but it had to be endured, and moreover
it demanded the relief of laughter which according to Baudelaire is something which the true sage does not permit himself.[1]
Even in the midst of carving the tree of Jesse the artist was
sometimes overcome by a sudden sense of the ridiculous and
moved to insert the head of a fool.[2] (As Rigollot comments,
"On dirait un membre de la famille.") The fool of proverbs
was the epitome of what man condemned, the antithesis of the
wise man. But other late medieval compositions presented
him in ways which emphasized his potentialities and developed
the paradox that what seemed to be wise might prove foolish.
They expressed the vast human fear of death as the end to
all delights and the irrepressible rebound of the mind in satire
and parody, in which the fool played a leading part. The fools
not only did not fail; they triumphed.

Solomon himself was known during the Middle Ages both as
a wise man and as a fool. As the Sage of the Book of Kings[3]
he naturally enough became the mentor to whom all instructive
aphorisms might safely be referred.[4] But he was credited too
with the composition of Ecclesiastes which questioned the ultimate value of both wisdom and folly, and, most surprising
of all, he became the butt of a story whose hero beat him at
his own game of sententious phrase-making.

A late fourteenth or early fifteenth century translation into English of the Book of Proverbs presented its selections in a form much more resembling the style of the *Cato* than that of the Hebrew teacher as we know it. Its author of course was advertised as the paragon of wisdom. The doctrine began with praise of God's greatness and with commands to love him. It proceeded with the familiar sequence of brief orders to do or not to do this or that.[5] Chastise your children for the good of their souls, honor your parents, choose yourself a true bailiff and pay him well, do not chide and do not go to law with the wealthy, do not associate with fools nor tell them your counsel, make your will wisely for the benefit of your friends, and so on. Reduced to these terms the metaphorical Hebrew proverb was turned into the sententious maxim and Solomon and Cato became interchangeable names for the author of elementary moral precepts, to whom the fool was simply a creature to be scorned and ignored.

But in the face of death the wise man and the fool were equals. The author of the Book of Koheleth chose the pseudonym of Solomon to give dignity and perhaps orthodoxy to his review of human life and his praise of the life of the spirit that seeks eternal truth. Although this book culminated in praise of wisdom and of the Creator, it poignantly expressed the sense that all is vanity and that the wise man perishes even as the fool. In one instance at least a fifteenth century translator attributed the sermon directly to Solomon:

Kynge Salomone sais, in his buk of his contemplacione and detestacione of this warld, that al this warld is bot vanite of vanitez, specialy of all lawbore that man makis, to conquest riches and landis in this warld, wyth al besy cure, nocht wytand quha Ioies thai landis and guids efter hyme, quhilk is gret vanite.[6]

He found that "frawart men and hard to coryke and that of fulys the maner is but end Infinyte,"[7] yet he set about to study ethical precepts to find what led straightest to the satisfaction of man's desire:

Item, I said in my mynd and thocht, that I suld absten me fra vice, & at I suld set al my hart to wysedome, and umbethow all erouris and foleys, quhill I saw quhat war maist spedfule to manis sone in erde. ...

Item, than I beheld that baith the wisman & the full deis, and ȝeldis the saul is lykwyss: than thocht I, gif our ded by elyk, quhat profitis It me to set my hart and besynes to al wisdome, mar na hyme quhilk set his mynd cur and besynes till al foly?[8]

Taken out of its context in this way the pessimism of Ecclesiastes stands out more strikingly than it does in the book itself. Yet in spite of the fact that in conclusion the author

considerit . . . and fand that wisdum precellis foly, as far as the lychtnes of the sone passis the myrknes of the mirk nycht[9]

the statement of the vanity of human achievement and the equivalence of wisdom and folly before death remains the point of emphasis in the argument. Solomon in sponsoring these words became a less convincing teacher of dogmatic wisdom than the bland king of Proverbs. The fool though condemned was dignified by his equality with the wise man in common mortality.

The possibility that deficiency and ignorance may prove more effective than wisdom, or than apparent wisdom, was demonstrated in the poems and stories of Solomon and Marcolf, where the great King and magician himself was made a fool of by a hairy clown, ignorant and obscene.

Marcolf did not apparently begin his career in literature as a fool. Whatever its origin, the story of his encounter with Solomon at first involved either a serious debate or a serious romantic story. Kemble mentions the fact that Pope Gelasius in the fifth century expelled from the Canon a *Contradictio Salamonis* and that a monk of St. Gall writing in the eleventh century reported that among the "haeretici" fables were current, *seculares literae:*

Quid est enim aliud, quum dicant Marcolphum contra proverbia Salamonis certasse? In quibus omnibus verba pulchra sunt, sine veritate.[10]

A German romance of the early twelfth century told of an emperor named Solomon who had a fair wife; she fled with her lover King Faro and was pursued and brought back by the King's brother, Morolf.[11] This romance seems to have had little to do with the formation of the Solomon-Marcolf debate, but it may have contributed to the character of Marcolf some of its reputed shrewdness and resourcefulness.[12] The mention of the *Contradictio Salamonis,* however, suggests that the dogmas of the wise met early with some sort of opposition which perhaps survived in the tenets of the heretics of the eleventh century. Since Solomon was explicitly known as "wise," anyone opposing him in dialectic or in the solving of enigmas would naturally become known as "foolish." At any rate by the early thirteenth century Marcolf, if not yet a fool, was at least known as the parodist of Solomon's wisdom.[13] In some verses he was the serious competitor with the King in the utterance of useful commonplaces, but during the fifteenth century he became known chiefly as the impudent outcast who humbled the wise man. A poem remains entitled *Proverbes de Marcoul et de Salemon* which suggests a combination of the French *Cato* and the *Proverbes du Vilain:*

> Por largement doner
> Puet-l'en enpris monter,
> > Ce dist Salemons;
> De poverté user,
> se fait-l'en fol clamer,
> > Marcol li respont.
>
> Qui saiges hom sera,
> Jà trop ne parlera,
> > Ce dist Salemons;
> Qui jà mot ne dira,
> Grant noise ne fera,
> > Marcol li respont.[14]

This is the type of *débat* which probably prompted Leroux de Lincy to suggest that Marcoul is an adaptation of the name of Marcus Portius Cato himself.[15] A disputation more frequently copied is that headed "Veez cy une desputacoun entre Salamon ly saage, et Marcoulf le foole"—"Salamon þe wyse, and Marcolf þe more foole"—in a manuscript from the time of Henry the Sixth of England.[16] This poem is one of the more ribald contributions to the literature abusing women.[17] But the version of the encounter between the king and the lout which was most popular at the end of the fifteenth century was a less monotonous prose story, of how Marcolf came to the court of Solomon, entered into contention with him and defeated him, returning to his home well rewarded for his shrewdness. This story is followed in some versions by a group of Jest stories describing the further intercourse of Solomon and Marcolf and how Marcolf continued to outwit the wisest man in the world.

In these prose stories Marcolf was definitely represented as one whom the world would take for degraded and ignorant. The title-page of an edition published in Copenhagen in 1488 described the contest of wit as taking place between

Rex Salomon sapientissimus, et Marcolphus, facie deformis et turpissimus, tamen ut fertur eloquentissimus.[18]

The King is seated in his audience chamber in state when news is brought to him that a strange man and his wife are coming up to him out of the east. When the man approaches, Solomon sees that he has a broad forehead full of wrinkles and frowns, ears hairy and hanging to the middle of his cheeks, running eyes, a nether lip like that of a horse, a goatish beard, hands short and black with thick fingers, and a face like an ass. His wife is another of the same kind. The king asks the man who he is, and the man replies by returning his question to the king. Solomon promptly recites his complete genealogy, which is pompous and impressive. But Marcolf is not to be so

easily quelled, and when his turn to give his pedigree comes he
answers:

I am of the .xij. kindred-[s] of Corlys. Rusticus gat rustam Rusta
gat rustum | Rustus gat rusticellū | Rusticell[us] gat tarcum | Tarc[us]
gat tarcol | Tarcol gat pharsi | Pharsi gat marcuel | Marcuel gat
marquat | Marquat gat marcolphū & that is I.[19]

In a Latin version from a Strasbourg press Marcolf does not
claim kindred with the Churls but states simply, "Et ego sum
Marcolphus Follus."[20] Solomon promises to reward Marcolf
if he can reply to all his questions; to each proverb he speaks,
or to each maxim which he pronounces, Marcolf is to make a
fitting rejoinder. The king begins boastfully and Marcolf
counters with a disparaging proverb:

Salo. If thou kāst answere to alle my questyons I shall make
the ryche | and be named above all othre withyn my reaume.
Marcol. The phisician promyseth the seeke folke helthe whan he
hath no power. *Salo.* I have iuged betwixt two light women whiche
dwellyd in oon house and forlaye a chylde. *Mar.* were erys are there
are causys where women be there are wordys. *Salo.* God yawe
wysdam in my mouth. for me lyke is none in alle partys of the
worlde *Marcolf*[us]. He that hath evyll neighborys praysyth hum self.[21]

The major part of the dialogue is made up of the familiar
truisms of the didactic poems and the Biblical proverbs, with re-
sponses which point out the sarcastic applications of the maxims
—or sometimes simply sound as if they had a connection with
the first proposition.[22] The contest is sustained through pages
of juggling. We hear again that it is proper to educate one's
children in the fear of the Lord, to cherish one's parents, not
to associate with the litigious, nor to fight with the strong,
nor to put off a loan to a friend when one is able to make it
on the spot. Marcolf is not to be defeated, and Solomon finally
admits that he deserves the reward. The courtiers are angry—
"Ut quid iste follus infestat dominum Regem nostrum?"[23]—but
Marcolf returns to his hut in the woods in triumph.

Solomon in this story is a pompous braggart who is defeated at his game of being the wise man by the foulest creature in his kingdom. In the jests which follow the dialogue in some editions the same situation is continued, in action instead of in a contest of words. Marcolf points out the moral of the story to Solomon when the king comes riding by his hovel and pauses for more conversation:

Sal. Sic me Deus adivvet in Gabatha mihi apparuit Deus, et replevit me sapientia. *Mar.* Talis dicitur esse sapiens, qui seipsum habet pro stulto.[24]

The wise man and the fool have changed places; Solomon is thwarted at every turn, and the fool by a shrewdness beneath the accepted code of the king accomplishes his purpose. As the Eiron defeated the boaster in the end,[25] the humble and ignored proved to hold the key to success, the rightness of orthodoxy was called in question and the high were humbled.

That the fool may prove wiser than the wise man was a commonplace less often reiterated but as well known in late medieval times as the other commonplace that fools are condemned to shame. The contest of Solomon and Marcolf was printed many times during the last years of the fifteenth century and the first of the sixteenth. Even as late as the seventeenth century it appeared, appended to the 1643 edition of the *Epistolae obscurorum virorum*[26] where it neatly supplemented the general thesis that all that glitters is not gold. Certain French proverbs of the sixteenth century, too, treated Solomon as more fool than sage.[27] As late as the eighteenth century he was to be found appearing in Punch-and-Judy shows in company with other demoted heroes.[28] In the Paris to which Erasmus came as a student in the 1490's it seems possible that Solomon's popular reputation was chiefly that of fool, for Michel Menot had put him in his place:

Si fieret chorea de omnibus fatuis qui fuerunt a principio mundi, Salomon tanquam praecipuus ferret marotam.[29]

Marcolf the fool, on the other hand, had risen to the position of counselor to the king. In an English poem attacking the sloth and avarice of the clergy, he speaks plainly to the authorities in the name of the poor and oppressed:

> I Marcol the more fole, mon, on my mad wyse,
>   I send the brod Salamon to say as I here,
> Hou homlé hosbondmen here hertys thai aryse,
>   Thai woldon thai wroʒton wysely that schuld
>   ham lede and lere.
> Do thi message mekely to pryst and to frere,
>   Thai are the lanternys of lyf ye lend men to lyʒt,
> Bot thai be caʒt with covetyse, with conscious unclere,
>   Aʒeyns the lauys of here Lord reson and ryʒt,
>   hit is noʒt unknow;
> Comawnd hem in al wyse,
> Never on other dai dar dyspyse,
> Fore here cursid covetyse
>   here horne is e-blaw.[30]

He recites the injuries to which the negligent priests subject the people and begs his "blessid broder Salamon" to take steps at once to remedy the situation. Otherwise more trouble will ensue:

> Cujus finis bonum ipsum totum bonum.
> Thus Salamon hath sayd the soth verement,
>   As Marcol, the more fole, warned hym I wene,
> Bot ʒif this draʒt be draun wel thai goune wil
>   be schent,
> And schal turne treulé to torment and to tene.[31]

The inversion of status that has taken place here is complete. The wise are no longer wise, their methods no longer lead to the accomplishment of their desires, and the foolish now speak with wisdom to those in authority.

The folly of Marcolf, however, was not true dullness or ignorance, it only appeared so to a blind court; in defeating Solomon, Marcolf used the same kind of wit that had built up the king's own reputation. The triumph was really for pov-

erty and ugliness rather than for witless ignorance. The story
is a burlesque, of which Marcolf the fool is the hero. But the
hero is not the centre of interest; Solomon the victim is its
focus and the source of its humor. Other triumphs of folly
however were recorded in literature in which the victim was at
once the hero and the fool. Gregory the Great, with Augustine,
Jerome and Ambrose, was one of the builders of the church
familiar to clerks who advanced through the arts course at the
university into the course in theology. His eloquent indictment
of the wisdom of the world denied that right conduct like that
described in Solomon's proverbs and the *Cato* would win man
the bliss of the eternal life, and he pleaded for an opposite way
of life which it was only logical to call folly. The fool to him
was both victim and hero. This heroic fool, contrasted to the
worldly wiseman, appeared frequently in literature from Gregory's time to the age of Erasmus.

Many of the precepts inculcated by the *Cato* and the proverbs are countermanded in Gregory's description of the innocent and pure life:

Huius mundi sapientia est, cor machinationibus tegere, sensum
verbis velare, quae falsa sunt vera ostendere, quae vera sunt fal-
lacia demonstrare. Haec nimirum prudentia usu a juvenibus scitur,
haec a pueris pretio discitur, hanc qui sciunt caeteros despiciendo
superbiunt; hanc qui nesciunt, subjecti et timidi in aliis mirantur,
quia ab eis haec eadem duplicitas iniquitatis, nomine palliata, diligi-
tur, dum mentis perversitas urbanitas vocatur. . . . At contra sapientia
justorum est nil per ostensionem fingere, sensum verbis aperire,
vera ut sunt diligere, falsa devitare, bona gratis exhibere, mala
libentius tolerare quam facere; nullam iniuriae ultionem quaerere,
pro veritate contumeliam lucrum putare. Sed haec justorum sim-
plicitas deridetur, quia ab huius mundi sapientibus puritatis virtus,
fatuitas creditur. Omne enim quod innocenter agitur, ab eis procul
dubio stultum putatur. . . . Quid namque stultius videtur mundo
quam mentem verbis ostendere, nil callida machinatione simulare,
nullas injuriis contumelias reddere, pro maledicentibus orare, pauper-

tatem quaerere, possessa relinquere, rapienti non resistere, percutienti alteram maxillam praebere?[32]

The injunctions of the precept books to be careful what you say, reticent and if need be deceptive, to stimulate stupidity if it is to your advantage, to guard your possessions carefully and to flee poverty as a mark of shame are the direct contradictions of Gregory's commands. Yet if the worldly who consider themselves wise have risen to power and honor and yet are really fools, how can their present situation be squared with the verse from the eleventh chapter of Proverbs: "Qui stultus est, serviet sapienti"?

Sed sciendum est quia contra sapientis vitam, dum stultus praeeminens terrorem potestatis exercet, dum hunc laboribus fatigat, contumeliis lacerat, profecto hunc ab omni vitiorum rubigine urendo purgat. Stultus ergo sapienti etiam dominando servit, quem ad meliorem statum premendo provehit.[33]

Gregory's distinction between the wise and the foolish was a genuine distinction in kind. Marcolf was simply a hideous creature who turned out surprisingly to be cleverer than Solomon at Solomon's own game; he looked like a fool but he proved to be wise. The wise and the foolish of Gregory's words, however, could neither of them ever outdo the other in his own field of activity, nor would either try:

Stulti cum prudentium facta conspiciunt, haec eis omnia reprehensibilia esse videntur; qui, suae imperitiae atque infirmitatis obliti, tanto intentius de alienis judicant, quanto sua profundius ignorant.[34]

The wise of this world were fools in the very methods by which they pursued that "end" of man which everyone, even if hypocritical about it, must assume as his real objective, and the pure in heart might be fools, but they were not, like the worldlings, ignoble fools:

Sciendum nobis est quod alii intra sanctam Ecclesiam vocantur stulti, sed tamen nobiles, alii vero sunt stulti et ignobiles. Stulti namque dicuntur, sed esse ignobiles nequeunt, qui carnis prudentiam contemnentes, profuturam sibi stultitiam appetunt, et ad novitatem internae prolis virtutis nobilitate sublevantur; qui stultam sapientiam mundi despiciunt, et sapientem Dei stultitiam concupiscunt. . . . At contra sunt stulti et ignobiles, qui dum supernam sapientiam, seme-tipsos sequentes, fugiunt, in sua ignorantia quasi in abjectae prolis vilitate sopiuntur. Quo enim id ad quod conditi sunt, non intelligunt, eo etiam cognationem acceptae per imaginem generositatis perdunt. Stulti sunt ergo ignobiles, quos ab aeternae haereditatis consortio repellit servitus mentis.[35]

The very futility of man's efforts to make his mark upon a constantly dissolving world was a proof of his folly:

Omnes qui cogitatione terrena huic saeculo conformantur per omne quod agunt huic mundo relinquere sui memoriam conantur. Alii bellorum titulis, alii altis aedificiorum moenibus, alii disertis doctrinarum saecularium libris instanter elaborant, sibique memoriae nomen aedificant. Sed cum ipsa ad finem celerius vita percurrat, quid in ea fixum stabit, quando et ipsa celeriter mobilis pertran-sit? . . . Recte ergo stultorum memoria cineri comparatur, quia illic ponitur, ubi ab aura rapiatur.[36]

Gregory had formulated and illustrated the Christian doc-trine of the triumph of the humble fool. After him, medieval laments at the evil of the world and of those who win power in it were nearly always sure to stress the folly of the good, or the goodness of folly:

Mundi libet vitia cunctis exarare;
Nam in mundo video multos nunc errare,
Spernere quod bonum est, quod malum est amare,
Et ad mala saepius sponte declinare. . . .
Quod ad lucrum pertinet nimis affectatur;
Lucra quisquis prospicit, cautus judicatur;
Res qui servat strictius, sapiens vocatur;
Sua qui dat largius, stultus reputatur.[37]

This foolish life is seductive and is no place for the man strug-gling to be wise for eternity:

Vita mundi, res polluta,
garrula, vaga, soluta,

cum sis tota plena nugis,
contra me cur stulta rugis? . . .
Si volebam esse largus
tu dicebas: Esto parcus,
quia cito dilabuntur
quae de longe conquiruntur. . . .
Idcirco, Vita inepta,
solis fatuis accepta,
cum sis tota plena sorde
te refuto toto corde.[38]

The satirical poems rebuking the avarice of the bishops and the Roman curia rang the changes on the ideas of the evil devices of the wise and the vanity of worldly success.[39] But the solution of the problem was hard to find. It is difficult to forego the satisfactions of this life, and yet as Audelay, the poet who made Marcol the spokesman of the people, pointed out, the Lord will no more be satisfied with a failure to follow his will zealously than will an earthly lord.[40]

In this dilemma there were some who, throwing overboard the conventions of right conduct and foregoing wealth, even turned to a way of life simulating the abandon of real madness, idiocy, or folly, as a means of approaching genuine satisfaction. The members of the Franciscan order foreswore the enjoyment of the goods of this world, humbling themselves to the level of the destitute. They did not seek a similar poverty of spirit, for the spirit was to be their instrument for wise living, but they cultivated a humility of the intellect which should keep their approach to God simple, innocent and direct. They took upon themselves the title of "Mundi Moriones," and Erasmus, making fun of them in the days of their deterioration, remarked that they only needed asses' ears and bells to make their hoods look like professional fools' hoods.[41] But their theory of humility and simplicity in one case, taking root in an ardent, logical and realistic mind, produced a fool-of-God who could defend his folly articulately while he acted it out convincingly, and who in his outpourings of rapture in the divine love gave evidence that his way of life had brought beatitude close to him upon this earth.

Ser Iacopo de' Benedetti da Todi did not live upon a plane that many simple people could reach, but in theory his method of approaching man's goal should have been available to the simplest and most ignorant. The highest wisdom according to him was to be thought a fool, but not an ordinary fool:

Como e somma sapienza essere reputato pazo per
l'amor de Cristo

Senno me pare et cortesia—empazir per lo bel Messia.
Ello me sa si gran sapere—a chi per Dio vol empazire:
En Parige non se vidde—ancor si gran filosofia.
Chi per Cristo va empazato,—par afflicto et tribulato;
Ma è maestro conventato—en natura et teologia.
Chi per Cristo ne va pazo,—a la gente si par matto;
Chi non ha provato el facto—pare che sia fuor de la via.
Chi vol entrare en questa scola—troverà doctrina nova;
La pazia, chi non la prova,—già non sa che ben se sia.
Chi vol entrar en questa danza,—trova amor d'esmesuranza.
Cento di de perdonanza—a chi li dice villania.
Ma chi va cercando onore—non è degno del suo amore,
Chè Iesù fra doi latrone—en mezzo la croce staia.
Ma chicerca per vorgogna,—ben me par che cetto iogna.
Ia non vado più a Bologna—a imparar altra mastria![42]

St. Paul's instruction to become a fool for the sake of Christ found its literal interpretation in the case of Jacopone, and other arguments for it or embodiments of it reappeared from time to time. At the beginning of the fifteenth century, a wave of assertion that the way to salvation was through simplicity or folly rather than through learning and the efforts of the reason manifested itself. Nicholas de Cusa, in his treatise *De docta ignorantia,* and Jean Gerson, chancellor of the University of Paris, taught that pure love seeking the road to God can reach a transport which is "within reach of the most simple."[43] The *De imitatione Christi* exulted to pour out the author's be-

lief in and love for Christ mixed with protestations of his abject
weakness, and urged faith to press on ahead of knowledge and
reason.[44] One of the *Miracles de Nostre Dame* told the story of
an emperor's son who laid aside his state and became a fool,
seeking in the deprivation of all physical and mental goods of
the world, even including the human reason, a greater consciousness of the world to come. He went to ask advice of a saintly
hermit in regard to his plan:

> Car tant hé celle joie vaine
> Et tant l'ay au cuer desplaisant
> Qu'aler le fol contrefaisant
> Vueil en povreté, nuz et las,
> Sanz penser aus mondains solas,
> Traveillier, pener et despire
> Ma charogne, si qu'adès pire
> Li soit demain que le jour d'uy.[45]

The hermit approved his scheme, and told him that it would be
acceptable to God:

> Amis, quant tu as tel desir
> Que ton cueur a ce s'humilie,
> Tu feras plus sens que folie,
> Se le fol par descongnoissance
> Fais ou lieu ou preis naiscence
> Afin que nulz ne t'aperçoive,
> Mais que pechié ne te deçoive.
> Dieu, qui toi bien appercevra,
> La foleur pour sens recevra
> Que tu feras par ficcion,
> En fuiant la decepcion
> Qui est es fausses vanitez
> Des temptables humanitez.
> Faindre estre folz et conme sages
> En Dieu et en ses sains messages
> Qui sont lumieré de dottrine,
> C'est usages qui endottrine
> Maint cuer de celer et couvrir
> Sa penance au monde, et ouvrir
> Son cuer a Dieu par oroison.[46]

The prince-fool, stoned through the streets of his capital city, became a saint through whose intercession the Virgin Mary will interest herself in the most perverse sinners.

It was of course only in the most extreme cases that those who found a rational search for a way to salvation unproductive abandoned the outward decorum of action in this world and disguised themselves as Poor Toms. But to question the conduct of the avowedly wise and visibly wealthy at all was to suggest that if accomplishment and foresight fail, possibly degradation and ignorance, or, more soundly, humility and innocence of the mind, may succeed. Perhaps man cannot struggle too consciously toward his "end." Such thoughts as these recognized that man's mortal nature differed from the celestial one attributed to him by Aquinas, and sought within the unanalyzed depths of that lesser nature new sources of strength which the reason had overlooked.

The son of the emperor of Alexandria sacrificed the pleasures of this world and embarked upon a saintly masquerade of folly in the depression following an intimate experience of death, yet in the belief that the destiny of man would be fulfilled after death. To him, as to all those who believed that the consummation of life comes after death, his assumption of folly seemed merely a temporary phase of the more miserable portion of his true existence. Even to those who in addition believed that dignity and wisdom on earth were not incompatible with dignity and wisdom in heaven, earthly life had to be looked upon as the lesser part of true existence, with death the gate through which one passed to a higher state of being. But death in itself is a grisly thing, and its horror was constantly presented to the people of the fifteenth century, in carvings, paintings, wood-cuts, poems and sermons. Did not doubters wonder at times if death was not really the dissolution it seemed, and, passing from the inertia of seeing all desires extinguished in death, resolve to profit by the satisfactions of this life, since, foolish or not, they were at least satisfactions of a sort?

Most medieval verses on death's cruel imminence, whether in Latin or in the vernaculars, implied or stated explicitly that man after the perilous adventure would embark upon eternity. Otherwise the natural fear of death became too undignified an emotion to write about. Man must think that he fears death because of the judgment to come:

> Celle vie est mauveis
> La ou home dit en la fin: Alas!
> Fole est qui sist en l'estate
> Ou il ne ose morrir pas.[47]

Ripeness is all, to be sure, but ripeness for admission to eternal blessedness:

> Mors, a celui qui s'asseure
> En gloutrenie et en luxure,
> Di lui por fol se puet tenir;
> Car riens ne vaut et petit dure,
> N'a vieil, n'a jouene n'est seure.
> Dont se fait-il boin astener,
> Quant a le fin estuet venir
> A Mort, et ne puet espenir
> D'infer, ki tant est pesme et deure;
> Boin fait en jouvent devenir
> Tel c'on puist a Diu avener;
> Petit vaut fruis qui ne meure.[48]

But in some of the comments on death this emphasis upon the future life was lacking. One of the popular tales of death in the later Middle Ages was the story of the *Trois vifs et les trois morts,* recounting how three young kings riding in the forest came suddenly upon three corpses stretched across the way in their coffins. The versified narrative gave a hideous picture of mortality but nevertheless held out the illusion of the good man's escape from destruction beyond the grave.[49] In the pictures, however, the reward of the good was not represented.

What held the attention was the sudden encounter of the young kings with the decaying corpses, the gruesomeness of decomposition itself.[50]

The Dance of Death, the most inclusive of these medieval representations of mortality, whether expressed in plastic form or in words, made little reference to the life to come but threatened all mankind, section by section, with inevitable extinction.[51] During the fifteenth century when its currency was greatest, this processional was represented on tapestries and in stained glass, in manuscripts and block-books.[52] It was worked into the series of initial letters known as the Alphabet de la Mort.[53] It was painted in frescoes like that preserved for several centuries on the walls of the Dominican convent at Basel.[54] At Paris, too, in the Cimetière des Innocents, a now vanished representation of the dance had existed in paint or in wood-carving since the early fifteenth century. Explanatory verses may have accompanied this Parisian dance, possibly those afterwards printed at Troyes as *La Grande Danse Macabre des homes et des femes*.[55] A Dance of Death was also one of the curiosities of old Saint Paul's in London. Lydgate, whose sequence of verses on death and the estates is the chief English poem on the dance, stated in his prologue that he found "thensample . . . depict ones in a Wall" at Paris and it has been suggested that his verses, copied perhaps from verses designed to accompany the Paris dance, were intended as commentary upon the scenes represented in Saint Paul's.[56] The mood of the poem is unrelieved ominousness!

Death speaketh to the Marchant

Ye rich Marchant ye mot look hitherward,
That passed have full many divers lond,
On horse and foot, having most regard
To lucre and winning as I understond;
But now to dance ye mot give me your hond,
For all your labour full little avayleth now,

Adue vainglory both of free and bond,
　　None more covet than thei that have ynough.

The Marchant maketh Aunswer

By many a hill, and many a strong vale
　　I have travailed with many marchandise,
Over the sea down carrie many a bale,
　　To sondry Iles more then I can devise.
Mine heart inward ay fretteth with covetise,
　　But all for nought now death doth me constrein,
For which I see by record of the wise,
　　Who all embraceth little shal constrein.[57]

This poem certainly did not suggest that man should eat
and drink since he died tomorrow, but neither did it help him
to face death by holding before his eyes enticing glimpses of
a life of security in eternity. The whole concept of the Dance
of Death emphasized man's defeat. A black-letter broadside
preserved from the sixteenth century shows in prints the miser
with his gold before him, the prisoner fettered to an iron ring,
the judge seated upon the bench, and the lovers in the bower,
all with Death leering at their elbows. In the centre of the sheet
a figure labeled "syknes Deathes minstrel" sits upon mattock,
shovel and crossbones, and plays the pipes, while Death leads
the dance of the king, the beggar, the old man, the child, the
wise man, the fool, with these lines:

Come, daunce this trace, ye people all,
　　Both prince and beggar, I say;
Yea, old, yong, wyse, and fooles I call,
　　To grave, come, take your way.
　　　For sicknes pipes thereto
　　　By griefes and panges of wo.[58]

Such concentration upon the fact of death slighted the idea
of the "animula vagula blandula" which was to arise out of
the perishable body, and focussed upon the sad truth that the
wise man dies even as the fool.

The fool himself appeared as a member of the estates in

several of the pictures of the Dance, but he seems to have been of no particular importance. It was not his death, but the death of the wise and powerful that was tragic and humiliating. The pictures did not hint that the fool died happier than the wise man because he had lived more irresponsibly. In the Dance attributed to Holbein, he is drawn as an idiot, like one of those in Velasquez' paintings;[59] in the Alphabet de la Mort, too, he looks more witless than merry.[60] He was, in fact, simply the objectification of dullness and ignorance. He might be dressed in the cap and bells of the jester, as in the reproductions of the Gross Basler Totentanz, but he wore them as the badge of his condition. But in these same pictorial Dances the death itself frequently wore the cap and bells.[61] It was a gruesome joke that in spite of all her honors the queen should be captured by that mortality which she had perhaps despised and ignored. Death, like Gregory's fool, was a figure disregarded and mean which rose up from its obscurity and triumphed over the great in this world. If death was the end of all activity, then man's effort on earth was indeed a joke, and the irony of its sudden end pure tragedy—unless life on earth were in some way an end in itself.[62] The skeleton, in that case, might well become a symbol of warning to man to enjoy the passing hour by satisfying his desires on earth as best he could. Petronius records that Trimalchio placed upon his banqueting table the dancing figure of a skeleton bearing a wreath and a wine cup, and inscribed "Take and enjoy."[63] The existence of a mood in which death itself could be represented in so facetiously sinister a fashion as in these Dances of Death may have prepared the way for a revival of what the *Book of Wisdom* called the creed of the ungodly:

For the ungodly said, reasoning with themselves, but not aright, Our life is short and tedious, and in the death of a man there is no remedy: neither was there any man known to have returned from the grave. For we are born at all adventure: and we shall be hereafter as though we had never been: for the breath in our nostrils is as smoke, and a little spark (?) in the moving of our heart: which being extinguished, our body shall be turned into ashes, and our spirit shall vanish as the soft air. And our name shall be forgotten in time, and no man shall have our works in remembrance, and our life shall pass away as the trace of a cloud, and shall be dispersed as a mist, that is driven away with the beams of the sun, and overcome with the heat thereof. For our time is a very shadow that passeth away; and after our end there is no returning: for it is fast sealed, so that no man cometh again. Come on therefore, let us enjoy the good things that are present: and let us speedily use the creatures like as in youth. Let us fill ourselves with costly wine and ointments: and let no flower of the spring pass by us: Let us crown ourselves with rosebuds, before they be withered: Let none of us go without his part of our voluptuousness: let us leave tokens of our joyfulness in every place: for this is our portion, and our lot is this.[64]

"Quid stultius," said the church fathers, than to forsake the pleasures of heaven for the sorry delights of this world. But the constant contemplation of death's overthrow of all that man struggled to accomplish while alive, without a corresponding concentration upon what he might get by way of reward later, might well have encouraged man to forgive his own weaknesses—even to indulge in them—and to take what he *could* know as equivalent to what he *ought* to know. In such a mood, the fool, formerly condemned by the reason, might be accepted by it as after all what man was and had a right to be.

The "ungodly" had of course always existed, whatever the official theology of the times, and had left a trail of written remains behind them throughout the centuries. They had crowned themselves with roses and filled themselves with wine, to the tune of such rollicking verses as "Mihi est proposito in taberna mori." The members of the Ordo Vagorum, or Goliards, expressed this attitude in the twelfth century:

> De Vagorum ordine
> Dico vobis jura,

Quorum vita nobilis
 Dulcis est natura,
Quorum placet animis
 Pinguis assatura
Vere plus quam faciat
 Hordei mensura.[65]

Clearly this order was not devoted to the development of the reasonable faculties, and one of its members frankly and joyfully proclaimed himself as "stultus":

Cum sit enim proprium
 Viro sapienti
Supra petram ponere
 Sedem fundamenti,
Stultus ego comparor
 Fluvio labenti,
Sub eodem tramite
 Numquam permanente.[66]

The fool here is the defiant and happy rebel, the pleasure-seeker who deviates from, even burlesques, monkish piety. He is a member of a mock order, though not a mock order of fools. Various defects in clerical character provided slogans for the foundation of other burlesque orders, the order of Bel-Eyse, for example.[67] But the poems in which these orders occur do not mention any order of fools. Even in the famous *Speculum stultorum* the members of the order of the ass were not called fools themselves; the readers of the book were divided by the author into the wise, who recognized the true sublime goal of man, and the foolish who did not.[68] But in later vernacular literature of a popular type the idea of the mock order was found combined with the idea of the gay though erring fool. *Colyn Blowbol's Testament* might have been the work of a vulgar English fifteenth century Goliard. Colyn made his will after a night of tippling and, according to the tradition of testament-writing, left his body and his soul to the gods of his creed, Lucina and Bacchus,

> And I byqueth unto my secrytory
> Regestered a brother in the order of foly,
> For his labour and his diligence,
> Six marke of bruce to have for his dispence,
> To this entent, that he bistow it shall
> Upon good drynk, and on no mete at all.[69]

He then gave orders for a banquet to be held upon his death, and, in the style of descriptive listing which characterized the poems on the follies, enumerated the types of "dronken fooles nyce" whom he hoped would attend it. In *Jyl of Breyntfords Testament,* twenty-four heirs, listed in similar fashion, were named by Jyl to inherit her contempt. Almost all of them came straight from the earlier lists, or were familiar from the instructions in *Cato.*[70] Jyl did not, however, refer to them as fools nor specifically organize them into an order. But both these devices appeared, combined with suggestions of the triumph of the fool, in Lydgate's poem, *The Order of Fools.*[71]

The Order of Fools dates from some time near the middle of the fifteenth century, later than the longest of the Anglo-French lists of follies. Unlike the simple catalogues that preceded it, it is clearly satirical. It suggests both the gaiety of the fools, their freedom and their ease, and their failure to achieve the proper end of man on earth or in heaven. It combines with its rebuke of folly a recognition of the pleasures of folly. While both attitudes are traditional, and while the combination of them has since likewise become traditional, it is this combination, in different proportions, which makes the fool in the fifteenth and early sixteenth century literature a symbol of a more or less ironic view of man. To the reader of French and English literature, Lydgate is in a limited sense the precursor both of Brant and of Erasmus.

The poem begins with a description of the patrons of the order:

> The ordre of folys ful yore ago begonne,
> Newly professyd, encresithe the couente;

> Bacus and Iuno hath set abroche a tonne,
>   And Brouthe ther braynys vn-to exigente,
>   Marcolfe theyer foundyr, patron, and presidente;
> Noumbre of thys frary, iij score and iij,
>   Echone registred by grete avysement,
> Endosyd theyre patente that they shale never the.

Bacus and Iuno are appropriate patrons for a merry company,
whether foolish or wise. Marcolf was a fool, but as we have
seen a fool who triumphed over the wisest of kings in the jest-
book and became the spokesman of the people in Audelay's
poem. His presence here brings up a passage in the history of
fools which contradicts the prophecy of the patent, "that they
shale never the"—which is however reiterated in each stanza.
The poem continues with the catalogue of fools in the familiar
order:

> Chyffe of folis, men yn bokys redythe,
>   Able yn hys foly to holde residence,
> Ys he that nowther god lovethe nor dredethe,
>   Nor to his chyrche hathe none advertence,
>   Nor to his seyntes dothe none reverence,
> And hathe dysdeyne to folke yn pouerte,
>   To fadre and moder dothe none benyvolence:
> A-sele hys patent, for he shal never the.

The repertory includes him who gives away his goods keeping
nothing for himself, who holds himself wise when he possesses
no experience, who comes to counsel before he is called, who
bears a double heart with a fair-feigned countenance, who tells
his own private business, who desires war when he himself is
not strong enough to fight, who when old marries a young wife,
who is gullible, who fights in a quarrel that is clearly unjust,
and so on throughout the tale. "Prudence cypryane" is called
in as authority for the folly of him who

>   sellythe a fatte swanne
> For a gosselyng, þat grasethe on bareyne clowrys,
> And he þat castythe hys cloke yn showrys
> Oute of the tempest whan he may flee,

> Or whan þat spado lowythe paramours,
> Is oon of hem that shalle never the.

Seneca too is invoked, to bear witness that he is a fool who delays in the execution of his purpose. The concluding stanza returns to the idea of the liberty of fools, combined with their sustained failure:

> Lete thys frary a confirmacioun,
>   And som worthy byshoppe nullatence,
> And graunten hem a general pardoun
>   And a patent to be-gyn her dispence,
>   Erly and late to walke with licence
> With opyn walet frely en eche countre,
>   Her bul enselyd, concludyng in sentence
> That none of al þys ordyrs ys never like to the. Amen.

Lydgate's poem is a satirical picture of society, written in the familiar form of a descriptive list of actions predicated of the fool. It is in the direct line of descent from such French and English didactic pieces as the vernacular *Catoes,* the lists of follies, or the book of Solomon's wisdom. In tone, however, it is different from these, for it connects with the fool a variety of attitudes according to which he is not purely despicable. It assumes an "order" of fools, and that assumption in itself raises an image of Goliardic gaiety, or at least of the comforts of Bel-Eyse. It invokes Bacchus and Juno to sponsor the festivities of the order, and further it places the whole order under the patronage of Marcolf, who was not a character to be despised, considering his triumphant history. With this introduction, it is impossible to take too seriously the list of errors that follows, although each stanza reiterates that the fools shall never prosper. The chief fool of all, of course, is still he who neither loves nor fears God, and it is assumed that man's goal is in heaven. But the reader of Lydgate's poem who knows Marcolf and remembers the pictures of the Dance of Death cannot condemn the fools as severely as he would had he confined his reading to the works of the moralists who taught that folly was explicitly sin. The occasional defeat of one wisdom by another shrewder wisdom, the different sets of moral codes at war in the world, the inevitability of death and the need for levity all gave the apparently witless or ignorant fool a chance of triumphing.

CHAPTER IV

THE FOOL IN PERSON

Le rire est un des nombreux pépins contenus dans la pomme symbolique.
—*Baudelaire*

"Fool" may be a term either figurative or actual. The fools condemned or applauded by the writers of moral guidebooks, tributes to innocence, semi-facetious lists of follies, were not seriously thought to be genuine half-wits, nor had they intentionally assumed an appearance of half-wittedness. The critical observer contrasting their behavior with other types of action dubbed it foolish. In so doing he spoke metaphorically, referring the mistaken or ludicrous act to a genuinely defective human being. During the years when the term "fool" was a popular metaphor standing for "indiscreet," "sinful," "innocent," or "carefree," these genuine defectives, or other sane people masquerading as fools, were however really visible in towns, in cloisters, in manor houses. They supplied living illustrations of the fool's ignominy, of his irresponsible wantonness and hilarity, of his occasional rise to power from low estate, and of the freedom which his "innocence" won for him. The real fools were cared for by individuals or communities. They were harbored by noblemen as harmless dependents and butts of merriment, playing aimless pranks and uttering confused talk. Or they remained in their villages, regarded with a mixture of disdain and superstitious awe as the privileged children of God, "sacred beings having some mysterious connection with the unknown."[1] Masquerading fools took advantage of the blend of disdainful tolerance and awe with which the real fool was regarded and claimed in the name of folly the particular privileges of high spirits and irresponsibility. Villagers perpetuating ancient traditions included fools in the cast of characters of their spring games and dances. The lower orders of the clergy made use of the title of fool to cover their ribaldries in the festivals of defiant high spirits with which they too celebrated Christmas and early spring. Some early groups of semi-professional French actors adopted the costume and name of fool and so obtained a particular satirical and moral effect in certain of their plays, as well as the freedom to rough-house and to criticize the authorities. The outcast condition of the tolerated domestic fool—his failure—and his occasional seasons of triumph were real facts, made apparent in the persons of jesters, festival fools and actors. These facts, as one can gather them from miscellaneous narratives and records and from the history of the companies of actor-fools, all played a part in the emergence of the fool as a symbol of man's nature.

The domestic fool, either in country house or court, may have been either a real half-wit or "natural," more or less cunning and sarcastical, or an "artificial" fool.[2] The essence of his folly was that it should be harmless. The folly of the feudal baron who let his estate fall into ruin was the failure of a reasonable person to do what society expected of him. But the family jester was not supposed to be able to make a coherent response to the demands of society. If he was really an idiot, his stupidity amused and diverted his master. If he was an artificial fool, his assumed "innocence" lowered him beyond the reach of vengeance and left him free to speak his mind, a freedom which he sometimes used to criticize his master.

The practice of keeping domestic fools had long been popular when Lydgate wrote his *Order of Fools*. The records of fools retained at the courts of the kings of England and France begin in the early days of both monarchies. Rigollot finds one in

France in the reign of Hugh Capet.[3] The English line probably began with Hitard, the fool of Edmund Ironside, who left
his property, received from the king in payment for his services,
to the cathedral of Canterbury.[4] From that time on, an un-
broken line of men and women served as fools to the sovereigns
of the two countries. Less is known of fools kept by private
persons than of the fools of royalty, but that they were generally kept is likely. In 906 it was forbidden on canonical
authority that any churchman should keep a domestic fool,[5]
perhaps because, as the song records

> Les fables d'Artur de Bretaigne
> E les chançons de Charlemaigne
> Plus sont cheries e meins viles
> Que ne soient les evangiles.
> Plus est escoutés li jugliere
> Que ne soit saint Pol ou saint Pierre,
> E plus est hui cest jor li fol
> Oïz que saint Pierre ou saint Pol.[6]

In the early sixteenth century, however, no less a churchman
than Wolsey kept his fools;[7] Sir Thomas More retained a
household fool, an ex-mummer crazed by a fall from a church
steeple,[8] and a series of famous fools, real and artificial, served
the royal houses of France and England. One wonders who these
men can have been who consented to make sport of themselves
for the powerful. Triboulet, fool of Louis XII, was apparently
a shrewd half-wit; Caillette, fool of Francis I, is supposed to
have been really imbecile, and Brusquet, the cruel jester of
the French court in the mid-century, was a deformed rachitic.
The stories told of him show a malignity which appears in none
of the other well-known fools of the time.[9] In England, Will
Somers seems to have been a kindly and amusing innocent.
After him, little is heard of English fools except of those who
"play the fool" on the stage, like Tarleton, and both in France
and England the practice of keeping fools fell into disuse in

the seventeenth century. Perhaps the growth of humanitarian sensibility combined with a preference for considering man as a reasonable animal to make the spectacle of the domestic fool intolerable.

The fool's actual lot in the household must have been a miserable one, however well he was treated in comparison with the other creatures in whose class he was supposed to be—the hounds and the horses. We read, to be sure, of kings who appreciated the services of their fools[10] and the "epytaphye of Lobe, the kynges foole" reflects an affectionate appreciation of his qualities, while it shows as well how the jester was the symbol both of the fool-condemned and the fool-tolerated:

O lobbe Lobe, on thy sowle God have mercye,
　　For as Petre ys *princeps apostolorum,*
Soo to the may be sayd clerlye,
　　Of alle foolys that ever was *stultus stultorum.*
　　Sure thy sowle ys yn *regna polorum,*
By reason of reason thow haddest none,
Yet alle follys be nott ded, Lobe, thouȝh thou be gone.

The losse of the, Lobe, maketh many sorye,
　　Thouȝhe ytt be nott alle for thyn awn sake,
Butt the kyng and the quene thou madyst so merye,
　　With the many good pastimes that thou dydes make.
　　Thy lyfe to be bought, I dare undurtake,
Gold nor sylver there shuld lake none;
Yet foolys be inoghe, thouȝhe thou be gone.

Thow wast a foole, withowten fraude,
　　Shapte and borne of very nature,
Of alle good follys to the may be laude,
　　For every man yn the hade gret plesure:
　　For owre kyng and quene thou wast a tresure.
Alas for them! wher shuld we have suche on?
Yet alle foolys be nott deed, thouȝhe thou be gone.

Thow wast nother Erasmus nor Luter,
　　Thou dydes medle no forther then thy potte!
Against hye matters thou wast noo dysputer,
　　Among the Innocentes electe was thy lotte!

Glade mayst thow be thou haddyst that knotte,
For many folys by the thynke themselfe none,
Yet alle be not deed, Lobe, thouȝhe thou be gone.

Tyt Apgnyllamys, prepare his obsequi,
  Nature constrenyth yow to doo hym good,
The mad ladye Apylton offer the masse penye,
  And ye as chefe moerner yn your own folys hode.
  Your wyttes were myche lyke, thouȝe nothyng of blode.
Save yn hym was muche goodness and yn yow ys none,
Yet ye be a foole and Lobe ys gonne.

Now lobbe Lobe, God have mercy on thy mery noole,
  And Lobe, God have mercye on thy folyshe face;
And Lobe, God have mercye on thy innocent sowle,
  Whyche amonges innocentes I am sure hath a place,
  Or ellys my sowle ys yn a hevy case;
Ye, ye, and mo foolys mony one,
For folys be alyve, Lobe, thouȝh thou be gone.

Nowe God have mercye on us alle,
  For wyse and folyshe alle dyethe;
Let us truly to owre myndes calle,
  And to say we be wyse owre dedes denyethe.
  Wherfore the ende my reason thys aplyethe,
God amend alle folys that thynke themselfe none,
For many be alyve, thouȝhe Lobe be gone.[11]

But the innocent led a hard life in the execution of his duty:

Once engaged, the poor slave—for he was little else—could not
sleep out of the palace unpermitted, without danger of a whipping
when he returned. Neither could he lay aside his dress, without sanction of his master; and even then, were he to clap a sword on his
thigh, and so try to pass abroad for a gentleman, and this offence
came to the ears of the "king of the ribalds," the provost marshal
of the King's household, the fool might reckon on being scourged
till the blood ran down to his heels. Further, it does not appear
that the fool could at will divest himself of his office. He was
bound to serve, and it was only the royal word that could set
him free from his bonds.[12]

King Robert of Sicily, who failed to humble his spirit at even-
song upon hearing the words "Deposuit potentes de sede et

exaltavit humiles," was punished for his pride by being transformed into a fool and set to caper in his own palace. He ex-
perienced to the full the degradation that accompanied the
rôle of jester:

> He was evyr so harde bestadd,
> That mete nor drynke noon he had,
> But hys babulle was in hys hande . . .
> Honger and thurste he had fulle grete:
> For he myght no mete ete.
> But howndys ete of hys dysche,
> Whedur hyt were flesche or fysche.
> When that the howndes had etyn ther fylle,
> Then my3t he ete at hys wylle. . . .
> Ther was not in the court grome ne page,
> But they of the kyng made game and rage:
> For no man myght hym not knowe,
> He was so dysfygerde in a throwe.[13]

To chastise him for continued insubordination, an angel gave
him for counsellor an ape, and decreed that his head should
be shorn. The conclusion of the sympathetic chronicler was
that,

> At lower degre he myght not bee,
> Then become a fole, as thynketh me.[14]

Whatever the privileges of the fool, his position must have
been deeply humiliating to any jester who had ambition for
worldly respect. One is glad that the stories of domestic fools
seem to indicate that they were most often mentally defective,
and that the greater number of fools of whom we read,—the
folk fools, the fools in plays, and the fools of carnivals,—were
mock fools who could abandon the rôle when it wearied them.

The stories told of the domestic fool are all similar, from
whatever time they date. They preserve incidents showing his
unreason in situations which can almost always be moralized
upon, or comments of his which can be satirically interpreted.

The *Speculum Laicorum* used stories of fools to illustrate religious axioms. For instance:

De amore mundi et ejus fallaciis. . . .
   Fertur quod in domo cujusdam divitis fuit quidam stultus nomine Philippus, Cui una die dominus suus dedit novam tunicam. Qua induta, discurrit per aulam et ceteras domus officinas requirens quis esset, Philippus stultus non cognoscens seipsum propter novam tunicam, Sic est de amatoribus mundi qui propter divicias et honores seculi excecati non respiciunt corporis fragilitatem, nec anime salutem.[15]

Or again:

De avaricia et ejus effectibus. . . .
   Stultus quidam habens nova calciamenta abscondit eo in sinu quo vadens per loca aspera et cum graviter pedem lesisset, gaudebat eo quod calciamenta essent illesa. Sic avarus omni lesioni corporis et anime exponit se, ut res suas conservet illesas.[16]

An epigram of John Heywood preserves a saying of "Patch, my Lord Cardinal's Fool" which has no more sense than these actions of the fourteenth century fools:

> Master Sexton, a person of unknowen wit,
> As he at my lord cardinal's board did sit,
> Greedily caught at a goblet of wine.
> "Drink none!" said my lord, "for that sore leg of thine."
> "I warrant, your Grace," quoth Sexton, "I provide
> For my leg; for I drinke on the tother side."[17]

Sir Thomas More's fool was not much wittier.[18] But one of the chief pleasures to be enjoyed by those who watched the fool arose from the satirical interpretations which could be put upon some of his prattlings.

   The fool's prattle was his chief means of amusing his employers, aside from awkward acrobatics and practical jokes. The piquancy of his nonsense lay in the gleams of truth which his simplicity or his wit allowed at times to come through the main stream of babble. His "happy unhappy answers" were the source of his success.[19] But records of the spontaneous chatter of household fools of course do not exist. Our idea of that chatter comes from records of the talk of pseudo-fools, persons who for one reason or another played the rôle of fool.

To impersonate the dullard, the booby, the dupe, the silly fellow, is a commonplace with comic entertainers at all times, and in the thirteenth century, as today, men amused themselves and their companions by playing the fool:

> L'uns fait l'ivre, l'autre le sot,
> Lis uns chante, li autres note,
> Et li autres dit la *Riote*,
> Et li autres la *Jonglerie* . . .[20]

Traveling players continued to include impersonations of the fool in their repertory up to the sixteenth century anyway, for one such actor, Verconus, has recorded in the prologue to his entertainment the different characters which he was prepared to represent. They included the court dandy, the falconer, the lawyer, and the fool:

> Si j'ay ung chaperon à fol
> Passé au travers de mon col
> Je contrefais le bien disant,
> Abordant a menuz flajolz:
> Onc on n'en veit de si plaisant.[21]

The simplest kind of fool's talk is probably that simulated by the emperor's son in the miracle play, who made himself a fool out of penitence and sorrow:

> Tureluru, va, turelu:
> Jouer m'estuet d'anchanterie:
> Non feray pour l'enchanterie
> De la feste sainte Susanne.
> Querre me convient dame Osanne,
> Qui m'endort par nuit à filer.
> Mes ongles me fault affiler
> Au bec d'un coq de blanc plumage:

> J'ay plus chier lait cler et humage
> Que burre mol.

The reaction of the hearers to this speech is probably much like the reaction met with by many fools in actuality:

> En sa sotie se deduit
> Moult joliement, ce li semble.
> Empognons boe et terre ensemble
> Et quanque pourrons amasser;
> Si le faisons avant passer
> En li ruant.[22]

The impersonation of the fool by the emperor's son in this play was an integral part of the action and was genuinely motivated by the idea of sanctity through humility which is the thesis of the play. But in other religious plays, especially the mystery plays, fools' rôles appeared which had nothing much to do with the action, or which were distinctly a facetious comment upon it. In these plays fool's chatter frequently conveyed a crude satirical comment upon either actors or audience.

The mystery plays required some form of comic relief to lighten the strain they put upon their audience's attention. These day-long dramas, still given all over Europe during the fifteenth and early sixteenth centuries, narrated the mysteries of faith while utilizing the play instinct of the villagers and bourgeois who sponsored their production. They were conceived for the most part in a solemn mood, with proper attention to the supernatural end of man. As Saint Genevieve admonished the citizens of Paris in one play:

> Laissiez le rire et le juouer:
> Joiaus, chancons, dances, karoles,
> Dex n'a cure de telz frivoles;
> Pleurer fault qui veult avoir joye.[23]

But no such mood could be sustained throughout a three-day play like the *Passion* given at Amiens in 1445.[24] Comic relief was a necessity. The various villains of the Scripture story, Herod, the devils, the executioners, certain groups of Jews, were humorously represented, but the producers evidently felt the need of introducing some entirely irrelevant diversion. The text of a *Nativity* given at Rouen in 1474 bears the direction: "On placera ici quelque récit propre à récréer joyeusement l'esprit des auditeurs."[25] Although the fool is a "personage assez déplacé" in a saint's life or in a scriptural episode, his sheer irrelevance makes him a suitable variation by way of interlude. In the *Mystere de Saint Bernard de Menthon,* the fool amused the crowd during the exit from the first day's performance.[26] In the Troyes *Passion,* his part, added in the margin of the text in a different hand, was made up of hits at local characters and places.[27] His function was to afford complete relaxation to spectators who had been following attentively a story of serious import for them.

The relaxation afforded by the fool's babble was increased in some of the plays by the facetious criticism which he leveled at the action or at the world in general. In the *Mystere de Saint Didier* he delivered himself of a long and playful monologue while the saint's body was being exposed for reverent observation:

> Je me veul faire enluminer
> De fine couleur de Beaulne,
> Je vous dis que pour choppiner
> J'y suis docteur, non pas bec jaulne.
> Scavez-vous point pourquoy un asne
> A si grans oreilles, beau pere?
> Non dea. C'est pour ce que sa mere
> Ne luy myt point de beguynet
> Pour sarrer ung petit sa teste.
> N'est-ce pas une saige beste
> Que d'ung asne? Mydieux! ouy!
> Il m'a maintes fois resjouy
> Par ses deoulx et gravieulx chants.[28]

He had something to say about the current fashions:

> Dea! appertient-il que Robin
> Ou Jehannyn, Jehannet de villaige,
> Soit fourre de divers plumaige,
> Comme s'il estoit de bon lieu?
> J'y pourvoyray, par le sang bieu!
> Puisque je l'ay mis en ma teste.
> Vous semble il qu'il soit bien honneste
> De porter ces robbes trainans?
> J'ordonne qu'aux gentilz galans
> Qui les traynnent parmy l'ordure,
> Qu'on leur retranche, a bout taillans,
> Deux doiz par dessoubz la saincture. . . .[29]

In the *Saint Bernard* he expressed his views on marriage while the saint was praying to be delivered from his impending nuptials.[30] Like Marcolf, he made the realistic comment upon the solemn or idealistic efforts of the heroes. The deeds of the wise or saintly are after all the deeds of fools. In *Saint Christophe,* the fool frankly burlesqued the actions of the saint. Christopher lies by the river asleep, waiting for inspiration; the "fol" comes by, finds "la folle," and attempts to carry her across the river, but succeeds only in dropping her in.[31]

This freedom to indulge in parody and unexpected truth-telling, and the additional freedom to be wantonly licentious without incurring blame are the two privileges of the fool which made it worth the while of normal men occasionally to assume his rôle. Upon these two freedoms, therefore, most of the activities of the mock fool were based. The privilege of free criticism is of course the more interesting. Marot, perhaps, claimed it when he assumed the name of Triboulet, the royal fool, to cover his attack upon Marguerite de Navarre.[32] The pseudonym of Chicot, fool to Henry IV, was used by pamphleteers under the League,[33] and many fools of the Elizabethan drama were counsellors in disguise. The type of such criticism is preserved in *The Sage Fool's Testament,* a prose piece contemporary with the *Order of Fools*. It tells the story of a fool who fell ill, and made a testament leaving his soul to the devil, his bed to his mistress, his bauble to his master's almoner, his hood to his master's steward, and his money to his master. When his master, the young heir of the house, asked him why he disposed of his property in this way he replied:

"I have lovyd so well your fadyr, þat I Covett & Dessyre to be in hys Company Above All thyngis, for he lovyd me so well. And I know well þat he ys in hell; wherfor I wolde be with hym. And I gyve to my lady your wyffe my Bedde, be Cawse þat she myghte lye on hyt; for now she lyethe so softe, þat hyt ys All-moste none every day or þat she Ryse. And to your Steward, my hode; be Cawse hyt hathe iiij erys. for where ye put All your truste in hym, to pay your Credytour & the pore pepyll, he may not here. And to your Amner, my Babyll: Be Cawse when he de-lyveryth your Almys A-monge the pore pepull, they prese on hym, & thene he betis them with hys Staffe, þat the Blode Ron Abowte there erys; & my babyll ys Softer. And, my lorde, to yow I geve All my money þat I have gatheryd, bothe in your servyse & my lord your fadyrs, to geve in Almus."

"Whye," seyd the lorde, "thowe knoweste þat I have money more then thow." Then sayd the fole "All that money þat ye have, & I to, wyll not Restore the wronge þat your fadyr hathe don, whyche ys in hell. And thedyr ye goe withowte Amentement; & therfor I geve yow All my money."[34]

The privilege of telling the truth to one's master in this way was utilized by the Joyous Societies whose pieces were played in Paris and other cities of France during the reigns of Louis XII and Francis I. It produced the series of plays known as "sotties" in which the fool characteristically served as the vehicle of a crude but lively satire. Louis XII at least knew the value of this outspoken comment, and protected the play-ers. But before studying those plays in which the mock fool took advantage of his temporary liberty to criticise the powerful, we must look at examples of that other liberty, the freedom to in-dulge unrestrained exuberance in incontinence of all sorts, which is expressed in the rôles of the fools in the degenerate remains of primitive cult, in folk plays and carnival revelries.

"Cult," says Chambers, "the sum of what man feels it obligatory upon him to do in virtue of his relation to the unseen powers, is notoriously a more enduring thing than belief, the speculative, or mythology, the imaginative statement of those relations."[35] Cult represents vitality making an effort to survive. It is a commonplace that since survival depends in part upon fecundity, one phase of any cult is likely to involve some form of sexual licentiousness. Barrenness and the extinction of the race, death and the extinction of the individual, are two fundamental human fears. The wantonness of the idiot or half-wit, "the great natural who runs lolling up and down to hide his bauble in a hole," fits him for a rôle in this cult. The outstanding characteristic of the folk fool is his power magically to revive himself and to propagate. He represents the most elementary biological wisdom, shared by men and animals alike.

The Dance of Death was a pageant of human defeat, and in that sense a pageant of human folly. Neither the fool nor any of the other mortals in the paintings of the Dance had any power over his fate. Stage representations of this history of man must have driven home its point with solemn emphasis. Twice during the fifteenth century, in eastern France, a "certain jeu, histoire et moralité sur le fait de la danse macabre" was acted,[36] and the mood seems to have extended to other types of plays as well, for in *La Mort de Narcissus,* a morality from the first decade of the sixteenth century, a fool, symbol here of humility, delivers an epilogue in the manner of the *Danse* moralizings:

> Bourgeoises, filles et pucelles,
> Fuyez de tout outrecuidance.

. . . .

Ne soyez pourtant cruelles
Vers vos servants d'humble souffrance;
Vous pouriez danser a la danse
A laquelle Narcissus danse,
Qui est mort par son orgueil.[37]

The performance of such plays might move the audience to philosophical resignation, but it would have no power to affect the forces of death. The plays of the carnival season, however, and in general all the springtime games, were in their origins a kind of sympathetic magic prophesying, encouraging and even coöperating with the rebirth of fertility in the land. If the death of the individual could not be prevented, at least man could assist in killing Winter and in bringing in Spring. Remains of these agricultural festivals persisted in fifteenth and sixteenth century England in the various morris dances, May-games, mummers' plays, on the continent in carnival customs in the country districts, and in the German carnival plays or Fastnachtspiele. The chief patterns of these traditional cult-games are familiar:—the marriage of the vegetation deities, or of the earth and sky, which goes back into the earliest known remains of cult and survives in the various May-day pairs, Robin Hood and Maid Marion, the Lord and Lady of the May, the May King and the May Queen; the death and resurrection of the fertility god—Attis, Adonis, Osiris and Balder—which is preserved in the sword dance; and the driving out of Death, Winter, or evil, which also found one of its embodiments in the sword dance. In most of these game-narratives of the cycle of life the fool is present, sometimes as protagonist, sometimes as hanger-on. Sometimes he is frankly lecherous; sometimes he is distinguished only by his childish babble and the animal attributes of his costume, but he is evidently considered indispensable, and he seems to bear witness to the fact that life itself must exist before the reason can function.[38]

The fool is a constant figure in the various versions of the morris dance, and is apt to be the central figure of the pantomime. In the Durham arrangement he is named Tommy, has a wife Bessy, and is accompanied by five dancers. In one of the Yorkshire versions he is called Thomas the Clown, his wife is Bridget, and they have a son Tom. Another Durham version describes him simply as the fool, makes him treasurer of the group, and gives him as a companion one Bessy, who wears a tail.[39] A morris dance from Bampton-in-the-Bush, near Oxford, was described in 1897 as consisting of eight dancers, a fiddler and a clown "called the Squire, dressed in whatever motley is available, who carries a staff with a calf's tail at one end and a bladder at the other, with which he belabors the bystanders."[40] This bladder, often combined with a fox's brush or a cow's tail which hangs from the other end of the club, is the distinctive equipment of the folk-fool. In the descriptions of the "ridings" of the Guild of St. George, the fool is referred to simply as the "club-bearer," and in later ridings of the Guild down into the eighteenth century, "Dick fools" in motley, with cats' tails and bells attended.[41]

In the Revesby Sword Play, into which the plough boys who gave it have condensed most of the features of the fertility-ritual survivals, the fool represents the god, and is slain, revived, and woos the woman Cicely.[42] In other sword dances his rôle is less important. He appears, however, in all mutations of the St. George plays, even though he has no more to do than to conduct the quête. In a Staffordshire version he is named Bellzebub, and comes in carrying a club and a ladle, with a bell tied at his back:

> Here comes one as never come yet,
> With a large head and a little wit.
> Although my wit it is so small,
> I've got enough to please you all.
> Ah, ah, ah, how funny!
> All these fine new things and no money!

> My name is called old Bellzebub,
> And over my left shoulder I carry a club,
> And over my right shoulder a small dripping pan,
> And I call myself a jolly old man.

He then sings:

> My coat is all pitches and patches,
> And when shall I get new?
> As I find my old worthy my slaver,
> Brave boys, if I'm ragged I'm true.[43]

Although named for a devil, this character is evidently a fool
—perhaps an unsuccessful devil sunk to the level of a fool—
he is witless and ragged, but he gets the money.

In May-games too the fool appeared, for, as Laneham's letter witnesses, where there was a "Mawdmarion" there was a
fool.[44] He was present doubtless at the May-game which
Machyn saw in Fanchurch Street on May 30, 1557, where
there were drums and guns, and a procession of the Nine Worth-
ies, "and they had speches evere man, and the morris dansse
and the sauden, and a elevant with castyll, and the sauden and
yonge morens with targattes and dartes and the lord and the
lade of the Maye."[45] A fifteenth century wood-cut reproduced
by Douce represents the figures of a morris dance in an ara-
besque of foliage. In the midst of the picture is a tree in which
stands a female, presumably the Lady of the May, while at the
foot of the tree below her a personage wearing a capuchon with
long ears makes gestures of devotion in her direction.[46]

The Church which in early days had encouraged the trans-
formation of pagan shrines into Christian places of worship,[47]
was rigorous in condemnation of these dramatic remains of
pagan custom. The Christian cult of chastity would evidently
be unable to admit the primitive and paradoxical wisdom of
incontinence, and the church authorities very sensibly distrusted
the effect of such performances upon the players themselves.

Most obnoxious of all was probably the presence in these plays of the professional actor, against whom the church had fought since its early years. Obscenity of language and gesture became the folk fool in his ritual rôle particularly well, but it also was and is the common property of all performers of low comedy. Since the serious propitiatory purpose of the rituals themselves must have been extinct long before the thirteenth century, no hangover of religious significance need have excluded the traveling player from taking part in the folk-plays along with the villagers. The task of the actor was entertainment, largely through horse-play, acrobatics, more or less gross witticism, and impersonation. We know from the monologue of Verconus that the rôle of fool was included in his repertory and that he was at times hired to play that part in the performances of the townspeople.[48] If this were the case, a part of the opprobrium visited upon the mime by the Church might have been passed on to the folk game itself, and its participants.[49] But the attack of the Church aimed also at the plays themselves, in so far as they were survivals of an unconquered religion, and was probably dictated in part by prudence, since we are told that a favorite device of the mimes was the parodying of Christian practices.[50] There were many good reasons why the Church, in the name of wisdom, would condemn the celebrations in which the folk fool took part. But the impulse to see and to take part in shows was ineradicable. Actors flourished, although outlawed by official society, and delighted their audiences with buffoonery and repartee. University students and the lower orders of the clergy continued to indulge their naïve vitality in outbursts of rowdy gamboling and to relieve the tedium of sustained reasonableness by playing the fool. The freedom to be irresponsible is at times a better reward for good conduct than the promise of heaven. One sees with amusement the clergy of the fifteenth century struggling to suppress the clerical "mimi" who within the Church itself had cultivated a mock ritual, a recurrent cult of unreason, featuring the fool.

Yearly, during the period of the Christmas liberties with its reminiscences of the Saturnalia and the Kalends of January, a festival took place in the church which had for its motto the words of Solomon: Deposuit potentes de sede et exaltavit humiles. This feast was not long dead on the continent by the time of Rabelais and Erasmus, and was not unknown even to Dekker. The hopeful humility of its text establishes a slight connection between it and Gregory's idea of the final triumph of the innocent fools of this world. It is, however, far more closely connected with the celebrations in which the folk-fool took part, and like them it takes us from the study of reasoned reflection upon conduct into the dimmer regions of folk-custom. It banishes the judging mind and turns to imprudent gaiety to enhance the passing moment.

The Feast of Fools, from the twelfth century when we begin to hear of it until long after it had been officially suppressed, fell somewhere in the season of revelry lying between St. Nicholas' day, December sixth, and Candlemas. Neither its name nor the date of its celebration was constantly the same. Although it was the definite prerogative of that fourth order in the church, the sub-deacons, and followed similar but less notorious festivals of the other orders—priests, deacons, and choir-children—it was variously referred to as the "festum stultorum" or "fatuorum," "follorum," "subdiaconorum," as the "festum baculi" or as the "asinaria festa." Joannes Belethus, a Paris theologian and dignitary of the cathedral of Amiens who is one of the first to mention the feast, says that it was held either on the day of Circumcision (January 1), on Epiphany (January 6), or on the octave of Epiphany.[51]

Like the secular festivals in which the folk fool played, it was constantly under attack. Between 1400 and 1450 the faculty of theology of the University of Paris, following the precedent of various bishops of times past, undertook to root out what they described as

quem superstitiosum et scandalosum ritum quem quidem festum fatuorum vocant, qui a ritu paganorum et infidelium idolatria initium et originem sumpsit.[52]

Gerson, in 1400, had also denounced the festival as "impious and mad . . . a relic of pagan sacrileges and idolatrous rites." Indeed, said he,

fatui sunt ipsi, et perniciosi fatui, nec sustinendi, opus est executione.

He goes on to describe the celebration as one

ubi fit irrisio detestabilis Servitii Domini et sacramentorum: ubi plura fiunt impudenter et execrabiliter quam fieri debent in tabernis vel prostibulis, vel apud Sarcenos et Judaos. . . . Hae enim insolentiae non dicerentur coces in eorum culina absque dedecore aut reprehensione, quae ibi fiunt in eclesiis sacrosanctis.[53]

The order of service for the feast of the sub-deacons is preserved in a missal from Sens, attributed to Pierre de Corbeil, a twelfth-century prelate.[54] It does not seem to justify the indignation of Gerson and the Paris faculty. The feast should take place on the first of January. On the Eve, vespers were to be sung "in ianuis ecclesiae" and included an invitation to rejoicing:

Novus annus hodie
Monet nos laetitiae
laudes inchoare.

The order for the day closed with a Conductus ad Poculum and a Versus ad Prandium.

This description does not give us a great deal of satisfaction as to the exact nature of the celebration, and does not at all explain the presence of the Prose of the Ass in the ritual. More light is shed by the negative description of how the feast in Paris was *not* to be kept, after the reforms of bishop Eudes de Sully, the contemporary of Pierre de Corbeil, went into effect in 1199. In the first place, the bells for vespers on the eve of Circumcision were to be rung in the usual way. There were to be no songs, no masks, no extra lights. The lord of the feast was not to be led in a procession with singing through the streets to the cathedral and back to his home, but was to put on the cope in the choir and with the "baculus" in his hand to start the singing of the Prosa—the interpolated *Laetemur gaudiis*. All was to go on as usual during the Hours and at Mass on the day itself, except that the Epistle at the Mass may be "cum farsis," but at vespers on the day of Circumcision the *Laetemur gaudiis* was to be sung again along with *Laetabundus*, after which the *Deposuit* was to be sung five times at the most. Then, if the "baculus" had been handed over to the new representative of the sub-deacons, the regular officiant was to close the service.[55]

This again seems a mild performance to have brought down such wrath upon itself, but the accusations of the Paris faculty at the time of its attack upon the feast show what it could turn into when the clerical revelers gave rein to their spirits:

Priests and clerks may be seen wearing masks and monstrous visages at the hours of office. They dance in the choir dressed as women, panders or minstrels. They sing wanton songs. They eat black puddings at the horn of the altar while the celebrant is saying mass. They play at dice there. They cense with stinking smoke from the soles of old shoes. They run and leap through the church without a blush at their own shame. Finally they drive about the town and its theatres in shabby traps and carts; and rouse performances, with indecent gestures and verses scurrilous and unchaste.[56]

With this riotous coursing through the town went, naturally enough, the giving of playlets. In 1490, on the day after the Feast of the Innocents, the deacons, sub-deacons and choir boys of the cathedral of Reims, at the instigation of the lord of the Bazoche, gave a play on a stage erected in front of the church, in which certain rhymes of Coquillart, ridiculing the women of the city, were recited. The husbands of the insulted ladies took offence and put on a retaliatory farce ridiculing the members of the chapter.[57] At Tournai in 1498 more scurrilous farces were presented, again in connection with the Festival of the Innocents. The bourgeois, exasperated by the suppression of the feasts, took matters into their own hands and elected one of the vicars "evesque des sotz," baptized him by torchlight with three buckets of water at a fountain and led him about with them for three days while they did their plays. It was the turn of the chapter to protest, and the affair took on the aspect of a row between it and the town. The Parlement at Paris judged the proceedings and found that at the end of his reign the mock bishop had distributed fools' hoods to his "suppotz" and had awarded some to members of the chapter who disliked the implication of the nodding ears.[58] As well as expressing his high spirits, the bishop had made use of the liberty of the fool to criticize his letters.

Chambers has made the important comment on these celebrations when he calls them "largely an ebullition of the natural lout beneath the cassock." The clerical louts celebrated much like any others, with eating, drinking, dancing, dicing, masquerading and making a general nuisance of themselves. The concept "fool," by its connection with them, was visibly extended beyond the image of the idiot to the vision of Bacchus and Juno setting abroach the tun while the orders of fools gather around for revelry. Their performances were candid displays of riotousness. The clerical celebrators took advantage of the freedom of the domestic fool to be his animal self. They also made use of his freedom to criticize, and gave plays whose asperity now and then got them into conflict with other groups in the community. They greeted the turn of the year by gamboling through the streets and churches as the folk fool gamboled a little later in the season, in the carnival and May-games. Although the Church condemned the feast, it could not obliterate the impulse from which it sprang. Feasts of Fools continued to be held in England up through the reign of Henry VII, dying out finally in the early years of the sixteenth century.[59] In France too they disappeared gradually, but their spirit and their particular concrete representation of the fool survived in the activities of the Joyous Societies, whose members like the sub-deacons were able to accept the natural lout as the natural man upon occasion, and who developed the use of the freedom of the fool to cover extensive attacks upon other fools.

Chapter V

THE JOYOUS SOCIETIES

Il y a moins d'inconvénients à être fou avec des fous, qu'à être sage tout seul.

—*Diderot*

The simplest triumph of the fool—the victory of impulse over reason—distinguished the riotous celebrations indulged in seasonally by the mock fools of the organized fool societies, some of which descended from the celebrators of the Feast of Fools. Under the guise of obeying pure impulse these mock-fools too could take liberties in criticizing their contemporaries which were denied to the avowedly sober. They stood in a sense like the folk fool for a licence and abandon opposed to the regular order of things but having about it the sanctity due simply to the sheer gusto of unorganized vitality. The folk fool and his analogue, the clerical fool, had represented outcroppings of subrational nature, and the Church in condemning them was trying, like the logical mind, to seize upon this vitality and canalize it into streams of effective conduct. But in spite of reason, human beings need to indulge

cet esprit de relâchement après le travail sérieux, relâchement effréné, l'abandon de soi-même à la folie, au charme de l'irresponsabilité, à un état qui a l'attrait irrésistible du contraste et de la nouveauté.[1]

When the Church finally suppressed the disorderly feasts they broke out again in a new form. In Dijon, the association presided over by Mère Folle inherited directly the tradition of the Feast of Fools.[2] Similar societies in Paris and Rouen, connected not with the Church but with the law courts, expressed also in their carnival stunts the same mocking and irrepressible gaiety. These societies and the many others like them continued to act out visibly the rôles of the fool-triumphant. In their plays appeared for the first time the figure of Mother Folly, the female jester who is also the approved censor of morals. She proved a genial mouthpiece for the utterance of satire, for the critics who through her drew attention to the folly of others had themselves claimed the rights of folly to unrestrained laughter, riotousness, and the giving of unasked-for advice, and she kept the figure of the fool present to the eyes as well as to the minds of the people who saw her.

The Church opened its last, and most successful, attack upon the Feast of Fools through the Council of Basel in 1435. It definitely prohibited the celebration of the feast, and was shortly afterwards supported, for the kingdom of France, by the so-called Pragmatic Sanction of Charles VII in 1438.[3] But both the Council and the King encountered opposition in the powerful province of Burgundy.

The Holy Chapel of the dukes of Burgundy at Dijon had been the seat of the Order of the Golden Fleece during the twelfth century. Although its chaplains were officially under the control of the diocese of Langres, they had been practically independent, had been received at table with the Burgundian dukes as "commenseaux à feaulté de bouche," and had furnished their religious directors. The officers of such a chapel were consequently in a position to oppose the dictates of their superiors at the Council with some chance of success, and to make a stand for the retention of their old privileges. Their duke, Philip the Good, a feudal dictator in his own regions, conceded to the members of his chapel in 1454 a Privilege allowing them to continue their accustomed celebration in spite of the decree of the King. The text of this Privilege gives a lively reality to the almost legendary festival:

Voulons, consentons, accordons,
Pour nous et pour nos successeurs
Des lieux ci-dessus dits Seigneurs,
Que ceste fête celebrée
Soit à jamais, un jour l'année,
Le premier du mois de janvier,
Et que joyeux Fous, sans dangier,
De l'habit de nostre chapelle
Fassent la fête bonne et belle,
Sans outrage et derision;
Et n'y soit contradiction
Mise par aucun des plus sages;
Mais la feront les Foux volages,
Doucement, tant que l'argent leur dure,
Un jour ou deux. Car chose dure
Seront de plus continuer,
Ni les frais plus avant bouter;
Par leurs finances qui decroissent
Lorsque leurs depenses accroissent.
Si mandons à tous nos sujets
Qu'en ce ne soyent empeschés;
Mais les en souffrent tous jouir
Paisiblement à leur plaisir.[4]

The members of the chapel therefore continued their annual feast, and had their privilege confirmed by Duke John of Amboise and the local governor, Baudricourt, in 1482.[5] This illegitimate celebration of the feast survived for nearly a hundred years, throughout the lifetimes of Erasmus and Brant. But in 1552 the ecclesiastical feast was abolished by the local parlement of Dijon and a new organization, the Mère Folle, inherited its privileges and its costume and the right of public criticism which the sub-deacons of the chapel royal had probably exercised in their day.

The new society masqueraded in the familiar equipment of the Feast of Fools. It was administered by a chief, Mère Folle, her lieutenant the "procureur fiscal" or Griffon vert, and a complicated subordinate organization. Admission was by examination. Meetings were held in the "tripot de la Poissonerie," where "six cent fols, a l'aise et bien assis" could foregather. They were summoned to

compaistre

Apporteant de quoy pour repaistre,

like a Sunday-school picnic, and this was the roll call:

> Fol folastrant, fol lunatique,
> Fol chimeric, fol fantastique,
> Fol jovial, fol gratieux,
> Fol courtisant, fol amoureux,
> Fol gaussant, fol contant goguettes,
> Fol gaillard, fol baisant fillettes,
> Fol fin et fol escervellé,
> Fol altéré, fol gabellé,
> Fol à la caboche legère,
> Fol cherchant faire bonne chiere,
> Fol aimant les morceaux choisis,
> Fol verd, fol teint en cramoisi,
> Fol en plein chant, fol en musique,
> Fol faisant aux sages la nique,
> Fol riant, fol gai, fol plaisant,
> Fol bien faisant, fol bien disant,
> Fol eventé, fol humoriste,
> Fol cault, fol pantagruéliste,
> Fol leger, fol escarbillat,
> Fol en folie esberlucat,
> Fol sur la terre, et fol sur l'onde,
> Fol en l'air, fol par tout le monde,
> Fol concluz, fol assis, fol debout,
> Fol ça, fol là, fol tout par tout.[6]

These "fools" evidently inherited the tradition of facetious public comment exercised by some of the groups of sub-deacons in their festivals—the right of the mock-half-wit to speak his mind. No early plays by Mère Folle remain to prove this, but a play still exists which in 1579 attacked the local superintendant of waters and forests, a certain M. Du Tillet, Parisian, who beat his wife. In certain parts of France wife-beating was only prohibited during the month of May[7] but in Dijon it was forbidden throughout the year. The Dijonnais therefore set out to satirize the wife-beater in a series of skits played by the Mère Folle. The first presented a plea to the wood spirits to rise up against the master of the forests, for,

> Le malheur a voulu qu'il a battu sa femme,
> Encore en ce pays, en estrange maison,
> Encore devant les gens, encore en tel saison!
> La battre au moys de may! n'est-ce pas ung difame?

Then came a discussion of the crime between two vine-growers and two fools, followed by an argument between Mère Folle, two of her suppôts and two Parisians, who claimed the right to discipline the offender because he himself was a Parisian. Finally Mother Folly received from Jupiter the decree that Du Tillet should be placed backward upon an ass and paraded through the town, and the piece was completed by a song by the satyrs upon courtesy to women.[8]

Later pieces by the society created the figure of Bontemps, a combination-symbol of peace and prosperity, whose acid reflections upon the policies of the governors of the province drew from Louis XIII an edict which crushed the society.[9] Its history nevertheless remains to show the intimate connection between the feast of fools, which fostered merry-making and allowed satirical play-acting, and the later lay societies which called themselves fools, wore the costume of folly, and specialized in playlets where the fool was both licentious and critical.

Petit de Julleville suggested that the Mère Folle of Dijon after 1552 was the result of a collaboration between an active bourgeoisie and a vigorous new law organization, the local Bazoche.[10] Such at any rate were the groups making up other societies who also practiced the fundamental wisdom of indulging their high spirits while exercising the fool's prerogative of free criticism. Paris, Rouen, Bordeaux, Poitiers and many other towns possessed in connection with their local courts brotherhoods of lawyer's clerks, known sometimes as the Kingdoms of the Bazoche, sometimes by more fanciful names, which enjoyed special liberty of comment at the holiday seasons. In addition to these brotherhoods—perhaps identical with them in personnel, perhaps recruited from another social level—existed non-professional Joyous Societies, whose most general title is that of the Paris order, the Enfants sans Souci. The exact relationship between the companies of the Enfants sans Souci and of the Bazouche is obscure, but everywhere they vied with one another over, or collaborated in, the carnival and mid-summer masqueradings and plays.[11] The Bazoche organizations throve in those central and southerly portions of France which had been Roman Gaul and had carried on the Roman legal tradition.[12] Northern France and Flanders, on the other hand, teemed with Joyous Societies. Martin Le Franc wrote:

> Va t'en aux festes de Tournay,
> A celles d'Arras et de Lille,
> D'Amiens, de Douay, de Cambray,
> De Valenciennes, d'Abbeville.
> La verras tu des gens dix mille,
> Plus qu'en la forest de Torfolz,
> Qui servent par sales, par villes,
> A ton duc, le prince des folz.[13]

The names of the societies in each of these cities, with the exception of Tournai and Abbeville, have been preserved. At Arras flourished "le Serment des Cannonniers," with a king, a constable, ten sub-officers and the brothers themselves.[14] "Le Rois de l'Epinette" in Lille went in for jousts and other exercises at arms.[15] Amiens had the "Sots" with their prince, who wore the fool's headdress and rode upon "chevaux d'osier enjupponnés." They held their celebration on the first of January, most generally supposed to have been the day of the ecclesiastical Feast of Fools.[16] Douai had three societies.[17] Cambrai, which itself had a number of companies, issued a yearly invitation to all similar orders in its vicinity to hold their mid-January gatherings in the town, and entertained as many as a hundred and fifty societies at once.[18] Valenciennes was represented by the "Compagnie du plat d'Argent" and the "Capitaine de l'Estrille."[19] The names of these companies suggest that, like the lodges and societies that flourish in America today, they gave their "suppôts" opportunity for dressing up and clowning as well as for jousting and marching in processions. The dates of their meetings and other bits of information about them connect them with the church feast, and, in France at least, the lay feasts seem to have retained the spontaneous rowdiness and the tradition of using in some way the idea of the inversion of status and the liberty of the fool which distinguished the church celebrations.[20] There is no evidence that the members of the Joyous Societies were as well educated as the members of the Bazoches must necessarily have been, or that they were a born breed of courageous critics; but when Bazoche and Joyous Society coöperated, as they did in Paris, Rouen and Dijon, high spirits, independence and a critical sense combined to satirize misguided conduct from under the protection afforded by the traditional irresponsibility of folly. Erasmus himself, one feels, might have enjoyed taking part in one of their satirical masquerades.

The Enfants sans Souci and the Bazochiens were, with the exception of the tellers of jest-anecdotes, the people who laid, as it were, the largest deposit of "fool" literature in French or English. They were not simply actors who were automatically called "fools," as the leader of the intrigue in later sixteenth century English plays was automatically called "vice." Their use of the idea of folly in their plays makes it clear that they intended their name to refer to a variety of attitudes toward weak and ignorant man. And each group contributed its special ability to the production of the style of play that remains as its comment on society.

With their cultivated pose of nonchalance and their insistence on the wisdom of making the best of things, the Enfants sans Souci set the tone of the holiday maskings of the city. The *Regrets et complaintes des gosiers altérés* apostrophized them thus:

> Facécieux Gens-Sans-Soucy,
> Vous passez temps joyeusement;
> Pleust à Dieu que feussions ainsi!
> Par vous fascherie est au vent.
> Hélas, et jouez plus souvent,
> Pour chasser deuil aucunes fois.
> Rejouissez honnestement
> Le pauvre monde qui n'a croix.[21]

The *Repues franches* took the same tone of wistful appreciation for the carefree if poverty-stricken company:

> Une assemblée de compagnons,
> Nommez les Gallans sans Soucy,
> Se trouvèrent entre deux ponts
> Pres le Palais, il est ainsi.
> D'autres y en avoit aussi
> Qui aymoient bien besoigne faicte
> Et estoient de franc coeur transi
> A l'abbé de Saincte Souffrette.[22]

They were poor, they were gallant, and they won the battles of Love, if not those of Luxury and Lucre, as the American Tiger Man is advertised to do.[23] Two opinions prevail as to the quality of their personnel: that they were mostly young men of good family whose professions allowed them ample time for gallivanting; or that they were not necessarily of good family but belonged to the "libre bohême de tous les temps, aussi riche de gaieté que pauvre de pécune."[24] But that in a period of rapid economic and intellectual change these two, the "libre bohême" and the "jeunes gens de famille" should have been one and the same, might not be impossible. An overproduction of students, or at least of those in whom some experience of education has aroused a capacity for social observation and greater self-consciousness, has today filled the ranks of the metropolitan theatrical companies with young people who could qualify in either of the two groups.[25]

Marot's ballade summed up what the Enfants had come to stand for by the early sixteenth century, during the time when Rabelais, or Erasmus, or the older Estiennes, may have seen their performances:

> Qui sont ceulx là qui ont si grand envie
> Dedans leur cueur, et triste marrisson
> Dont, ce pendant que nous sommes en vie,
> De Maistre Ennuy n'escoutons la leçon?
> Ilz ont grand' tort, veu qu'en bonne façon
> Nous consommons nostre fleurissant aage:
> Saulter, danser, chanter à l'advantage,
> Faulx Envieux, est ce chose qui blesse?
> Nenny, pour vray, mais toute gentilesse,
> Et Gay Vouloir qui nous tient en ses laqs.
> Ne blasmez point doncques nostre jeunesse,
> Car noble cueur ne cherche que soulas.
>
> Nous sommes druz, chagrin ne nous suyt mie;
> De froid soucy ne sentons le frisson;
> Mais dequoy sert une teste endormie?
> Autant qu'un boeuf dormant près d'un buysson.
> Languards picquans plus fort qu'un herisson,
> Et plus recluz qu'un vieil corbeau en cage,
> Jamais d'autruy ne tiennent bon language,
> Toujours s'en vont songeans quelque finesse,
> Mais entre nous nous vivons sans tristesse,
> Sans mal penser, plus aises que prelats.
> D'en dire mal c'est doncques grand' simplesse,
> Car noble cueur ne cherche que soulas.

> Bon cueur, bon corps, bonne phyzionomie,
> Boire matin, fuys noise et tanson;
> Dessue le soir pour l'amour de s'amyie
> Devant son huys la petite chanson;
> Trencher du brave et du maulvais garson,
> Aller de nuyct, sans faire aulcun oultrage,
> De retirer, voyla le tripotage;
> Le lendemain recommencer la presse.
> Conclusion: nous demandons liesse;
> De la tenir jamais ne fusmes las,
> Et maintenons que cela est noblesse;
> Car noble cueur ne cherche que soulas.[26]

. . . .

Such a group of intelligent and carefree "noble hearts," eager for "solace," was in an excellent position to criticize the existing order. Through the Bazoche they were connected with the law courts, and though the Bazochiens would certainly have been familiar with the public persons who from time to time became notorious, their rank in the service was yet humble enough so that they were in no way responsible for the failures or successes of the great. In such a set of circumstances, opinion is peculiarly free to comment on the passing show, provided the censor does not suppress it. And one of the most direct forms of comment is the little "act," the short dramatic skit, which is as popular today as in 1500.

Both Bazochiens and Enfants had been given to acting or masquerading of some sort from the beginning. On the second day of May, "l'an mil lllç. lllllxx et cinq," the "Galans sans souci, de la ville de Rouen" were paid eight pounds "tournois" for a performance at Reims before the Duke of Orleans.[27] In 1401 the account books of the town of Cambrai recorded on the ninth of January, "ce jour presenté au Prince des Folz du Palais, au Soupper, sur le marchiet ou il souppait desoubs une tente, VIII los de vin de XVI los."[28] But while the Joyous Societies alone may have been only "gosseurs," as Durand called the Conards of Rouen,[29] the dramatic activities of the

Bazoche seem to have been satirical from the start. Members of the association were sent to prison on a diet of bread and water for having played "satiras" without permission in 1442.[30] In 1476 the Parlement issued a grave warning:

La Cour a defendu et defent à tous clercs et serviteurs tant du Palais que du Chastelet de Paris, de quelque état qu'ils soient, que doresnavent ils ne jouent . . . farces, sotties, moralités, sur peine de bannissement de ce royaume et de confiscation de tous leurs biens.[31]

One year later, when Jehan l'éveillé was king of the Bazoche, the Court proclaimed that the playing of farces and moralities in any place whatsoever would be punished by a public beating.[32]

These satirical plays of the Bazoche were evidently similar to the plays given by the celebrators of the feast of fools in their offensive criticism of authorities or personalities. They were also probably similar to them in being given by actors dressed in the particular costume symbolic of folly. We know at least that in 1470 farces and moralities were acted in fool's costume, although the evidence applies to plays by students at the Paris Faculty of Arts rather than by the law clerks. The Faculty, meeting "ad providendum remedium de electione regis fatuorum," decreed "quod nullus scolaris assumeret habitum fatui pro illo anno, nec in collegio nec extra collegium, nisi forsan duntaxat ludendo farsam vel moralitatem."[33]

Clothes, it appears, often made the fool. The outstanding mark of the usual "habitum fatui," more familiar to fifteenth century Parisians than the skins and tails of the folk fool, was the bonnet or hood. This bonnet, either fitting the head closely or hanging loosely about the face, was garnished with two long ears, one on either side. The hood itself was a familiar piece of medieval apparel which did not become particularly associated with the fool until the fifteenth century, when it seems to have taken on the ears.[34] It had, rather, a monkish suggestion, suita-

ble to the learned professions. Marot's *Epître à Lyon Jamet*
proves that the members of the Bazoche, in their rôles as "sots,"
wore these hoods:

> Attache moy une sonnette
> Sur le front d'un moine crotté,
> Une oreille à chaque costé
> Du capuchon de sa caboche.
> Voilà un sot de la Bazoche
> Aussi bien painct qu'il est possible.[35]

Varieties of these hoods appear in Brueghel's print of the Fête
des Fous. The merrymakers all wear bonnets with small, ter-
rier-like ears on either side. Some of the fools have coxcombs
running down the middle of their bonnets; some wear hoods
which terminate in broad scalloped capes covering their should-
ers, while others seem simply to have on close-fitting jerkins
which continue up into a cap-like headpiece out of which sprout
the two little ears. The gowns are various also; some resemble
ordinary monkish robes, some are cut into points that hang
loose below the waist, others are plain peasant coats and still
others are adaptations of the long dress-like garment that was
the proper habit of the idiot. Bells are attached on elbows,
around ankles and knees, on hanging points of coats, and in one
or two cases on the ends of ears.[36] The revelers carry baubles
with heads like their own on the ends, and seem chiefly engaged
in playing musical instruments and in tossing about large, soft-
looking balls. The same type of bauble appears in two other
prints of carnival fools, but the ears in these pictures are much
longer than in the Feast and all terminate in bells.[37] Clothes
very like these were probably the acting costumes of the Bazoche and Enfants sans Souci, for the emblem of Gringore,
chief of the Enfants during the time of their greatest prestige,
represents three fools dressed in variations of this costume.[38]

The Brueghel pictures do not give any indication of the parti-
colored dress which we associate with the costume of the fool,

nor does the description of the suit made for Will Somers, the English court fool, suggest that any particular colors were *de rigueur* for professional fools.[39] But it is possible that the Enfants sans Souci and the other companies of the kind favored the combination of green and yellow for their costume as Sots. In a sonnet upon them, Jean Passerat describes the Enfants:

> L'un a la teste verte; et l'autre va couvert
> D'un joli chapperon, fait de jaune et de vert;
> L'un s'amuse aux grelots, l'autre à des sornettes.[40]

The appearance of this combination of colors may be accidental in some cases,[41] but as late as 1614, in the province of Champagne, a yellow and green costume was used in circumstances which made it appear the traditional color device for fools or "sots." The treasurer-general of the province had offended the Duke of Nevers by some official act. The retainers of the duke came to the treasurer's house

> environ les 6 heures du matin, comme nous étions encore au lict.

They got him up, made him dress in certain garments of disgrace and led him around all day. The undignified costume was

> faict par bandes de serge, moitié de couleur verte et l'autre de jaune; et là ou il y avoit des bandes jaunes il y avoit des passemens verts, et sur les verts des passemens jaunes: entre les bandes, il y avoit aussi du tafeta jaune et vert qui estoit cousu entre les dites bandes et passemens. Les bas de chausses cousus avec le haut estoient, l'un tout de serge verte et l'autre de jaune: et un bonnet aussi, moitié de jaune et vert, avec des oreilles.[42]

If yellow and green were indeed the most generally approved colors for the costumes of the Joyous Societies, the symbolism attached to them made them particularly fitting for companies claiming as their right the freedom of humility—licence in body and in mind. Yellow is said to have represented both gaiety and dishonor, while green stood both for ruin and for hope. "Crocum edisse," according to a collection of proverbs published in Paris in 1531, meant to burst out laughing; but the fool did not need the stimulus of safran—"Croco stultus non eget." On the other hand, yellow was the color of the avaricious, the cowardly, and the wanton in love, as well as of the deceived husband. Green, from Roman times, was a symbol of mourning as well as of hope, and Alciati's *Emblems* preserve evidence that these color symbolisms were still current in the early sixteenth century.[43]

One more perquisite was essential to the fool—his bauble.[44] Of these indispensable clubs there were two chief kinds, those that made a noise and those that served to strike with. Those that rattled—"une vessie de porc bien enflée et résonnante à cause des poys qui dedans estoient"[45] for instance—may have pleased the fool himself, and represented the hollowness of his babbling talk. The scourge, which one can take as the symbol of the satiric comment of the fool, was perhaps the instrument described in the fifteenth century word-books as "babulle" or "librilla."[46]

The hood with ears or cockscomb, the gown, perhaps of yellow and green, and the bauble—such was the "habitum fatui" against which the Faculty of Arts thundered. But the costume must have protected the clerks from the penalties threatened by the courts, for in spite of the decrees against them, the Bazochiens celebrated May day, 1486, with the performance of a morality attacking the ministers who were abusing their power during the minority of Charles VIII. The anonymity of the fool's costume would have been appropriate to this play, though there is no record that it was used. The royal authority is likened to a fountain of pure water which has been muddied by impurities,

> Herbes, racines,
> Roches, pierre, boue, et gravois,

terms uncomplimentary to the ministers. The leading spirit of this exploit, Henri Baude, was not unnaturally pursued, and when captured thrown into prison. The Parlement, however, interceded for him and obtained his freedom.[47]

Henri Baude has left two poems which express the attitudes of philosophical flippancy and facetious criticism which the Joyous Societies affected and which they embodied in their plays. Gaily, they say, man makes a hopeless fool of himself; and conversely, the hopeless fool is made free of the kingdom of carefree idleness and gaiety presided over by Bacchus. The *Moral Poem* explains itself:

> A l'estourdy, sans y veoir goutte,
> On fait souvent mainte follye;
> On va, on vient, on se marie,
> Et ne sçait-on ou l'on se boutte.

> On tire l'un, et l'autre on boutte,
> On menasse et apres on prye
> à l'estourdy.

> On parle assez, mais on n'escoute,
> Si ce n'est quelque menterie.
> On dispose, et puis on varie.
> On mesdit de tous somme toute
> à l'estourdy.[48]

The other poem calls up images of the paraphernalia of the *Order of Fools*. "Cadier, serf des serviteurs Bacchus," by right of his episcopacy over all those "de foi legiere et de sens indiscret" however they may be dressed, confers a cardinalcy in the order upon

> . . . un nostre filz que la lune a formé
> Que s'il avoit un bonnet enformé
> A oreilles, on verroit sa science.

The description of the candidate is brief, but includes many of the traditional weaknesses and ignorances of the fool:

> Bien confians de l'inlicterature,
> Engin cornu, cornue voulenté,
> Vouloir trop prompt, sans avoir soing ne cure
> Contre raison de sa propre nature,
> Riz sans propoz, propoz entallenté,
> Tallent, vouloir sans etre contenté,
> Content tousjours de dormir à toute heure,
> Posé travail, qui sans cesse labeur.

What he wins for these virtues is, as in Lydgate's poem, a patent "that he shall never the":

> La nuict veiller, ou dormir sur ung banc
> Et, au reveil, ne trouver pas un blanc
> En ta bourse, par grant humilité,
> Et pour pourvoir à la necessité
> Tu t'en iras bien souvent, sans lanterne,
> Te colloquer au fons d'une taverne.[49]

These poems, and the plays given in the costume of folly by the Paris societies and their fellow-actors in Rouen and other cities, combined gaiety,—sometimes, with the help of Bacchus, hilarity,—with the ordinary critical purpose of satire. They seemed to excuse and laugh at offenses against the established order because they called the offender only fool, and were themselves in fool's costume. Sometimes however too great acidity betrayed their serious intention. Louis XII treated the players kindly and found their critical activities useful to him,[50] but under later kings the liberty of the Bazoche and the Enfants was less well received and finally censored. Presumably when plays by the Bazochiens were suppressed, plays by the Enfants were too. But they left such a reputation behind them that the Abbé d'Aubignac a hundred years later seriously stated that "les Bazochiens furent comme les premiers comediens de ce royaume."[51] When they perished, the visible figures of Folly and the fool in cap and bells lost their most familiar representation and began to recede into that literary limbo where they languish at present.

Chapter VI

THE FOOL'S ROLES IN THE SOTTIES

I must have liberty
Withal, as large a charter as the wind
To blow on whom I please; so for fools have;
And they that are most galled with my folly,
They most must laugh.

—*Shakespeare*

The semi-professional actor-fools of the Joyous Societies put the figure of the fool to a variety of uses in their playlets. They presented him as a failure and as a success, as a lusty animal, as a critic, as an irresponsible mirthmaker. Dressed in tunic and long-eared hood, they simulated the fool now as a harmless amusing innocent, now as a creature to be condemned, now as both at once. In the rôles which they constructed for him to play, the metaphorical significance of "fool" to the moralist and theologian was embodied in the person of the jester, and he himself appeared as a dramatic formula denoting contrasting aspects of man's nature. From these living dramatic expressions of the qualities of the fool was abstracted the symbolic figure of Mother Folly herself. She emerged as the personification of all folly, grave or gay—the archetype of fifteenth-century cynicism.

The plays of the societies were called without careful distinction of genre either farces, moralities or sotties.[1] Modern scholarship has attempted to sort out from the remains of the repertories a group of "sotties" in which the content has some connection with the idea of the "fool" or "sot."[2] Various bases of differentiation have been suggested,[3] but the most plausible explanation for the use of the title is that the actors in "sotties" wore the costume of fools, the "habitum fatui" that the records show was often used in the playing of farces and moralities both.[4] If any play bears in its text signs of exploiting the fool-condemned or the fool-critic—of requiring the fool's costume—that play, whatever denominated by the printer or scribe, may legitimately be included among the sotties.[5] The fool's costume was suited to actors in farcical stunts, in dances and verbal patter, and pointed the satire in any skit upon contemporary events, however demurely performed. It gave a realistic explanation to the incoherent badinage which was one of the accepted literary forms of the times, the "fatrasie," and legitimately accompanied the other characteristics according to which M. Picot established his canon of the sottie repertory:

Les sotties se reconnaissent d'abord à leur titre, puis à leurs personnages désignés sous les noms de sots, de fous, de galants, de compagnons, de pèlerins, d'ermites; elles se reconnaissent enfin à leur dialogue dans lequel nous trouvons toujours des traces de la fatrasie.[6]

The style of broken badinage which appeared in the speeches of the fools in miracle and mystery plays and which was supposed to be a fair imitation of the real fool's talk had been admitted as a verse form for some time. It had appeared in the New Year's "concours poétique" at Amiens, and in other towns of Flanders and Picardie, as a "sotte amoureuse" or a "sotte chanson," and its chief excellence was described in the *Doctrinal de secunde retorique* of 1432:

Tant plus sont de sos mos et diverses et estranges rimes, et mieulx valent.[7]

The term "coq-à-l-âne" or "fatrasie" was used for this chaotic type of composition in the fifteenth and sixteenth centuries.[8] Sibilet in his *Art poétique* recognized that the coq-à-l'âne was a kind of satire, although he did not note its connection with the fool or its use in the sottie:

Sa matiere sont les vices de chacun, qui i sont repris librement par la suppression du nom de l'autheur. Sa plus grande elegance est sa plus grande absurdité de suite de propos, qui est augmentée par la ryme platte et les vers de huit syllabes.[9]

The author of the *Quintil Horatian,* two years later, pointed out the use of the verse form in playlets:

Parquoy, pour leurs propos ne s'ensuyvans, sont bien nommez du coq à l'asne telz enigmes satyrics, et non satyres, car satyre est autre chose; mais ilz sont satyrez, non pour la forme de leur facture mais pour la sentence redarguante à la manière des satyres latines, combien que telz propos du coq à l'asne peuvent bien estre adressez à autres argumens que satyricques, comme les *Absurda* de Erasme, *la Farce du Sourd et de l'Aveugle,* et *l'Ambassade des Conardz de Rouan.*[10]

That is to say: something like the conventionalized speech of the fool is used both in Erasmus' collection of "happy unhappy" juxtapositions of ideas, in the matter of a farce and in the pronouncement of a Joyous Society.

The actors of the sotties, then, amused their audiences with running talk into which swift bits of satire could intrude. They took advantage too of the obvious pun upon their name— "sot" equals "saut," and the play of *Les sobres sots* is really "les soubresauts." Acrobatic antics eked out their efforts at entertainment. Like the Trompettes-Jongleurs of Chauny, they needed to be both "grands jaseurs et beaux bailleurs de balivernes" and to be skilled in "gestes, ruses et sobresaulx."[11] They must be able to turn a hand-spring in the midst of their "fatrasie:"

> Voicy celuy qui passe tout;
> Sus, faictes le sault, hault, deboult,
> Le demy tout, le souple sault,
> Le faict, le defaict, sus, j'ay chault,
> J'ay froid; est-il pas bien apris?[12]

This acrobatic capacity, combined with patter, was the simplest element in the concept of the fool which provided material for sotties.

While the gaiety or the guilt of the fool, his failure or his triumph, his criticism of his masters or the triumph of folly itself all played occasional parts in the sotties, the amusement of nonsensical metrical jabber—a "grande absurdité de suite de propos" without any particular concern with the "vices de chacun"—is made use of in some part of almost all of them. The *Menus propos*, from Rouen, jogs along in a style of confused proverbial statement which resembles the fool's talk:

Le Tiers.	Or me dy par quantes manieres On doit commencer son latin.
Le Premier.	Soleil qui se lieve matin A grant peine fera ja bien.
Le Second.	Figues de chat, estront de chien Si sont assés d'une figure.
Le Tiers.	C'est bon menger que d'une heure, Entendés vous bien? de sanglier.
Le Premier.	Par sainct Jehan, qui la veult sengler, "C'est aultre chose," dit la vache.
Le Second.	Qui bien bat ung sergent a mache, Il gaigne cent jours de pardon.[18]

There may be obscene innuendoes, concealed references to local Norman absurdities here, but they are hidden as deep from our eyes as the circumstances which gave rise to the *Absurda* collected by Erasmus. The patter is the main thing.

In the *Farce nouvelle tresbonne et fort recreative pour rire. Des cris de Paris* the patter is elaborated by the familiar farce procedure[14] of the intrusion of unexpected contradictory statements into a sustained argument. A definite folly, however, is the subject here, and in the argument a humbler fool, like Marcolf, routs the opinions of his superiors. Two "gallants" are discussing marriage, although their introductory badinage would never lead one to suspect it:

Le premier Gallant *commence.*	Et puis?
Le Second.	Et fontaine?
Le Premier.	Et rivieres.
	Se sont tousjours de tes manieres.
	Tu te gaudis.
Le Second.	Je me gaudis
	Et en povreté m'esbaudis
	En passant ma melencolie.
Le Premier.	Melencolie n'est que follie.
Le Second.	Jamais charger ne t'en convient.
	Comment te va?
Le Premier.	Comme il me vient.
Le Second.	Comment te vient?
Le Premier.	Comme il me va.
Le Second.	Jamais gallant mieulx ne resva.
	Feras tu tousjours le mauvais?
	Comment te va?
Le Premier.	Comme je voys.
Le Second.	Comment vas tu?
Le Premier.	Comme je peulx.[15]

The talk continues at last with the real subject of the playlet:

> C'est grant pitié, je te prometz,
> Que de pouvres gens mariez.
> Ilz sont bien souvent hariez;
> On m'a dit que c'est une mort.[16]

The Sot, a peddlar, is heard crying his wares near by, but the gallants pay no attention to him until his shouts become too irritating. Then they turn their attention to convincing him of the advantages of matrimony, forgetting their own previous doubts about the perfect happiness of marriage in their persuasive zeal. He, however, has the last word in the bout of proverb-speaking with which the argument closes:

Le Second.	De grant follie ung homme est prins
	Qui se fuyt pour femme espouser.
Le Premier.	Grande follie veult user
	Qui tant se veuil faire appeller.

Le Second.	De follie se veult mesler
	Qui a soy marier omet.
Le Sot.	De grant folye s'entremet
	Qui se chastie par aultruy.

Since this is the final stand of the peddlar, the gallants give him up, for he is only a beast, and because

> . . . à laver la teste d'ung asne
> On n'y pert rien que la lescive.[17]

The actor-fools in the *Cris de Paris* mock at marriage in detached fool-proverbs. The *Farce moralle et joyeuse des sobres sots* makes fun specifically of the victims of the female bullies of Rouen, analyzing them into classes according to a form of "list of fools." The cast of characters consists of five "sots" and a "badin," into whose mouth the list is put. He begins his criticism of society with the remark that a hen-pecked husband is nothing but a "sot" whom the public dares to deride before his very face. But his fellow-actors are evidently meant to represent "sots" of this kind themselves, and beg him in embarrassment to get on with his story about "fos," not "sots." With this encouragement he proceeds to his enumeration of local types in terms of Folly. The *dangerous fool* is he who may strike a blow at you with his hammer or make a pass at you with his guarded rapier point if he meets you in the street— the irritable, suspicious citizen. The *joyous fools* are the ordinary domestic articles whose heads are no bigger than apples:

> De ceulx la on en a vendu
> Cent escus ou deulx cens la piece.
> Ces fos la sont plains de lyesse;
> Ce sont singes en la maison;
> Ils ont moins de sens c'un oyson,
> Toutefoys si sont les meilleurs,
> Et volontiers les grans seigneurs
> En ont qu'i gardent cherement.[18]

These fools enjoy a security which the "sots" avow they wish they might share. There are other fools, "acariâtres, estourdis et opiniâtres," who talk like herring-vendors and are apparently plentiful in the town, for the "badin" hints that if they were known by their dress at least a hundred might be seen in any street. Leaving this ticklish ground, he goes on to speak of the "glorieulx cocars," the boasters whom you gratify by listening to, but at whom you must not laugh. More ridiculous, perhaps, but less well known, are the "folz subtilz":

> Ilz trouvent des inventions
> Sy parfondes en leurs espritz
> Qu'en donnant foy a leurs escriptz
> Y sont cousins germains de Dieu.[19]

The "badin" particularly disapproves of the foolish conduct of certain sullen, obstinate people:

> Ces fos, sy bien le retenés,
> Se sont ceulx, ainsy que l'on dict,
> Qui se font bruller a credit
> Pour dire: 'C'est moy qui babille;
> 'Je suys le reste de dix mille
> 'Qui pour le peuple voys mourir.

These are the Protestants. Like Rabelais, the "badin" feels that to survive is more important than to believe:

> Ny Grectz, ny Ebreutz, ne Latins
> Ne me feront croyre au parler
> Qu'i se faille laiser bruller.
> Bren, bren, bren! y n'est que de vivre.[20]

Finally there are the "fos nouveaulx," the half-fledged lawyers newly come from Orleans and Poitiers and very forward in airing their learning. With them the "badin's" enumeration ends, and the first "sot" closes the argument with the proverbial comment:

> Tout homme qui s'estime sage,
> Il doibt estre fol reputé.[21]

The "badin" of the *Sobres sots* believes in living and in letting live. He condemns the various bourgeois fools merrily, as the minstrel in the *Des sis manieres de fols* condemned the erring feudal knights, extracting a laugh from their failings. Yet he safeguards himself from condemnation by proclaiming himself a fool, too, and a more complete fool than any of the rest. The difference between a "badin" and a "sot," according to this play, is the difference between "inscius" who knows nothing at all and "ignorans," "insipiens" and "stultus" in the definitions of the *Catholicon*. The "wise" and "foolish" of moral terminology are neatly separated from the "innocent":

> Les badins ne sont pas vrays sos,
> Mais ils ne sont ne sos ne sages.

The distinction is not labored, but it is clear:

Le Badin.	Vous estes tous sos, n'estes pas?
Le. Ve. Sot.	Ouy vrayment.
Le Badin.	A! voiecy le cas.
	Si vous estes sos en tout temps,
	Fault que soyés, comme j'entens,
	Sos par nature ou par usage.
	Un sot ne sera pas un sage;
	Vous ne le serés donq jamais.
Le .IIIe. Sot.	Povre badin, je te promais
	Qu'il ne t'appartient pas de l'estre.
Le Badin.	Non vrayment, car il fault congnoistre
	C'un badin, qui ne pense a rien,
	Scayt plus d'honneur ou plus de bien
	C'un sot ne scayt toute sa vye.
Le .IIIe. Sot.	Pour ce mot j'airoys grand envye
	De te soufleter à plaisir. . . .
Le Badin.	Un badin vault myeulx en chiant,
	Mangeant, buvant, dansant, riant,
	Que ne font tous les sos ensemble.[22]

This use of the liberty of the pretended "inscius" to call the rest of the world "stultus," the combined assertion that the fool is both innocent and erring, wise and unwise, is one

method of those sotties which aim both to amuse and mildly
to edify. The *Sobres sots* is a mild satire, concerned mainly with
what all the world takes for a joke, the hen-pecked or deceived
husband. Pure edification, however, is the purpose of some of
the sotties which discuss more widely social questions. In them
the story is told without emphasizing the paradox of the wise
and the foolish; the costume, chatter and acrobatics of the
actors are used to point out the folly, but the culpable folly,
of the personages presented. The "farce joyeuse" of *Le Monde
qu'on faict paistre,* for instance, deals like many other sotties
with the exploitation of the many by the few. Three gallants
wish to despoil the World, blind it, make it into a beast—of
burden, presumably—and lead it off to grass. They come upon
the stage talking in the usual fragmentary fashion, explain that
they are out to seek their fortunes, and approach the World
with gambols. The World resists the compliments by which
they try to wheedle his possessions away from him, calling the
gallants "sos radotés" and insisting

C'est mon, mais vous ne l'arés pas.

Order overhears the argument and comes to the support of
the World whom he advises to buy off his persecutors. The
piece ends with the moral, pointed out by Order, that one cannot live off of the World without working, and the actors all
join in a final song.[23] There is no paradox nor innuendo here.
The gallants are as clearly fools-to-be-condemned as the unwise borrowers or lenders of the *Cato* or the *Proverbes du
Vilain.*

A number of sotties point out in this way the misery of the
world, and the unsocial ignorance and weakness of those who
keep it miserable. It may be the heartless rapacity of the "mod-
erns" which is to blame, as in the *Farce nouvelle moralisee
des gens nouveaulx qui mengent le monde et le logent de mal
en pire.* The "gens nouveaulx" consider themselves masters of

the present and inheritors of the wealth of the past. In their fantastic plans for the future they show themselves boastful, as well as avaricious, fools:

Le Second.	Faisons oyseaulx voller sans elles,
	Faisons gens d'armes sans chevaulx:
	Ainsi serons nous gens nouveaulx.
Le Tiers.	Faisons advocatz aumosniers,
	Et qu'ilz ne prennent nulz deniers,
	Sur la peine d'estre faulx:
	Ainsi serons nous gens nouveaulx.
Le Premier.	Faisons que tous couars gens d'armes
	Se tiennent les premiers aux armes
	Quant on va crier aux assaulx:
	Ainsi serons nous gens nouveaulx.[24]

Their actions immediately betray that they have no intention of working for the Utopia they have been describing, for after complaining that the wealth of the past has been poorly distributed in useless foundations like nunneries and abbeys, they themselves turn upon the World. Unable to resist their despoiling, he is taken to lodge at the sign of Mal, then at that of Pire. Or it may be the more closely defined companions of Abuse who put the World to sleep, pluck the fruit of the tree of Dissolution, build a new world out of Hypocrisy, Treason, Anger, and similar materials, set up "sot glorieux," a soldier, "sot corrompu," a lawyer, "sot trompeur," a merchant, as their officers and woo "sotte folle," the populace, until their world topples down upon them and annihilates them all.[25] Most effective of all, perhaps, is the representation of *Tout le monde*. The three "gallants" who open this play are far from being "gallants sans soucy." They are seeking Passetemps, to be sure, but cannot find him:

Le Premyer.	Vous cherches donques Pase Temps,
	Est il pas vray?
Le .IIe.	Il est ainsy.
Le Premyer.	Comme vous je le cherche ausy.

Le .IIe.   Pase Temps? Las, il est transy.

                  .   .   .   .
                  Avarice l'a tins en serre
                  Sy long temps qu'il est toult remys.
Le Premyer.   Faulte d'Argent encor l'enserre,
                  Et Erreur l'a a luy submys.[26]

Failing to find Passetemps, the companions turn their attention
to Tout le Monde, who arrives in a curious disguise:

Le .IIe.   Onc en telle sorte ne vis
                  Le Monde. Ou il est afollé
                  Ou c'est quelque sot avollé
                  De nouveau qui vers nous s'adresse.
                  Y porte l'estat de Noblesse,
                  De Marchant, Labeur et l'Eglise.[27]

This curious figure proves really to represent the ambition of
Every Man to profit at the expense of Every Other Man, and
he explains in detail his desires as nobleman, merchant, lawyer,
and churchman. The "companions" find him unsuitably
dressed, and though the text does not show what garment they
thought fit to clothe him in, the concluding ballade suggests
forcibly that it was the fool's costume:

                  Mais encore pour abreger,
                  Messieurs, pour la conclusion,
                  Tout le Monde à l'heure presente
                  Est fol et plain d'abusion.
                  C'est luy qui malheur nous presente;
                  D'estat jamais ne se contente,
                  Et s'estime autant que sainct Pol;
                  Pour quoy je dis en nostre entente
                  Qu'aujourd' uy Toult le Monde est fol.[28]

In these sotties which lament the state of the world and
blame those human beings responsible for its misery the notes
of sadness and anger sound loudest, and the fatrasie, the acrobatics and the fool's costume seem merely devices for under-
lining the stupidity of the culprits. They were not incentives to

laughter, for the fools they signalized were positively dangerous to society. Where the prattlers of the *Menus propos,* the *Cris de Paris,* and even of the *Sobres sots* discuss fools whose weaknesses do not keep mankind from proceeding to the gratifications of its main desires, these plays set in action ignorant, weak, or malicious people whose activities jeopardize the life and wealth of the majority—guilty fools. The actors of the plays mean to say that the actions they are depicting are sins, but to make the pill more palatable they say, less emphatically, that they are due to folly, that is, to weakness and ignorance. Another group of sotties, however, deals with these same sorry conditions from a less somber point of view. The avaricious merchants, the boasters, the unscrupulous pillagers, the spendthrift husbandmen are fools, they say, not because society in general suffers from their actions but because they themselves suffer. They misjudge their own best good. And the man who knows that his reward is in heaven can afford to laugh at the pompous conceit of the worldling. The plays which express this point of view criticize mankind in general with the gaiety proper to a band of joyous companions who know the poverty of this world and seek only "soulas." They create, too, the generalized figures of various kinds of folly, conceived as the mother of all fools and the patron of the Joyous Societies.

The sottie of *Folle Bobance* is supposed to come from Lyon where Joyous Societies were plentiful[29] and to date from 1500 when the fashion of interpreting human nature in terms of folly was near its greatest currency. It evokes the figure of Folle Bobance, or Foolish Display. She opens the play with a summons to all her family similar to the later roll-call of the Mère Folle de Dijon:

> Ou estez vous, tous mes folz affollez?
> Sortez trestous et cy me venez voix.

Et qu'essecy? N'oyez vous point ma voix?
Despechez vous; bien tost cy avollez,
Affollez folz, de follie raffollez,
Rafollee suis que cy je ne vous voix.
Ou estes vous, tous mes folz affollez?
Sortez trestous, et cy me venez voix,
Borgnes, bossus, rabostez et follez,
Folz folians, de folie fault pourvoix.
Folz lyonnoys, myllanoys, genevoys,
Folz folastres, serveaux asservelez,
Ou estes vous, tous mes folz affollez. . . .[30]

The three fools who answer her represent the Estates gathered in general meeting. They agree to follow her counsels and commands, and proclaim their ambition to "passer temps joyeusement" as becomes good fellows:

Le premier Fol, *gentilhomme.*   Fy de travail!
Le Second, (marchant).   Fy, fy de peine!
Le Tiers, (laboureur).   Fy de soucy.
Le Premier.   Fy de chagrin!
Le Second.   Tel seme froment et aveine
         Qui n'en mengit jamais d'ung grain.

Le Tiers, *laboureux.*   Tel menge trop.
Le Premier.   Tel meurt de faim.
Le Second.   Tel se tue de labourer
         Sa vigne, mais il n'ose grain
         Sa gorge du vin arrouser.

Le Tiers *laboureux.*   C'est trésor de soy reposer.
Le premier Fol, *gentilhomme.*   C'est plaisir de vivre en liesse.

.   .   .   .

Folle Bobance.   Gentilz folz, vous debvez scavoir
         Qu'il n'est que de vivre en
                 plaisance;
         Et si pouez appercevoir
         Qu'il n'est vie que de Bobance.[31]

The fools admit that they have all tried living within their means and have found that without egotistical display they make no advance in worldly success. They are now prepared to spend what they possess and to mortgage their standing crops to enjoy and maintain Bobance. They will dress in the latest fashion, they will enjoy fair women, eat and drink their fill—claret, ypocras, sugared tarts and cheese, chickens, pigeons, coneys, all kinds of fish, spices, eels, crabs!—and then they will pull out their purses and pay their debts with ready gold. To accomplish this the gentleman must sell the steady income from his land for cash, the merchant must compass the ruin of other more honest merchants, and the farmer must sell his land outright. All this they do, and when they presently return to report to Folle Bobance that their resources are exhausted, she receives them with malicious joy and shuts them up in the castle of Tout-Y-Fault:

> La vivres en mendicité
> Jusques à la fin de vos jours.

It appears that all along she really had cherished the purpose of pointing out to them the inevitable end of their folly, and that she herself is a severely moral monitor:

> Je fais congnoistre la folie
> A tous folz de prime venue.
> Je leur montre chere jolie
> Tant qu'ilz ont rente et revenue;
> Mais quant ont toute dependue
> La rente, l'argent et les biens,
> De les bouter en ceste mue
> De Pouvreté, n'en donne riens.
> Quant hommes sont grans terriens,
> Riches marchans ou laboureux,
> Tant qu'ilz en ont, les entretiens,
> Tant qu'enfin les rens souffreteux
> Et en ce chasteau tenebreux
> Les enferme, tous mors de fain,
> Tous dessirez et malheureux.
>
> .   .   .   .
>
> Paier fault l'ouvrier selon l'oeuvre
> Et aux quoquars leur bienvenue.[32]

The play ends with an antiphonal chant by the fools lamenting their folly and with epigrammatic advice to the audience to avoid the same misfortunes.

Folle Bobance represents a special kind of conduct by which men think to achieve success in the world and actually compass not success but ruin. Sottie, who presides over the fate of her children Fine Mine, Teste Verte, and Chascun in another playlet, stands rather for a philosophical resignation to the real state of human affairs. Like Folle Bobance, she summons her children with a call. Chascun does not respond; he is busy "trompant le monde" with a "trompe" given him by the Time under whose orders he is carrying on his life. He is brought back to Sottie, stripped of his borrowed clothes in which he has been aping the condition of all the Estates except his own, and proves to be dressed in the garments of folly. When he has finally been claimed for the family and has laughed, grunted and capered with the two faithful "sots," he receives from the Time instructions as to how to get on in the world:

> Chascun, voicy le principal
> De ce qu'il vous conviendra faire.
> Se voulliez aller à cheval
> Et estre homme de grant affaire,
> Premier, il vous fault contrefaire
> Du saige et du bon entendeur,
> Dire le mal et le bien taire,
> Et estre tresparfaict menteur,
> Bourdeur, mensongier, rapporteur,
> Jurant fort d'estoc et de taille;
> Mais, se vous n'estes bon flateur,
> Vostre faict ne vault une maille.
> Dictes tousjours des maulx, sans faille,
> De quelc'un, voire en son absence,
> Et se celuy le scet: 'Je raille',
> Direz vous; mais, en sa presence,
> Blandissez le sans abstinence,
> Le servant de belle parolle.[33]

Sottie, that is, reigns in the world as mother of those who "get on" by the road described by Gregory as the foolish wisdom of the worldling. But the author and the audience know that the road to truer satisfaction is not that road.

Folly herself, so called, appears in the *Farce nouvelle nommee la Folie des gorriers* as the embodiment of the way of the world, and while she counsels her followers to the same anti-Gregorian code of hypocrisy, flattery, false promises, slander and opportunism, she pleads as her excuse that all men at the end will be accounted fools in one way or another, and that folly is the general lot of mankind. The tone of the skit is merrier than that of the others. Folly's victims are again braggarts, pretentious scoundrels who wish to live off of the world by the easiest means. The scene discloses them calling angrily for their servants, while Folly stands by unseen, whispering to the audience that in truth the boasters have no pages at all. The "gorriers" resolve to take steps to mend their fortunes, which are at lowest ebb. They will get to Paris and begin to make some sort of display that will catch the attention of the great. At this point in their discussion Folly steps forward, and they immediately make amorous advances to her. She receives their protestations casually:

> Je vous entens. Dea! je suis femme
> De plusieurs prisee et cherie.[34]

They ask her who she is and where she comes from, and she replies without giving her name, in a list of places and estates: France, Flanders, Picardy, Normandy, England, Rome, Italy, Spain and Germany, each is equally home to her. She is at ease in the courts of princes, with churchly dissimulators, with students and beggars, with lawyers and women and she understands theology and astrology. She goes so far as to confess her birthplace:

Folie.   . . . Je fuz née
Au fons du paradis terrestre.

Le Second.   Ce que dictes ne pourroit estre:
                Vous n'avez pas .xxv. ans.
Folie.   J'en ay plus de six mil vc.
                Je suis celle, pour toute somme,
                Par qui Adam menga la pomme.[35]

Her name is written across her sleeve but the fools cannot read it and agree to accept her guidance in seeking their fortunes. She dresses them in gowns with large sleeves, gives them hats and big slippers, and sends them out to face and outface the world. They are to provide themselves with money by borrowing, and are to deny their debts when called upon to make payment. "Baillez bourdes en payement" is her advice to her new admirers, and the credo she gives them is this:

> Qui vivre veult en grand prosperité
> Se doit garder de dire verité,
> Promettre assez et du tout rien tenir.
> Par mesdire se doit entretenir
> Selon le temps et l'oportunité.
> Mordre en riant par grand subtilité,
> La ou verra avoir gratuité,
> Pour son proffit chascun entretenir,
>   Qui vivre veult.
> Flater les grans par importunité,
> Complaire à ceulx qui ont auctorité,
> Ne payer riens et l'aultruy retenir
> Font les meschans aux grans estas venir
> Soubz le dangier d'estre decapité
>   Qui vivre veult.[36]

The "Gorriers," however, do not like their appearance in the new clothes, and suspect that a trick has been played on them. They demand to know whom they are serving, and Folly admits her identity:

> Je suis Folie naturelle,
> Plaisant Folie lunatique,
> Folie en folie autentique.
> N'en ayez ja plus de mesaise,
> Car plus grans, ne vous en deplaise,

> Que vous ont eu par mon service
> Et prelature et benefice,
> Et mariage en grans maisons.[37]

Here she takes off whatever she had on her head and reveals a bonnet with ears and horns. The account of her own
nature which she proceeds to give is complicated by an involved rhyme scheme and by the display of vocabulary which
it entails, yet in the course of it many of the qualities of Folly
with which we have become familiar in the proverbs and
sentences are indicated: her arrogance, her malice, her love of
slander and back-biting, her zest for discord, her hatred of
stability, her eagerness for authority, her obstinacy, her lying
flattery—

> Et, pour toute conclusion,
> Toute plaine d'abusion:
> C'est la commune renommee.[38]

And she closes the play by reminding them that so many men
have been governed by her that they need not be discontented
at having fallen under her spell in their turn.

The qualities which Folly attributes to herself here may
nearly all be found among the branches and twigs of the Seven
Deadly Sins as analyzed in the *Calendrier des bergers*.[39] They
are the repertory of humdrum human failings. In making them
culminate in "abusion", a mixture of "abuse" and "deception",
the author of the play blames them upon human ignorance and
weakness rather than upon human malice, and suggests that they
do man more harm than good. The braggarts are after all deceived by Folly; they do not profit by her ministrations and
they try to repudiate her service. She herself is not a genuine
allegorical figure but a literary device for performing effectively
on the stage three actions: for listing the variations from ideal
conduct by which the "average man" succeeds in the worldly
struggle, for dubbing those variations "folly" and thereby at-
tributing them to man's limited nature, and for laughing at

them. To say that folly is general and inevitable is not to say that it is good; but in a generation which sees death standing between itself and its supernatural destiny, to say that folly is the accompaniment of life on earth may generate an affectionate regard for it! The image of this coquettish Folie who sees through the braggarts and leads them on to their own undoing, taking the audience into her confidence, who remembers the garden of Eden and recalls gleefully how Adam ate the apple, is a more genial vehicle of satire on human nature than those fables which show Chascun or Tout le Monde as fools. It reflects both tolerance of what man is and consciousness of what he should be, and puts the symbol of the fool to a double function.

The costume of the fool, which in the *Folie des gorriers* conveyed these two supplementary attitudes toward human nature, was used in other plays to furnish that liberty of criticism which the fool may claim by virtue of his harmlessness. A group of plays produced probably by the Paris society under the reign of the lenient Louis XII commented freely upon the national situation through the mouths of the Prince des Sots and his children, or by means of "sots" appearing as pilgrims or astrologers.[40] In Rouen and Geneva figures similar to Folie and Sottie, christened Mère Folle, La Mère de Ville, or more indicatively, La Reformeresse, were used by the local Joyous Societies as mouthpieces for public criticism.[41] One such sottie, given as part of a program containing also a morality and a farce, combined the liberty of the fool to comment with condemnation of human folly and laughing extenuation of that folly as human weakness.

Gringore, in his *Sottie contre Jules II,* described on the title page as "Le jeu du Prince des sotz & de mère Sotte. Joue aux halles de paris le mardy gras," vindicated elaborately the policy of Louis XII in prosecuting his war against the militant Pope. The play sets before the audience an assembly of Sots summoned before their Prince by a "Cry" published through the

streets the day before. This "Cry" rehearses the familiar roll-
call of the fools with more inventiveness than usual:

> Sotz lunatiques, sotz estourdis, sotz saiges,
> Sotz de villes, de chasteaulx, de villages,
> Sotz rassotez, sotz nyais, sotz subtilz,
> Sotz amoureuz, sotz privez, sotz savages,
> Sotz vieulx, nouveaulx, et sotz de toutes aages,
> Sotz raisonables, sotz pervers, sotz restifz,
> Vostre prince sans nulles intervalles
> Le mardy gras jouera ses jeux aux halles.[42]

All foolish women, old and young, fair and foul, all "bons
viveurs" drunk or sober, are summoned to the Halles for the
occasion.

When the company assembled, the actors must have been
dispersed among the audience, for while three "sots" prepare
the stage and call for the different members of the Prince's
council, the ministers of the kingdom of Folly come down from
seats in the auditorium and take their places. Their names
show that they are colleagues of the Enfants sans Soucy: le
Seigneur de Pont Alletz, le Prince de Nates, le Seigneur de
Joye, le General de l'Enfance, l'Abbé de Frevaulx, l'Abbé de la
Lune, and others. When the Prince himself enters and looks
around at his *suppôts*, his gaze includes the audience as well as
the stage, and his comment is:

> Honneur, Dieu gard, les sotz et sottes!
> *Benedicite,* que j'en voy![43]

The state of the country and of the clergy is under discussion
when a grumbling voice is heard; Sotte Commune has made her
way into the group. She is discontented, ignorant, poor:

> Et! que ay je a faire de la guerre,
> Ne que a la chaire de saint Pierre
> Soit assis ung fol ou ung saige?
> Que m'en chault il se l'Eglise erre,
> Mais que paix soit en ceste terre?

Jamais il ne vint bien d'oultraige,
Je suis asseur en mon village:
Quand je veuil je souppe et desjeune.[44]

Although she sings part of the song "Faute d'argent est douleur
nonpareil," the assembly dismisses her from their minds because
her temper is uneven and her judgment unreliable. The point
of the conclave becomes clear when a personage enters in the
costume of Mother Church, attended by Sotte Fiance and Sotte
Occasion, and raises the question of loyalties among the *sots*.
The assembly is divided in its allegiance to Mother Church and
to the Prince. A general scuffle takes place, during which Mother
Church has her clothes torn from her back and is seen to be
after all only old Mère Sotte masquerading in a new guise.

In this play the external trappings of the fools' organizations are duly preserved and the various attitudes from which
man may be called foolish assembled. Petty vices, debauchery
and gaiety are jumbled together in the "Cry" as earmarks of
folly. The Prince in reviewing his *suppôts* sees them as nu-
merous as the citizens of the town. "Stultorum numerus infinitus est." The officers of his organization bear names suitable to
members of a Joyous Society and gambol and chatter in the introductory moments in the traditional manner of fool and mock-
fool. The common people are fools in their miserable dullness and limitation. The Prince of Fools, paradoxically, is
wise, and the supposedly all-wise church errs because she is
after all only Mother Folly from whom error is expected. All
these devastating truths may moreover be pointed out gaily by
those who themselves adopt the name of fool. Little remains
to be said on the subject of human folly after this review of its
omnipresence from one point of view or another, except to re-
call the power of unreasoning vitality to cope with earthly
problems or the power of unreasoning love to win the kingdom of heaven. But the business of the Bazoche and of the
Enfants san Souci in their rôles as fools was to deal entertain-

ingly with subjects accessible to the reason. And in the early sixteenth century the range of ideas currently connected with the concept of folly gave them, in its personification, a peculiarly supple instrument both for entertainment and for satire.

The sottie found its fullest use in providing a vehicle of criticism like that expressed in the *Sottie contre Jules II,* but the censorship soon suppressed it, and its other functions as pure entertainment and as general analysis of human nature were more acceptably embodied in the new comedy and tragedy developing under the inspiration of the classic revival. The confidence in man's reason which was fostered by the study of the classics made unreason and incoherence seem unworthy of the attention of princes and courtiers, citizens and counsellors. The agitation of the religious controversy of the Reform obliterated the traces of the Feast of Fools, and a period of open struggle between ideas made clear affirmation or open vituperation more useful than comment shielded by the liberty of the fool. By 1550 the sottie and its actors had been reduced to silence or the harmless displays of pageantry. But it had contributed to the literature of folly the chief substantial literary evidence of the liberty of the fool to criticize, which might otherwise have remained a legend connected with the vanished domestic fool. It embodied the conclusion that those who forsake the precepts of Cato are fools, as well as the paradox that the fool may be wise. It proclaimed too that folly was part and parcel of human nature, and moreover ruled the world:

> Me dis tu que dame Folie
> Est morte? Ma foy, tu as menty;
> Jamais si grande ne la vy,
> Ny si puissante comme elle est.[45]

These lines were written probably in 1513, two years after Erasmus' *Praise of Folly* had been printed. England, France,

Germany and the Netherlands were already familiar with Brant's *Ship of Fools*. Each of these books bore out the comment of the sottie, that Folly rules the world, but each conceived in different ways of the nature of the fool. Each in its way made visible the members of a world-wide company of fools. But knowledge of the sotties helps in the study of both books. Brant followed the proverbial list method, presenting Chascun in the whole repertory of his follies, stressing his unfitness for society and the damage he does to his own chances of salvation by his misconduct. He took a more rigorous position on the humor of folly than did the Enfants sans Souci, for he found only a bitter mirth in observing man's perversion of his own nature, and he desired to see man prosper in this world as well as in the next. He used folly as a simple symbol of opprobrium. Erasmus, without forgetting the disadvantages of folly, outdid the Enfants in his acceptance of its place in human nature and forced into the concept of the fool as many significances as the paradoxes of life provided to accompany it.

Chapter VII

THE SHIP OF FOOLS

Order is Heaven's first law.
—Pope

The most famous piece of European literature which used the fool as a literary symbol was a vigorous denunciation of disorder. Even during the years when the fool was a popular and handy expression of several different aspects of man's nature, the dominating interpretation of that symbol was in the tradition that condemned him. Wisdom and law, not folly, are the heroines of Brant's *Narrenschiff*, or in its English translation, *The Ship of Foles of the Worlde*. The book is a summary of all those rebukes which the preacher eternally addresses to his congregation, served up in the terms which in 1494 evidently seemed vivid—proverbial maxims illustrated by pictures of fools. The fool is the erring man, pitiful, inadequate, and as degraded in the eyes of the wise as King Robert of Sicily with shaven head among the hounds. Erring fools are comical just as jesters are comical, because the onlooker sage in his own sanity sees how misguided they are, how disproportionate their efforts to their ends. In this sense Brant's use of the fool-symbol is ironic. But the deeper disproportion between reason and the needs of life and the relation of the fool to that idea, the freedom of the fool, the triumph of the fool, these connotations of the symbol are not exploited in the *Ship of Fools*. The humor of the book lies in its descriptions of unwise conduct or in its explosions of contemptuous ridicule aimed at the offending fools. It shows, one fancies, what partisans of an existing order must always mean by "fool."

The *Ship of Fools* was a work of European importance. Its German editions during the sixteenth century ran into scores and it was translated into every language of western Europe. But outside of Germany the work known as the *Ship of Fools* and rendered into the local vernaculars was not Brant's lively series of tetrameter couplets expressed in terse proverbial language but the Latin hexameter translation first published in 1497 by his disciple Locher. Upon this the French and English translations were based. The more important English version, in addition, was much expanded by its author Alexander Barclay, both because he had a great deal to say about fools himself, and because he found difficulties in rendering Locher's hexameters into rhyme royal. The detailed effects of Brant's and Barclay's compositions are therefore very different. But the Latin *Navis stultorum* was sanctioned by Brant and he himself wrote introductory material to accompany it. The didactic purpose of the book, the use of the symbol of the fool, and the general subjects discussed are the same in the Latin as in the German. Therefore, although Barclay's version and the French of Pierre Riviere, the "child of Poitou" whose translation he used to help out his Latin, are more inspired by a Latin original than by Brant's own text, it is still possible in studying the use of the theme of folly to take Barclay's text as a fair translation of the spirit of the original.[1]

Brant's fools are consigned to Narragonia for disregard of fundamental regulations, earthly and heavenly. The "end" of man, according to him, was the orthodox Catholic one of salvation in heaven, to be reached by the exercise of that "sapientia" discussed by Aquinas as the chief intellectual virtue.[2] The world, said Brant, is a vain thing, and he bade farewell to it with eloquent melancholy:

Plurima quae sub sole patent vidi atque revidi
Et stabile inveni prorsus in orbe nihil.
Omnia cognovi vana irrita stulta caduca
Et labi in terras protinus instar aquae
Nil solidum firmumque nihil durabile parvo est
Tempore quicquid habes hoc brevis hora rapit
Praestes multa licet pecora aurum iugera natos
Coniugium et quicquid stulta libido cupit. . . .
Te (the world) fugiam linquam dimmittam et
deseram ab omni
Parte ita me superi me Deus ipse iuvet
Quin potius semperque velim pater optime, solum
Te colere, et solum te bone Christo sequi.[3]

Death to be sure stands horribly between this life and the after-life. *De periculoso scaccorum ludo inter mortem et humanam conditionem* shows us three episodes from the universal dance: the angel with the hour-glass watches while Death proclaims his power to Julius Caesar, to a certain rich man, and to Brant himself.[4] But the divine law is omnipotent and controls nature and man for its own supernatural ends, in which the vain world and death have their due places. Failure to recognize this order is what makes men fools:

Perspicimus cunctos (the fools) sine lege atque
ordine, remos
Traxisse: et velis non posuisse modum
Atque ideo in Scyllā, Syrtes, brevia, atque
charybdim
Vortice detrusos: naufragiumque pati.
E quibus, in summa, repetendo ab origine stultos
Invenio cunctos hoc periisse modo:
Quod praetergressi legemque, modumque, viamque
Quam deus et rerum dictitat ordo decens.
Omnia quae in caelo, aut terris, vel in aequore vivunt:
Ordine servantur: stantque vigentque suo
Quem si destituant: si vivere in ordine cessent:
Continuo intereunt, in nihilumque ruunt.
Ordine infirmo starent elementa, perirent:

Ordinem habent certum, tempus, et hora, suum
Ordo est nascendi: et vitae certissimus ordo:
Estque suum mortis tempus, et ordo placens:
Ordinis haec virtus: ut certa lege modoque
Cuncta gubernentur: subpeditata deo.
Atque ut quisque minor, maiorem observet: et illi
Pareat: atque libens iussa petita ferat.[5]

To follow order is the essence of wisdom. Brant's whole literary purpose was to teach obedience to the law of God and compliance with the code of man, and he made his personages fools in contemptuous ridicule of their inadequacies to these laws. His other works aside from the *Ship* are all concerned with instruction in order of one kind or another. He translated into German the *Cato,* one *Facetus,* and a *Moretus* which he recommended as supplying information about any details of conduct omitted in the *Cato,* as well as a *Thesmophagia* or guide to table manners.[6] Moreover, he intended his work to get into the hands of the people, of the "gens Theutonica" whose rise from "barbarism" he and his German fellow-teachers so greatly desired. His Latin poem on the life of St. Onofrius was issued in broadside form, probably for distribution by pedlars, along with ballads and tales, and it is even possible that chapters of the *Narrenschiff* were circulated in that form before they were assembled in the book itself.[7]

With popular instruction thus at heart, Brant made his chief work attractive to the public by presenting it in the familiar paraphernalia of moral exhortation enlivened by pictures and by some overtones of gaiety. The book, he said, was a "mirror" like the innumerable other mirrors from which the late Middle Ages were accustomed to take their instructions:

Contemplator age hoc speculum: quicunque cupiscis
Scire hominum vitas: interitusque graves.
Nam qui se, vitamque suam speculatur in isto
Codice: non dicet se facile esse bonum.

Quod si quis, sapiens sibi, se nusquam putet esse
Nos inter: cunctis se sciat esse locis.[8]

And like other mirrors, this "Speculum stultorum" is furnished
with references to the recognized authorities on conduct, the
Scriptures and the familiar Latin authors. The section describing the road to felicity and the pains that await the traveler
on the primrose path bears marginal references to Proverbs,
Psalms, the Book of Wisdom, Ecclesiastes, Ezeckiel, Matthew,
Luke, as well as to the works of Virgil and Seneca.[9] The condemnation of "disordred love" is supported by Ecclesiastes,
Proverbs, and Ovid's *De remedio amoris,* while the marginal
annotations present the terrifying information that:

Ob Venerem Troia crematur, Priamus trucidatur, tota
pene Asia conculcatur.
Marcus Antoninus a Caesare obtruncatur, & Cleopatra
amica sua.
Ovidius Epistola, i. Res est solliciti plena timoris
amor.[10]

This familiar equipment would suffice to assure the conscien-
tious reader that he had opened another *Summa vitiorum.*

But lest the erring should not care for a plain mirror, Brant
adorned his sermon with pictures. The truism that "pictura
est laicorum litteratura" was as true in the fifteenth century as
in the twelfth or the twentieth.[11] In Brant's own country, pictures, and pictures of fools too, had already been used for the
illustration of moral teaching. Vindler's *Blume der Tugend,*
published at Augsburg in 1486, drove home its instruction by
means of representations of the fools condemned in Proverbs
dressed in fool's costume,[12] and among the Swabian "fliegende
Blätter" of the 1470's and 1480's were broadsides of fools in
long dresses holding scrolls upon which appeared proverbs, each
introduced by the phrase "Der ist ein Narr."[13]

The device of embodying a symbolic teaching in a picture
with explanatory verses received new impetus in the late fif-

teenth century from the growing popularity of the "emblem," and the pictures with which the unknown master who worked in Van Olpe's printing house adorned the first edition of the *Narrenschiff* are "emblems" in the sense in which Charles Estienne many years later defined the genre:

L'Emblesme est proprement un Symbole doux & moral, qui consiste en la peinture & aux parolles par lequel on declare quelque grave sentence. . . . Le principal but de l'Emblesme est d'enseigner en touchant nostre veue par les figures, & en frappant nostre esprit par leurs sens: il faut donc quelles soyent un peu couvertes, subtiles, ioyeuses, & significatives. Que si les Peintures en sont trop communes, il faut quelles monstrent un sens caché, si elles sont un peu obscures il faut quelles soyent Analogiques ou correspondantes.[14]

Van Olpe's draughtsman succeeded in many cases in "declaring a grave sentence" in his pictures. His Venus shows a woman in the genre of Dürer's symbolic figures, with trailing skirts, flowing hair, great feathered wings, leading in ropes an ass, a monkey and several fools, while Death peers over her shoulder.[15] The devil too appears effectively with great ragged bat wings, enormous ears, hair streaming up in the wind over his forehead, a shaggy body, and for hands and feet, claws with which he is about to pull off the cap of the fool kneeling before his money bags.[16] In these instances the picture is more closely packed with meaning than the text. In other cases the illustration is merely a realistic presentation of the proverb which Brant's verses are developing. The vivid chapter describing how wealth may indeed promote you to the office of sergeant, bailiff, constable, justice or mayor but will certainly damn you if you do not give alms to the poor is preceded by a woodcut showing an interior with bed, shelves, table and plates, where a fool counts his money before a great chest, while outside in the immediate foreground a saintly king with begging bowl and cross lies in the dust with dogs licking his sores.[17]

But if Brant's book may truly be considered an early emblem book[18], it must however be distinguished from those of certain later makers of emblems—full of mythical birds, fish tied up in ribbons, animated pots and pans, chests with one eye-in which the cryptic character of the picture was chiefly emphasized. Brant's purpose was far less "precious" than that, say, of Sambucus or Catz, whose designs are as far-fetched as the literary conceits of Marini or Gongora. The vogue of the emblem was born of the fifteenth century discovery, by scholars, of late Egyptian hieroglyphics, and was sustained by the delight of complex minds in obscurity and concealment.[19]

Brant's purpose was not to conceal but to make plain, to furnish a text which should be legible to the untrained mind as well as to the scholar. Too great complexity in the pictures would have defeated his purpose. The mere fact of costuming his personages in fool's dress carried the burden of the simple symbolism of disparaging scorn which he wished to convey.

In placing his repertory of fools upon a "ship" Brant sounded an overtone of humor above the basic solemn harmony of his work and mitigated ever so slightly the weight of his disparagement. Earlier poems in the German vernacular had made use of the ship as a container for collections of undesirables[20] and a mock oration of which he may well have heard had been given before his friend Wimpheling at the University of Heidelberg, making use of the ship-motif in a similar fashion. The orator summoned into the "Lichtschiff" or ship of irresponsibility those members of all the estates who indulged their love of a good time at the expense of their social duties.[21] The mood of this oration was quite suitable to a carnival celebration or to a frolic of the Joyous Societies. The ship itself, it has been suggested, was not an ocean-going vessel but the "carrus navalis" or emblem of fertility which was dragged through the streets of German towns at Shrovetide.[22] These ships may have been the ancestors of our holiday floats. In such vehicles too the participants in the Fastnachtspiele or in the levities of the Nürnberg Schembartlauf may have been drawn through the streets[23], and often enough the players in these carnival shows were fools, or perhaps wild-men-in-green, whose gambols and stupidities suggested both the unreason of man and his natural high spirits. Such a connotation of carnival gaiety hidden in the title of his volume of instruction may have seemed to Brant a good bait with which to catch the popular audience he aimed at. His illustrator, too, drew for the title-page of the book two scenes, one representing the fools in a true boat, the other showing them huddled in a cart which may have been intended for no other than a carnival wagon.[24]

But if Brant meant the ship in which he placed his fools to suggest the hilarity of the carnival season, he did not intend it to extenuate their misconduct. He says nothing of carnival gaiety either in the book itself or in the introductory additions which he appended to later editions of it, and he does on the other hand harp on the metaphor which represents the life of the ill-governed man as a boat tossed oarless on the sea of life. It was in this latter sense that his friend, the Strassburg preacher Geiler, interpreted the image in his sermons upon the *Narrenschiff*. Quoting as text the words of Hugo of Saint-Victor:—

In navicula sedens per fluvium voluptatum descendis in mare amarum et mortuum. . . . In aquis deliciarum trahimus ratem grandem peccatorum,

he expressed a melancholy despair over the lot of the fools borne away upon the ship of aimlessness:

Schluraffen narren, die inen kein ander end und selikeit setzen dan dise welt, sie wolten sich mit disen zeitlichen dingen beniegen lassen. Es seint die, die inen kein port noch ort fürnemen zu den sie faren wöllen uff disem grosen meer d'welt.[25]

Whatever the overtones of carnival high spirits and the celebration of unreason hidden in the title of the book, it is clear that Brant did not intend his use of the symbols of the fool and the ship to glorify the natural man but to point out his failure to reach his true end.

Alexander Barclay proved a most sympathetic interpreter of Brant's serious message to mankind. Although Barclay claimed that the book had been translated by him out of "Laten, French and Doche," it has been shown that his sources were the Latin version of Locher and the French translation of it by Pierre Riviere.[26] But whether or not he had appreciated the detail of Brant's compact and vigorous denunciations of human failings, he fully understood and acquiesced in their didactic purpose. His version of Locher's prologue shows how soberly he accepted the work of reform and instruction. He brings out clearly the mirror idea:

For in lyke wyse as olde Poetes Satyriens in dyvers Poesyes conioyned repreved the synnes of ylnes of the peple at that tyme lyvynge: so and in lyke wyse this our Boke representeth unto the iyen of the redars the states and condicions of men: so that every man may behold within the same the cours of his lyfe and his mysgoverned maners, as he sholde beholde the shadowe of the fygure of his visage within a bright Mirrour.[27]

Apparently the ship-symbol had no carnival connotations to the English priest, or if it did he chose to disregard them for he maintained that the name of the book was simply a novelty, to express freshly the perilous course of man through the world:

This present Boke myght have ben callyd nat inconvenyently the Satyr (that is to say) the reprehencion of foulysshness, but the neweltye of the name was more plesant unto the fyrst actour to call it the Shyp of foles. . . . But bycause the name of this boke semeth to the redar to procede of derysion: and by that mean that the substance therof shulde nat be profitable: I wyl advertise you that this Boke is named the Shyp of foles of the worlde: For this worlde is nought els but a tempestous se in the whiche we dayly wander and are caste in dyvers tribulacions paynes and adversitees: some by ignorance and some by wilfulnes: wherfore suche doers ar worthy to be called foles. syns they gyde them nat by reason as creatures resonable ought to do. Therfore the fyrst actoure willynge to devyde such foles from wysemen and gode lyvers: hathe ordeyned upon the se of this worlde this present Shyp to contayne these folys of ye worlde, which ar in great nomber.[28]

Barclay therefore proceeded to transfer to an English ship the cargo of common types of fools assembled by Brant. He did not include the particular German eccentricities originally described by Brant, but to replace them he supplied vignettes of his own, drawn from English life as he knew it. In them Hans Narr became Robin ye foule, but they were comparable in quality to Brant's own, and the main burden of the vessel, the great common family of fools, was the same in German and English.

Admission to the ship of fools is gained in general by the transgression of human or divine law. Man's life on earth should be directed toward the evolution of a coöperative group existence on earth and toward the enjoyment of that salvation promised to the righteous in heaven. All but fools know this, and a life of prudence and reason on earth is practically guaranteed to bring man to bliss. Wisdom herself testifies to this when, quoting from the Proverbs of Solomon, she presents her case to the people. She commands "equity," she says; she is the root of chastity, casts out covetise, preserves men in authority, guides the sceptres of kings and keeps them prosperous:

> He that me folowyth shall avoyde all dolour
> I shall hym folowe promotynge in suche case
> That none shall be before hym in valour
> I godly ryches in my power imbrace
> Whiche man by me may esely purchase
> And he that wyll his way by me addresse
> I shall rewarde with hevenly joy endles.[29]

This is the familiar code whose medieval currency is attested by the popularity of the *Cato*. And since creatures in human

form are expected to be able to order their lives by this rule,
he is a fool who ignorantly or wilfully ignores it, as Barclay
has already pointed out. Ignorant fools are "caytyffes" and
"wretches" who prefer a "folysshe yest of Robyn hode" to the
word of God which contains all "mannys comfort and solace."
Among wilful fools are numbered those who sin, trusting in the
mercy of God to save them:

> Put case he (God) gyvyth nat aye lyke jugement
> On mannys mysdede, nor yet mundayne offence
> And though he be gode meke and pacyent
> Nor shortly punyssheth our inconvenyence
> Put case also he gyve nat advertence
> To all mundayne fawtes synne and fragylyte
> Yet none sholde synne in hope of his mercy
>
> But these folys assembled in a companye
> Sayth eche to other that oft it is laufull
> To perseverant synners lyvynge in iniquyte
> To trust in god syns he is mercyfull
> What nedeth us our wyttis for to dull
> Labourynge our synne and foly to refrayne
> Syns synne is a thynge naturall and humayne.

But supposing that God does for the time being overlook the
offences against his law committed on earth, he will eventually
check up on them:

> Remember Richarde lately kynge of price
> In Englonde raynynge unrightwisely a whyle.
> Howe he ambycion, and gyleful Covetyse
> With innocent blode his handes dyd defyle
> But howbeit fortune on hym dyd smyle
> Two yere or thre: yet god sende hym punysshment
> By his true servant the rede Rose redolent.[30]

The immutable divine order will eventually and inevitably re-
assert itself.

It is not necessary, according to this picture of life, to preach
the ecstasy of a Jacopone da Todi as an inspiration to seek

heaven; prudential motives should suffice man as an incentive. Man should bow before superior power, nor reprove "the workes of god omnipotent.[31]" He should accept God's will with reverence and not send up vain prayers for success, beauty, office and so on, all of which may, like Midas' gift of the golden touch (borrowed from Juvenal to adorn this passage) turn to his damage.[32] All those, of course, are fools who prefer earthly bliss to heavenly, the transitory to the eternal, but so close is the correlation between satisfaction on earth and satisfaction in heaven that the fate of man on earth seems to furnish an index of his immortal destiny.[33] It seems, in fact, as if Barclay deduced the necessity for prudence as much from the old conception of the whirligig of Fortune and the proper strategy for dealing with it as from his vision of the appropriate road to heaven:

> Labour nat man with to moche besy cure
> To clymme to hye lyst thou by fortune fall
> For certaynly, that man slepyth nat sure
> That lyeth lows upon a narowe wall
> Better somtyme to serve, than for to governe all
> For whan the Net is throwen into the se
> The great fysshe ar taken and the pryncipall
> Where as the small escapyth quyte and fre.[34]

Man is weak; he must keep his weather eye out for the gusts of Fortune and stand by ready to reef in his sail, if he is to bring up at the heavenly port, says Barclay, but the arrival in port seems the least interesting portion of the voyage. Fortune, which presides over man's lot on earth, is evidently the delegate of God's order, and it takes a wise man to manoeuvre Fortune into dealing justly with him. Neither Brant nor Barclay mention the fact that Fortune is popularly said to love fools.

With heaven remote and Fortune immediate and powerful, Death, man's visible final destiny which remorselessly equalizes success and failure in common ruin, bulks large in the pattern of man's life. The fall of the heroes of antiquity brings from Barclay the lament, *Ilz sont tous mortz ce monde est choce vayne*.[35] Death comes to rich and poor alike, bringing dismay to the one and peace to the other, but opening no door upon the beatific vision:

> O deth howe bytter is thy remembraunce
> And howe cruell is it thy paynes to indure
> To them that in erth settyth theyr plesaunce
> On wretchyd ryches, unstable and unsure
> And on vayne pleasours: yet every creature
> Must from this riches (though they be loth) depart
> Whan deth them woundeth with his mortall dart
>
> It is thynge Folysshe to trouble and encomber
> That man that restyth and slepyth quyetly
> His tyme was come, and we in the same slomber
> Shall be opprest: god wot howe sodaynly
> We all must therto, there is no remedy
> It hath to meny ben profyte, and gladnes
> To dye or theyr day to avoyde this wretchydnes.[36]

This view of man's life makes no appeal to those springs of vitality, physical or mental, which the gay fool symbolizes and which genuinely foster a vision of immortality. The condemned fools are all judged on a basis of whether or not they conform to a code. They do not, for instance, serve religion properly. And in dealing with man's relation with the church Barclay stresses matters of external observance and organization rather than the creation of fresh attitudes toward what is supposed to lead man to his desire. The laity is recommended to seek virtue by a proper observance of the Sabbath, by prayer, by honoring the Lord and his saints, and not frousting in taverns or reveling in the streets.[37] It is foolish to cry out to God that one's prayers for grace are not acceptable to him, for the way to avoid sin lies open to him who wills to follow it.[38] Do good works, preparing your soul in this way for its heavenly reward, and do not hinder others who attempt to do the same.[39] So shall you live "rightwisely," if it is possible for a weak man to do so. The faults of the clergy are presented as extremely serious, and both Brant and Barclay attack them with uncompromising courage, but they too consist in defective organization or lapses from dogma. "For the love of the peny and riches" foolish priests load themselves with more benefices than they can adequately serve.[40] Courtiers, all ignorant of the service of the church, are promoted to orders, to enjoy the riches thereunto pertaining. Pride, Riot and Venus consume the substance which should be used for the relief of the poor.[41] Not only is the priesthood full of persons who are in it for gain, but it is used as an asylum for sons of good families who are misshapen in body or in wit. The orders of monks and friars are no longer what they should be, and the whole fabric of the clergy, from the highest to the lowest, is rotten with bribery.[42] And as might be expected, the foolish priests misbehave in church as badly as do the laity, with the telling of fables, jests of Robin Hood, stories of battles in France, Flanders and "small brytayne" during the Mass.[43]

Order and reason are the laws offended against in all these transgressions, and order and reason too are attacked by the heretics who frowardly "the sentence do transpose" from its right sense, "though the wordes stryve and make great resystence," preaching the doctrine of predestination which is obviously counter to God's gift of free-will to man.[44] Other heresies too divert the believer from the three sources of his faith, the Bishop's words, the Scriptures, and the Doctrine of the Church.[45] And as dogma crumbles the physical frontier of Christendom crumbles. In the face of Mohammedans, Jews, hounds of Tartary, Scithians, Bohemians, devils of Prague and Toledo, negromancers and false witches (about whose activities Barclay is far from clear), and above all in the face of the encroaching Turk, the kings and governors of the Christian world slumber. The Pope sleeps in his see. The world is so lost in the worship of riches that it cannot awake to defend its faith:

> The Turke to his Idols hath gretter reverence
> And more devocion, to his fals lawe and doctryne
> Than we christen men without obedyence
> Have to our true fayth, and holy lawe dyvyne
> Concorde and peas ar fall into ruyne
> Unmekenes us pleasyth: disceyt and usury
> The pore, and good we, oppres by robbery.[46]

The erring fools outside the fold are on the eve of overwhelming the no less erring fools inside, and there is only one remedy—action. Just as what the individual needs for personal salvation is a vigorous will directed to the simple recognition of the authority of the prescribed codes and compliance in them, so what Christendom needs in this situation is sheer vigor and strength, supported by an unassailable belief in the rightness of the established order. Reason must seem to guide its acts, but reason must direct scorn to prevail over tolerance, aggression over submission, righteous anger over love for one's fellows outside the Christian fold. Any other conduct is folly. The individual may perhaps seek God through speechless raptures, but society in building the city of God on earth must have articulate and dogmatic explanations for its conduct in order to carry on group life this side of anarchy. The preservation of this group life is Brant's main preoccupation, and since it involves more organization rather than less, he cannot invoke the unorganized vitality of the fool to help towards it. He interprets folly only as that conduct which he unequivocally condemns.

The same concern with the life of the group appears in the discussion of those acts called Deadly Sins. Avarice, which destroys social justice, is to Brant the true fountain-head of evil, and by avarice he means simply unmeasured grasping after material things. He has nothing to say about that basic "cupidi-tas" or desire, which according to Aquinas is the root of sin.[47] In the picture of man's conduct, of course, he does include some mention of other sins. Gluttony, envy, pride, wrath, sloth all come in for description and rebuke.[48] But the desire for immoderate riches remains the chief motive of those "lousers of love and infecters of Charite" against whom he rails. In his invectives against it one sees again, as in the sotties, the picture of the oppressed and long-suffering world, and hears again Folie's ironic instructions as to how to prosper on earth.

Yet even in their profound dismay at the disorders arising from the lust for wealth, the authors of the *Ship of Fools* looked to the established order, rather than to change, for help. They were not prepared to preach the doctrine of leaving all and be-coming a fool for Christ's sake. They no more desired a di-vine anarchy on earth than they enjoyed the present results of man's weakness. They hoped that out of the maintenance of the established order might come some coherence in human af-fairs. Barclay is lamenting the golden age of feudalism when he criticizes the desire of "rude men of the country" for money and better clothes:

> Fye rurall carles awake I say and ryse
> Out of your vyce and lyfe abhomynable
> Namely of pryde, wrath, envy and covetyse
> Whiche ye insue, as they were nat damnable
> Recover your olde mekenes, whiche is most profytable
> Of all vertues, and be content with your degre
> For make a carle a lorde, and without any fable
> In his inwarde maners one man styll shall he be.[49]

The general welfare seems to him to have been better fostered under the old social system than under that which is coming into existence. He attacks the guild craftsmen for the covetous-ness, ill will, envy of their tribe in verses which seem to reflect an economic system in process of rapid change, yet he himself blames the change and the vices resulting from it without attempting the folly of understanding the forces at work in the background.[50] It is therefore perfectly fitting that the chapters of the book not concerned with rebuking avarice, or the confusion in religious affairs, should describe those lesser caterpillars of the commonwealth who exist in every established order, once it is established—those permanent types of erring human nature celebrated in the *Order of Fools* for their lapses from order.

The ship of fools therefore houses soft-hearted and negligent parents and ungrateful children, for a well-ordered society is founded upon the reciprocal duties of the generations.[51] "Folys without provysyon" make up a large group, for foresight is the tool by which the adult compasses his own survival, and improvidence gives birth to many of those acts by which the fool proves himself, as the *Catholicon* said, "temerarius" or "presumptuosus."[52] Other familiar fools include those who undertake to erect great buildings without sufficient means, or show an "over great and chargeable curyesyte" in interfering in other people's business, talk too much, are unable to learn from the example of others, give unwanted counsel and refuse to accept it themselves.[53] Foolish students collect libraries for the sake of looking wise as they display their beautifully bound books. Others meddle with the mysteries of the universe through the study of the stars, or play with logic before they have mastered grammar.[54] Those who "nought can and nought wyll lerne, and seyth moche, lytell berynge away, I mene nat thevys" illustrate the ways of him "qui rien scait et rien ne veult apprendre."[55] Avaricious and presumptuous lawyers and physicians despoil the people by the unscrupulous practice of their professions.[56] Wasteful messengers, night-revelers, "brybours and Baylyes that lyve upon towlynge," "courters and caytyfs begynners of frayes," those who misbehave at Mass, who use foul language and cultivate beastliness in their manners[57], all these and many others see themselves reflected in this "mirror" as fools.

The symbol of the fool himself, then, does not connote gaiety in this book. The humor of the composition lies in the tart realism with which Barclay describes some of the fools whom he condemns. The old fool who has sinned all his life and still trusts to train up his son to exceed him in villainy is exposed in his own monologue:

> I trust so crafty and wyse to make the lad
> That me his father he shall pas and excell
> O that my herte shall than be wonder glad
> If I here of may knowe, se, or here tell
> If he be false faynynge sotyll or cruell
> And so styll endure I have a speciall hope
> To make hym scrybe to a Cardynall or Pope.
>
> Or els if he can be a fals extorcyoner
> Fasynge and bostynge to scratche and to kepe
> He shall be made a comon costomer
> As yche hope of Lyn Calays or of Depe
> Than may he after to some great offyce crepe
> So that if he can onys plede a case
> He may be made Juge of the comon place.[58]

He who together will serve two masters is painted hastening to and fro on errands, bending low with his bonnet in his hand, scratching his master's back, ready with a jest for every occasion.[59] Those who dress extravagantly—the servants of Folle Bobance—and their pitiful destiny are relentlessly described:

> A fox furred Jentelman: of the fyrst yere or hede.
> If he be made a Bailyf a Clerke or a Constable.
> And can kepe a Parke or Court and rede a Dede
> Than is Velvet to his state mete and agreable.
> Howbeit he were more mete to bere a Babyl.
> For his Foles Hode his iyen so sore doth blynde
> That Pryde expelleth his lynage from his mynde.

Yet fynde I another sort almoste as bad as thay.
As yonge Jentylmen descended of worthy Auncetry.
Whiche go ful wantonly in dissolute aray.
Counterfayt, disgised, and moche unmanerly
Blasinge and garded: to lowe or else to hye.
And wyde without mesure: theyr stuffe to wast thus gothe
But other some they suffer to dye for lacke of clothe.

Some theyr neckes charged with colers, and chaynes
As golden withtthes: theyr fyngers ful of rynges:
Theyr neckes naked: almost unto the raynes
Theyr sleves blasinge lyke to a Cranys wynges
Thus by this devysinge such counterfayted thinges
They dysfourme that figure that god hymselfe hath made
On pryde and abusion thus ar theyr myndes layde.[60]

These gentlemen are unfortunately headed for the gibbet, but
for the time being Barclay summons them into the ship of
fools. And while no great hilarity can be aroused by the sight
of follies which bring in their wake such terrible consequences,
yet the precision with which Barclay does expose them induces
a satirical smile, perhaps not unlike that with which the fifteenth century baron regarded his doomed and dishonored jester.

Man's reason and the order of life already established on
earth and justified by reason are the limits within which Brant
and Barclay wished man's activities to fall. For reason and the
(theoretically) established order have shown man a way to gain
heaven and a way to live socially on earth with a certain
amount of satisfaction. To act in contradiction to those canons
is to show oneself weak and ignorant, a fool; or if one is revealed as wilfully rebellious against law, one is all the more a
fool. The laughter associated with such fools as these is the
scornful laughter that accompanies failures and sinners. But
while the mirror thus held up to erring man showed what humanity was, it did not suggest what man might be. It projected
no better picture of life on earth and no fuller vision of heaven

than that given by a sincere, pedestrian, static comprehension
of feudal and Catholic teaching. Barclay in fact even deprecated
the extension of man's knowledge of the planet. Pliny and
Tholomeus, he says, make mistakes in their descriptions of
the regions of the earth, and new lands, of whose existence no
man ever heard before, have recently been found for the Spanish
king:

> Syns these actours so excellent of name
> Hath bokes composyd of this facultye
> And never coude parfytely perfourme the same
> Forsoth it is great foly unto the
> To labour about suche folysshe vanyte
> It is a fuour also one to take payne
> In suche thynges as provyd ar uncertayne.[61]

The study of the classics gave him no new sense of man's
power over his environment, but only of his failure to achieve
the poise of certainty.

The use made of the symbol of the fool in this varied and
diverting document is limited to its negative function of condemnation. But in the idea of folly as expressed in other phases
of the life and thought of the fifteenth century was contained
a point of view which could give man's activities the wider
scope which the authors of the *Ship of Fools* denied them, and
free him temporarily from his sense of inadequacy. Brant's attack upon the follies of his time shows that he felt the terrible
discrepancy between the ideal outer order which man had tried
to project and the travesty of that order visible in western
Europe in the 1490's. When this sense of discrepancy becomes
too acute and the actual form cannot be wrenched into con-
formity with the ideal preserved in the reason, man's only re-
source is to turn away from the distorted external and social
forms of life to those inner personal springs of nature from
which new forms may be evolved. Already in 1494 Thomas à
Kempis had preached the quest for heaven through unreasoning

love, and the miracle plays had represented the fool as particularly acceptable to God. Other minds of a different bent from those of Barclay and Brant had found in the study of the classics a basis for confidence in man's nature and a source for a new formulation of an external order. In the brief time before that new interpretation of man and that order took on in turn the aspect of authority, Erasmus embodied its life-giving fluidity in the *Praise of Folly*.

CHAPTER VIII

THE PRAISE OF FOLLY

Contempt is a sentiment that cannot be entertained by comic intelligence. What is it but an excuse to be idly minded, or personally lofty, or comfortably narrow, not perfectly humane?
—*Meredith*

Folly is not the heroine of the *Ship of Fools*. Brant's sympathies were all with wisdom. He assumed, too, that some sort of wisdom was available which would protect men from their follies and furnish an active principle for the attainment of a formulated end. Wisdom in Barclay's version appeared more like a shrewd foresight, laboring zealously in an earthly field while carefully nourishing her desire for security in a heavenly home. But neither Brant nor Barclay really transported their readers beyond wisdom's knee into the carnival pageant of obstreperous and irresponsible life which they visualized while they penned their books to rebuke it. The *Praise of Folly*, however, first printed in Latin soon after the appearance of Barclay's *Ship*, led the reader into the market place in full carnival, where Folly herself attended by a rout of masquers mounted the mock pulpit and delivered him a sermon. But though this Folly, like Brant himself, seemed to speak to the populace—and Chaloner justified his English translation of the oration in part by the comfort it would bring to "meane men of baser wittes & condicion[1]"—her true audience was that smaller groups of minds prepared to enjoy a more varied irony and to follow the idea of folly from paradox to paradox. Assuming the liberty of the privileged fool, and evoking by her carnival surroundings the gay confidence in vitality which lends a keener edge to criticism of conduct, she preached a sermon in praise of folly which made generous allowance for the weakness of man's earthly nature and yet directed his aspiration to a more intensely spiritual heaven than that described in the *Ship of Fools.*

When Erasmus wrote the *Praise of Folly* he had not yet lived under the shadow of the great Dance of Death in Basel, nor had he yet embarked definitely upon the sustained labors which culminated in his editions of the New Testament and the Works of Saint Jerome. Instead of pursuing his studies among the humanists of the Rhineland, his native home, he had gone from his monastery at Steyn to Paris, exchanging a life of contemplation according to the Windesheim rule and the meditations of Ruysbroek and Thomas à Kempis for the life of a student of the more intellectual aspects of theology. Paris in the 1490's and early 1500's was still the centre of theological study in western Europe, in spite of the abuses in discipline at the University and of the sterility of the Terminist and Scotist methods of argument in vogue at the colleges of Montaigu, Navarre and Sorbonne. Since the visit of Bessarion, and since Fichet's institution of the study of Greek in the University, progress had been made in the knowledge of Plato and in the methods of the Italian humanists; even during Erasmus' first stay in the city Lefèvre d'Etaples was at work on his editions of Aristotle, and was teaching at the headquarters of Greek studies, the Collège du Cardinal Lemoine.[2] But Erasmus, until after his first trip to England and his crucial meeting with Colet, seems to have been affiliated rather with the group of humanists working in Latin than with the Greek scholars. From his membership in the Montaigu organization he must have been in touch with the movements for the reform of the clergy, secular and regular, initiated by the indefatigable Standonk; but by his friendships with Faustus Andrelini and Robert

Gaguin (whose poem *De fatuis mondanis* was appended to a French edition of the Latin *Ship*)[3] he was thrown with stylists and with moralists of the older order. The *Antibarbaros* which he showed to Gaguin during his first winter in Paris, and the first edition of the *Adages*, printed in 1500, represent his preoccupation with the elegancies of expression. His spiritual development, nourished by the mysticism of the Brothers of the Common Life and fertilized by his friendships with Colet and Batt and his studies under the direction of Jean Vitrier, flowered in the *Enchiridion militis Christiani*, in 1504, but it does not seem to have guided his associations in Paris until after his trip to Italy. His interest while in Paris seems to have centered about the study of expression, with theological labors in preparation for the doctorate thrown in, and in investigation of the life of the city.

Up to the time of the writing of the *Praise of Folly* (1509), France had not severely censored the activities of the Joyous Societies. The episode of Baude and the counsellors of Charles VIII was in the past, the performance of the sottie by Gringore against the militant Pope was still to come, but the absence of prohibitions and of records of performances by the societies during these years is as likely to prove that they were going on as that they were not, and we can assume that Erasmus saw the costume with cap and bells going to and fro in the streets on days of merry-making. He may even have heard one of the mock preachings or "sermons joyeux" which celebrated the virtues of Saint Onion or Saint Raisin, or which, like the "Cry" preceding Gringore's sottie, expanded the text "Stultorum numerus est infinitus."[4] He had, in any case, had the opportunity to observe the idea of "folly" interpreted, through Gaguin, as a generic name for undesirable conduct, and also to see the gaiety of those who disguised themselves as fools.

To a student of the classics the vision of Folly in person may well have suggested the figure of Momus, god of reprehension, particularly when Olivier Maillard in his Cordelier's robes was acting out the rôle from Parisian pulpits.[5] But Erasmus, after his studies in Greek were really under way, could round out his conception of Folly and her attitude toward man not only from the Parisian Folie of the sotties, if he chanced to see her, or from listening to the sharp-tongued reformer, but from the characteristic point of view of Lucian, with whose "educated insolence" he became thoroughly familiar. Shortly after his departure from Paris for Italy in the fall of 1506, the collection of dialogues translated jointly from Lucian by More and Erasmus was issued from the press of Badius Ascensius. It contained the *Toxaris, Alexander, Gallus, Timon,* the *Tyrannicide* with Erasmus' reply, *De eis qui Mercede degunt,* the *Cynicus, Menippus* and *Philopseudes.*[6] While Erasmus was waiting in Florence for the end of the siege of Bologna, he worked on still other dialogues, "so as not to be entirely idle."[7] From all these he learned to roam in mind through a heaven and hell peopled by the personifications of myth, and to attack erring human nature with a weapon lighter than the facetiousness of popular satire—light irony.

When Erasmus jolted back along the road to England in 1509 inventing the beginning of the *Praise of Folly* in his mind, he brought to its composition a wealth of association which inevitably turned his personification of Folly into a different figure from that either of the moralists or of the popular satirists. He had, in the first place, the tantalizing pun upon the name of his merry friend Sir Thomas More to build on. His sense of form, apparently a native gift, had been disciplined by his studies in elegant Latinity and already expressed in the early treatise *De conscribendis epistolis* as well as in the *Adages.* His command of classical references had been vastly broadened by the work of expanding the *Adages* which he had undertaken for the Aldine edition of 1508. The greater part of his translations up to the time of his return to England had been the dialogues of Lucian, whose rhetoric must have delighted him as much as their irridescent irony. He had as well some knowledge of France, surely some knowledge of French and of the popular literature in which the idea of folly was current as a symbol of man's behavior. (His scathing references to the aureate language of the Rhetoriqueurs in the beginning of the *Praise* bear out the opinion of Richter that he know French.)[8] Above all, he had a well-defined personal religious attitude, strengthened by his knowledge of the early fathers of the church and the teachings of the Windesheim group. This attitude, not yet under attack in the controversies of the Reformation, satisfied his own need for sincerity in reverence and in conduct, and also left him free to pursue his philological studies with the complete approbation of his conscience. His sermon on wisdom —or folly—then, beckons with one hand to Solomon and Ecclesiastes, as all meditations on wisdom or folly must, but stretches out the other to the whole "rout of poeticall gods." Condemnation of man's weakness and ignorance may be the object of his book, and the familiar figure of Folly the means, but the result is the creation of a symbol which shows how human nature bears present fruit indeed in ill, but yet contains the seeds of future good. The paradoxes which present themselves to minds aware of the real and eager to create the ideal must have risen up in his mind in the terms in which they were thought by Augustine and Gregory, and he related them to the symbolical currency which he found at hand, to the obvious descriptions of fools and folly. But by virtue of his faith in man he united the old feeling of mystery and freedom connected with the wanton folk fool to his picture of erring fools in society; he censured earthly morality in the double name of earthly and spiritual vitality. Although the central preoccupation of his thought remained the reform of human society especially as it was embodied in the church, he made his sermon intelligible to his contemporaries, and tasty too, by binding it firmly to the familiar lists of follies and by coupling the preaching of an unusually canny apostle of the ideal to the mock-preaching of a carnival masquer. He organized into his picture of Folly all the elements with which he was familiar and fused them by his supple rhetoric.

Rhetoric is the tool by which Erasmus makes his lesson attractive. Brant's readers were supposed to need the help of pictures to hold their attention upon what they read, but the audience to which Folly speaks is evidently expected to be stimulated to nimble-wittedness by the use of language alone. As soon as she opens her oration—the "vulgar" English version of Sir Thomas Chaloner catches the mood of the Latin skilfully—one perceives that she is genuinely at home with the Muses![9]

How so ever men commonly talke of me (as pardie I am not ignoraunt what lewde reportes go on Folie, yea even amongs those that are veriest fooles of all) yet that I am she, I onely (I saie) who through myne influence do gladde both the godds and men, by this it maie appeare sufficiently: that as soone as I came forth to saie my mynd afore this your so notable assemblie, by & by all your lokes began to clere up . . . me semeth evin, that all ye (whom I see here present) doe fare as if ye were well whitled, and thoroughly moysted with the Nectar wine of the Homericall Godds, not without a porcion of the juyce of that mervaillous herbe Nepenthes, which hath force to put sadnesse and melancholie from the herte: Where as before ye satte all heavie, and glommyng, as if ye had come lately from Trophonius cave, or saint Patrikes purgatorie. But lyke as when Phebus displaieth his golden bright raies uppon the earth, or whan after a sharpe stormie wynter, the new primetyde flourisseth with his caulme sweete Westerne wynds, than (loe) a new lykenesse, a newe hewe, and a newe youthe (as it were) retourneth unto all thynges: Even so, as soone as I appeared, ye all beganne to loke up lustily.[10]

The whole induction is gaily ornate, but ornate with a purpose; Erasmus believed that "sweet similitudes and sage sentences" afforded not only pleasure but definite and serious didactic effect:

Iam vero quis nescit praecipuas orationis tum opes tum delicias in sententiis metaphoris parabolis paradigmatis exemplis similitudinibus imaginibus atque id genus schematis sitas esse, quae quum semper vehementer honestant dictionem tum incredibilem adferunt ornatum et gratiam quoties iam communi consensu recepta in vulgi sermonem abierunt, libenter enim audit quisque quod agnoscit, maxime vero, si vetustatis commendatio quaedam accedit.[11]

The pictures with which Holbein illustrated the *Praise* were vivid sketches[12], but the rich rhetoric of the oration, not the illustrations, carried the burden of its moral meaning.

Chaloner responded to the challenge of Erasmus' vein by justifying his translation of the mock oration with some ironic rhetoric of his own. His motives in making the English version were all sobriety and altruism, he says, but still it may be thought a folly to have translated a book

whereas the name it selfe semeth to set foorth no wisdome, or matter of gravitee: unless perhaps Erasmus, the autour thereof, delited to mocke men, in calling it one thyng and meanyng another.[13]

Like Barclay, he wished to avoid the suspicion of dealing in "derision," although he confessed that he recognized that Folly was a general human characteristic, as much English as Dutch:—"will we or nill we, she will be sure to beare a stroke in most or our dooyings."[14] He really designed his translation to relieve common men of their envy for those in high estate, by painting the trials of kingship and the follies of those in authority. But he would like, for the benefit of those authorities, to disclaim any part in Folly's over-sour words, excusing himself with Erasmus' own plea:

So what excuse he maketh, the same I requyre maie serve for me: that thyngs spoken foolisshely, by Folie, maie be even so taken, & not wrested to any bitter sence or ernest applicacion. For surely if the crabbedst men that be, are wont to take a fooles woords as in sporte, for feare lest others myght recken they would not wynche without a galled back: than how muche more is a domme booke written generally to be borne withall? namely where the title pretendeth no gravitee, but rather a toye to stirre laughter, without offence in the boke, if the reader bring none offence with hym.[15]

But Chaloner recognized that the book was, partly at least, in the tradition of the mirrors of conduct, for he stated that in it a man may see his "owne image more lively described than in any peincted table." To make all clear, he proposed to guide his readers through the book by means of marginal notes to warn them when the first author was not speaking seriously— for in so far as the sermon deals with abuses of the time, "what knowe we, if Erasmus in this booke thought good betweene game and ernest to rebuke the same?"[16]

The general plan of Folly's harangue is: first to introduce herself and her attendants, and to state her claims upon mankind's attention. In doing this she discusses her version of the dictum that all is vanity and expresses her theory of the nature of man and her estimate of the respective wisdoms of the fool and the sage. Then glancing around the world she points out those whose condition is especially blessed, either through her own ministrations or through those of her chief handmaids, Self-love and Oblivion. Among these happy ones she finds poets and all devotees of the arts and sciences, none of whom thrive except in their own esteem, with the possible exception of doctors and lawyers, for whom practical human beings do find certain uses. From these lesser fools she passes on to the greater, to all officers of the state and to churchmen of all ranks, regular and secular. Their lives, she proves, owe all their security to the human cult of folly. She brings her oration to a close with a long justification of herself, illustrated by scriptural and classical texts, and climbs at the end to a praise of the unreasoning love of God which is worthy comparison with the words of Bembo in the fourth book of the *Courtier*.

In her roll-call of human vanities Folly introduces the familiar varieties of proverbial fool, but the vividness of her appreciation of their peculiarities makes them live as they never live in lists of proverbs. The unloved, and the love-sick, jealous husbands who imprison their wives needlessly, all those who sin against the group by covetousness—men who marry to acquire their wives' dowries, false executors who are guilty of mal-administration of their clients' goods, cheating merchants whose deceptions are forgiven by equally false friars when they make donations to the orders, dreamers who satisfy them-selves with the imagination of riches to be acquired through luck or through inheritance—she ridicules them all in a few droll words. She rebukes gluttons and sluggards and the falsely proud who build themselves great tombs and arrange the pomp of their funerals in advance, "with none other desyre in this poyncte, than if beyng made maiors or sherives they shoulde ordeine a midsomer syght."[17] Some of the pictures of these fools and their fellows in action have the gusto of scenes in the Flemish tapestries with which they are contemporary. The hunters, for instance, are puffed up with pride in the ritual of their sport:

what an incredible pleasure thei conceive, so often as thei here that foule musike, whiche a horne maketh, beyng touted in, or the howlyng of a meny of doggs: yea I thinke the veric stenche of the houndes kennell, senteth muske unto theyr noses.

And what a ceremony at the death—

Every poore man maie cutte out an oxe, or a shepe, wheras suche venaison maie not be dismembred but of a gentilman: who bare-headded, and set on knees, with a knife prepared proprely to that use, (for every kinde of knife is not allowable) also with certaine jestures cuttes a sunder certaine partes of the wildbeast, in a cer-taine order verie circumstantly. Whiche duryng, the standers by, not speakyng a worde, behold it solemnly, as if it were some holy Misterie, havyng seen the like yet more than a hundred tymes before.[18]

Dice players, real addicts of the game, feel their hearts begin

to beat in their stomachs if they so much as hear the sound of
dice upon the board, and having make shipwreck

upon the Dyserocke (a daunger farre more perilous, than is the
race of Britaine) theim selves hardely escapyng in theyr hose and
theyr doublets.

will nevertheless rather cheat their own brothers than their
opponents at the table, all for love of the game.[19] Poets, ora-
tors and rhetoricians make fools of themselves by feeding
"fooles eares with mere trifles and foolisshe fables,"[20] and
pardoners play upon the credulity of the people who love tales
of feigned miracles, and "surely suche fables are not onely
doulcet to passe the tyme withall, but gainfull also to theyr
practisers, suche as perdoners & limittours be."[21]

Gullers and gulled alike, the world is after all a kingdom of
fools. Folly makes rather bitter fun of those of her servants
who try to curry favor with other deities by offerings. Some
seek to cozen the Lord by the use of their "charmelyke Ro-
saries," or to get boons from the saints by prayers. Usurers,
warriors and corrupt judges display their "foolisshe wanhope,"
each one thinking that by dropping "one halfpenie of all his evill
gotten goods" into the alms box he will obtain forgiveness for
his deceptions.[22] Fools like these hang votive tablets on the
walls of the chapels of their favorite saints in thanks for benefits received, but none of them ever ask to be relieved of their
folly—which proves that she controls them:

Some one (perchaunce) was saved from drowning: an other striken
through with a pot-gonne, recovered. . . . An other, that dranke two
sortes of poyson at ones, through the conflict of theyr contrarie opera-
cions, beyng driven into a laxe, found theim rather medicinable, than
deadly, unto hym. . . . An other, beyng passhed with the fall of an
house, lost not (thankes be to the sainct) his life. . . . But none of
all these (I warrant you) yeldeth thanks for his folie laied asyde.
So sweete a thyng it is, to be cumbred with no wysdome, as men had
rather axe perdone of any other thyng, than that.[23]

Even the powerful on earth are subjects of Folly. When she comes to discuss the follies of courtiers, kings, bishops, cardinals, and popes, however, the gravity of the subject checks her merry-making and she speaks with dignity and brevity. She hits the courtiers off as "minion gaibeseen gentilmen" whose gay clothes belie their true natures; beauty of apparel should accompany wisdom and virtue in its wearer, whereas actually it conceals adulation, avarice, lust, and envy.[24] The magnificence of the garments of the king should reflect his beneficence to his people, for the king is magnificent either as a bright star or as a baleful comet. His clothes symbolize the ideal virtues with which he should shine:

Geve hym a chayne about his necke for token that all vertues woulde agreablie be enchayned in him: geve hym also a crowne frette with perle and stone, in signe he ought to excelle others in all princely vertues: than a sceptre in his hand betokennyng justice with an upright mynde on all sydes: lastly a Robe of purpre, whiche signifieth zeale & fervent affection towarde his subjectes: This maner apparaile (I saie) if that a prince shulde duely conferre with his livyng, I wene he wold be ashamed to weare it, fearyng lest some fine expositor myght tourne all his pompe and solemnesse of royall robes into a derision: namely whan he hath no maner part of a prince in hym, savyng onely the clothyng.[25]

In the same way, the robes of the bishops and cardinals and of the pope himself should properly betoken the purity and rectitude of their lives. Since it patently does not, and since even Folly may not attack the great too openly without fear of reprisals, she passes them over with this gesture of mournful reminder and devotes the greater part of her oration, not to the powerful who are in charge of the destiny of the external order of society, but to the members of the learned professions who supposedly preside over the activities of the reason—the book-makers, doctors of divinity, theologians. They too, she finds, are servants of Folly.

The verve with which Erasmus assails the battalions of the

supposedly educated comes from his conviction that their activities in many cases are futile in the promotion of man toward his true end; they are motivated by petty ambition, and they misuse the reason, the tool which after all is a necessary instrument for the liberation of the human spirit. His irony here is most explicit. Authors, for instance, "suche also as in makyng and publisshyng of new bokes, doe fisshe for a praise and glorie," are the happiest among writers: they do not harass themselves over their composition but set down anything that they happen to have in their heads, even their own dreams, and their books then appear in all the booksellers' front windows, with their "names, surnames and bynames, set in the fyrst frunts" of each copy; and they send each other epistles and verses in praise of each other's works, "from fooles, to fooles: and from asses to asses."[26] But the poor fellows who go in for solid scholarship live miserable and dull lives:

seyng how continually thei are faine to writhe their wittes in and out, in puttyng to, in chaunging, in blottyng out, in laiyng theyr woorke aside, in overvewyng it againe, in shewyng it to some for a prouffe, and yet kepyng it in theyr hands whole nyne yeres togethers, so that they are never satisfied with theim selves, whiles they goe about to purchase so vaine a rewarde as praise is, yea and that gevin theim by a few, onely so dearely bought with many nights labors, and losse of slepe, the sweetest thing that can be, & with so many travailes, and beatyng of theyr braines about it: besides the hurt thei susteine in their bodies, decaie of beautie, marryng of theyr eiesight, or also blindnesse, together with povertee, envie, forbearyng of pleasures, untimely age, hasted death, and suche like disadvantages, whiche natheles these wisemen sticke not at, so they maie have theyr writyng allowed at one or two of these blereied bokewormes hands.[27]

The richness and, it must be confessed, the occasional confusion of the *Praise of Folly* comes from the completeness with which Erasmus reviews the errors of the "mental workers" of his time. Alchemists, grammarians, natural philosophers, jurists, and logicians who let truth slip by them for the moon shine in the water, are all with rhetorical pungency scourged for their fatuous methods and inadequate objectives. All of them fail to use their reason properly for the discovery of accessible truth.

Methods which are foolish and sterile in the pursuit of the facts of inanimate nature are doubly useless in the search for spiritual truth. Yet Folly maintains that her chief subjects are the theologians and the friars whose business it is to search out spiritual truth and express it in action. The theologians use their reasons chiefly to generate definitions, and Folly doubts the value of unrestrained defining, for she considers it unlucky to try to bound, or to separate into parts, the universal.[28] But the whole delight of these doctors of divinity is in nothing else. They look down upon other men as upon worms creeping on the ground, while they themselves are

hedged in on all sides, with suche a gard of Magistral diffinicions, conclusions, corollaries, explicite & implicite, proposicions, with so many startyng holes, as not Vulcanes netts were hable so fastly to holde theim, but they wolde wynde theim selves out againe with Distinctions, wherwith thei carve al knottes asunder, as smothely as a rasour dooeth the heares of a mans beard.[29]

They argue how the world was created, by what channels original sin was driven into Adam's posterity, whether Christ might have appeared upon earth in the form of a woman, of a devil, or of a squash, and if he had chosen to do so how he would have been able to preach. They understand the letter of their faith but not the spirit, although to hear them talk you would think they knew more about Christianity and its meaning than those who were Christ's followers during his life. Folly's conclusion— for she herself has been indulging in definitions, distinctions and conclusions—is that the whole pack of theologians, Reales, Nominales, Thomistes, Albertistes, Occanistes, and Dunsmen, should be shipped off to fight the Turks and Saracens, for surely even a Turk would run from a doctor of divinity in full panoply.[30] And as for the monks and friars, the less said of them the better, though Folly for her part has a lot to say. They are ignorant and gross, they haunt the alehouses, roar out psalms which they don't understand "(lyke a meny of asses)," they beg from door to door in a great lowing voice, and think that they represent the apostles. Yet for all their apostolic charity, they fall to quarreling over the color of their gowns or to boasting of preserving themselves in a state of meritorious dirtiness. Their words are stupid and their actions are those of mere ignorant fools.[31]

So Folly demonstrates that all mankind is under her sway, dissecting it with greater or less asperity according to whether she is treating the conventional list of social misconducts or the deeper misuses of reason and power among the clergy and rulers of the people. But in spite of everything, she feels that man's nature is good, she knows herself to be benign, and after all she as overlord of the race of men is the moderator of its destiny. When therefore she comes to analyse her own relationship to men, her argument leads her to identify herself, Folly, with that wisdom which formulates anew man's desire. Unlike the fore-ordained wisdom whose goodness is preached in the *Ship of Fools*, the wisdom into which man's folly may grow emerges gradually from the chaos of appetites and is recognized by the reason as valid because it can be seen to satisfy the needs of man.

Folly explains first that with the wealth of images offered up to her she has no cause to be jealous of any other god:

But I take it, that so many images are erected in my name, as there be livyng men, bearyng the lively representacion and image of me about theim, will they, or will they not. Wherfore, I have no cause to be agreeved with the other Godds, though they be woorshipped sundrely, in sundrie partes of the earth: and that at tymes of the yere prefixed. As Phebus in the Isle of Rhodes, Venus in Cypres, Juno at Argos, Minerva at Athenes, Jupiter in Olympus,

Neptunus at Tarentum: and Priapus at Lampsacum, Wheras all the worlde universally offreth me daie by daie farre dearer, and more digne sacrifiics, than theirs are.[32]

Life itself, and its perpetual recreation upon the earth, are both due to her, she says; and those human beings who are most closely created in her image are best fitted for the business of living. Consider old men, children, and "naturals": their weakness or ignorance is tolerated by the whole world and brings them privileges denied to the rest of humanity. The domestic fools are particularly happy in their lot, for they are "free, and exempt from all feare of death, whiche feare is no small corrosive, to a mind that mindeth it I warrant you"; they do not dread impending adversity, nor hope for gifts from fortune, and they are cherished by the great, who allow them to speak their minds freely.[33] Outside of these particularly favored classes of mankind who have nothing to do, it appears that other lesser fools carry on the real business of the world and win success and renown. Who goes to the wars? Not the good father sages "who soked up with longe studie, leane, and colde of bloudde, maie scantly draw theyr wynde," but the bold young bloods with as little wit as possible.[34] And what human friendship can be established with a sage, requiring as he does a relationship based upon wisdom and proportion—able in fact to be friends with his like only? The pursuit of wisdom does not fit man for life but rather leads him hastily toward exhaustion and death:

For see you not (I praie you) how these wysemen, who are geven to philosophie, or some suche ernest and grave studie, dooe for the most parte waxe hore, before they be fully yonge men? Whiche undoubtedly cometh of cares, & incessant sharpe travailyng of the braine, by little and litle sokyng up the lively juice of the sprites: wheras my fooles on the other side, be slicke, and smothe skinned, yea & well trussed together, lyke hoglyngs of Acarnania.[35]

So far the irony of the picture is clear. But when Folly comes to discuss the failure of the wise really to live, one can no longer be sure that Erasmus through her is speaking only a part of his thought. Only experience of living can bring real prudence, she says:

A wyseman reports hym selfe to his bokes, and then learneth naught but mere triflyng distinctions of woords. A foole in jeopardyng, and goyng presently where thyngs are to be knowne, gathereth (unless I am deceived) the perfect true prudence.[36]

Those who ordinarily pass for wise are ineffective outside the study-room because they do not understand the forces that really motivate their fellow-men.

For if wisedome, accordyng to the Stoikes diffinicion, is naught els than to be ruled by reason: and folie to be ledde as affection will: Consider now (I praie you) how muche more Affection, than Reason, Jupiter hath put in men, to the end theyre lyfe shoulde not altogethers be heavy, and unpleasant. As if ye shoulde compare an ounce to a pounde. Furthurmore, he shutte up Reason within the narowe compasse of mans head, leavyng all the rest of the bodie to affections: settyng also, two most violent tyrannes against hir, that is to saie, Anger, raignyng in the fortresse of the hert: and concupiscence, whiche evin to the lowest part of the bealy, dooeth occupy a large possession.[37]

Thought therefore is weak; the "truth" of the sages may or may not be true in the realm of reason, but it will have little genuine power over mens' actions if it comes in conflict with their desires. Opinion, which rather than truth expresses what men think they want, is of chief importance to man.

But Philosophers saie it is a miserable thyng to be begyled, and erre so. Naie, most miserable is it (I saie) not to erre, and not to be deceived. For too too are thei deceived, who wene that mans felicitee consisteth in thinges self, and not rather in the opinion how the same are taken. In as muche as in all humaine thynges, there is so great darknesse and diversnesse, as nothyng maie be clerely knowne out, nor discouvered.[38]

Folly formulates freshly the ancient wisdom with which priests and psychologists encourage the groping mind:

For that is (saie they [the philosophers]) even the greatest miserie of all, to be blinded so with Folie, to erre so, to be deceived so, to be ignorant so. Naie verilier, that it is to be a man. And yet I see not why thei shuld call you miserable therfore, in as muche as ye be borne so, ye be ordeigned so, and made so, and such is the commen destiny lotted to every one of you.

For nothyng maie properly be called miserable, that agreeth with the kind it cometh of, unles perchaunce some woulde thynke a mans nature were to be lamented, because he can not flie as burdes dooe, nor go on all foures as other beastes dooe, nor fence hym with his hornes as bulles doe.[39]

In the golden age, when intellectual disciplines had not been invented, man managed to live in a condition of social equity, benevolence and understanding in spite of his so-called folly. In making this admission, Erasmus acknowledges the difference between the nature of man once-upon-a-time and now; but he goes quickly on to say that any satisfaction which man feels in his condition at any time is due to self-deception. Self-love, Folly's handmaid, encourages men in self-deception and in so doing gives them the power to live at all, and Adulacion, another of Folly's servants, teaches man the way of social intercourse more kindly than a rough honesty which blurts out unwelcome truths at inopportune moments. Adulacion

encourageth a weake sprite, comforteth one droupyng in sadnesse, quickeneth a langwisshyng thought, wakeneth a dulle head, reiseth up a sicke mynde, mollifieth a stubbourne hert.[40]

and performs many other benefits, and Self-love is absolutely essential for the individual's peace of mind:

I praie you, can he love any bodie, that loveth not hym selfe? can he agree with anybody, that discordeth with hym selfe? Maie he please others, that is displeasant, and tedious to hym selfe?[41]

The technique of mental adjustment described here rings familiarly in modern ears, all the fresher for its allegorical garb. Apparently the modern temper is not the only thing which can

knock the heroics out of man's idea of himself. Life, from the
vantage point of Folly, looks petty, crawling, dull. Borrowing
from Lucian, and so referring forward to another satirist who
with more pain and through other symbols expressed his sense
of the weakness of man, Erasmus reports what humanity looks
like seen at a distance:

Briefely, if one (as Menippus did) lokyng out of the moone, be-
helde from thence the innumerable tumults, & businesses of mortall
men, he shoulde thynke verily he saw a meny of flies, or gnattes,
braulyng, fightyng, begilyng, robbyng, plaiyng, livyng wantonly,
borne, bredde up, decaiyng, and diyng: So that it is scant belevable,
what commocions, and what Tragedies, are sterred up, by so litell,
and so short lived a vermyn as this man is. For sometimes a small
storme of warre, or pestilence, swopeth awaie and dispatcheth many
thousandes of theim togethers.[42]

Yet this same man is capable of an immense exaltation which
may as truly be called folly as the other aberration which leads
to all social ills, and while condemning that aberration Erasmus
pays tribute too to the happy madness which carries man beyond the bounds of reason:

But there is an other kynde of madnesse, farre unlike the former,
whiche procedeth from me wholy, and most is to be embraced. As
often as a certaine pleasant raving, or errour of the mynde, de-
livereth the herte of that man, whom it possesseth, from all wonted
carefulnesse, and rendreth it dyvers waies, much recreated with
new delectation.[43]

This supreme unreason is the final justification which Folly
advances for her sovereignty over man, but before she describes
it she finds many pleasant things to say about herself which
between them show the materials out of which she herself was
confected. She is the daughter of mythology, born of the young
Plutus and of the nymph Neotete or Youth itself. She was
brought forth in the classical Earthly Paradise, the Fortunate
Isles, where

neither labour, nor age, nor any maner sickenesse reigneth, nor in the fields there dooe either Nettles, Thistles, Mallowes, Brambles, Cockle, or suche lyke baggage grow, but in steede therof Gylofloures, Roses, Lilies, Basile, Violetts, and suche swete smellyng herbes, as whilom grew in Adonis gardeins, dooe on all sides satisfie bothe the sente, and the sight.[44]

She was nursed by Drunkenes, daughter of Bacchus, and Rudenes, daughter of Pan, so her bond with high spirits and fertility is attested by the best mythological witnesses. But for all her classical birth, her pedigree is best known among the schoolmen. She cites the familiar didactic texts of the Middle Ages as sponsors for her importance, *Cato*, then Horace— "myne owne good Horace, as a fatte and fayre fedde hoglyng of Epicure's herde"[45]—Homer, and Cicero. Among Biblical authors she finds her chief supports in Salomon the Ecclesiaste and Jeremiah, and in the New Testament in the works of Paul. But the words of Christ himself, turning to his Father with the cry "Thou knowest myne unwysedome" provide her with her highest patent, and with her transition from ironic condemnation of earthly fools to genuine praise of the godly folly of Gregory, of the fool who like Jacopone da Todi seeks God through unreasoning love. She reconciles the nature of man with his own highest aspiration, still with the point of rhetorical irony behind her words:

Now all these textes that I have alleaged, doe thei not plainly testifie, that mortall men beyng fooles, are godly also? and that Christ hym selfe mindyng the relefe and redempcion of mankynds folie, although he was the ineffable wisedome of the father, became yet a maner foole, wheras takyng mans nature upon hym, he was founde both in fourme & habite lyke unto other men?[46]

Has not the Christian religion, she asks, a "certaine sybship with simplicitee & devoute foolishenesse, in nothyng agreyng with worldly wysedome," for its devoutest followers are children, old folks, women and fools, her most privileged followers. Moreover, "no maner fooles are in apparence more ideote-like, than suche as are totally ravisshed, and enflamed with the ardent zeale of Christian charitee."[47] The codes of conduct of the worldly and of the true Christian, or of the true philosopher according to Plato, are totally opposed. The true Christian and philosopher meditate upon death, which no successful worldling can consider healthy mental exercise. The affections of the body govern the worldling, the affections of the mind—the exercise of the memory, the understanding and the will—occupy the efforts of the godly and the philosophical. It is not that the godly condemn what the eye can see, but that they set less store by it:

For as worldlyngs have richesse in best reputacion, next therto estemyng the weale of theyr bodies, and lest regardyng the profite of theyr soules, in case thei regarde it all, for some of them believe there is no soule, because they can not see it at the eie: So againe devout persons put theyr whole confidence in god beyng the simplest and most pure thyng of all others, and secondly do chearishe that, that draweth nerest to hym, I meane the sprite, bestowyng no cost nor tendance on their bodies, nor on pleasures belongyng to the same.[48]

So the oration climbs up to a vision of the love of God, into which the idea of folly still intrudes itself; for love is a madness, a being ravished away from oneself, beyond reason, and the love of God is the most intense ravishment, the truest folly.[49] After this there is no epilogue. The picture is complete, and the speaker abruptly takes her leave:

Fare ye well therfore, clappe your hands in token of gladnesse, live carelesse, and drinke all out, ye trustie servaunts and solemne ministers of Folie.[50]

The contrast between the *Ship of Fools* and the *Praise of Folly* is complete, yet both use the symbol of the fool to express their opinion of mankind. The differences between them show how effective this fool-symbol could be, when it had a literary context and a variety of physical images back of it. The *Ship of Fools* interpreted the figure in the traditional Old Testament manner, condemning fools as actual or potential sinners, making man's nature no excuse for his misconduct. Its concrete descriptions reflected the contents of the lists of secular nuisances, the arrogant huntsmen, the extravagant dandies, the pedantic scholars. Its criticism of churchmen expressed the hope of reform through the preservation of the established order. It did not mention any future blessedness for the fool-in-the-world, although the church fathers who reiterated the idea after Paul were cited as general authorities for the condemnation of worldly misconduct. By the ship device, by the procession-like parade of follies and by the pictures, it suggested the fool of the carnival season, but the liberty in criticism of the carnival fool or of the jester did not figure in the book at all. No feeling of freedom of any kind, indeed, is conveyed by the *Ship of Fools,* not even the freedom to damn oneself by folly if one will. Rather, one is conscious of pressures hemming one in and relentlessly pushing one upward and onward, a sense of the perils that this world holds for the unwary, of the ridicule of one's fellows, or of the spiritual rewards held out to one and of the probable pains awaiting the backslider. Erasmus gives one the freedom of folly. The traditional fools are duly present in his book, as well as the individualized follies of the age; the carnival fool, too, is invoked by the mechanism of the mock sermon. But his Folly is free, with the license of the jester, and she thinks not of rewards and punishments but of man's nature, weak as it is, expressing itself in life, and of the reality which cannot be approached by the strictly reasonable and prudent. Out of this admission of the weakness of human devices comes a sense of power. One no longer feels that provision for the future is the object of life, that the fool is only he who either does not see or wilfully ignores future dangers.

The fool is strong and gay, strength and gaiety in their way bring power. By these expansions, the symbol of the fool becomes a stimulus to benign laughter. Not the hysterical laughter arising from the "philosophy of the Broad Grin, hesitating between the skeleton and the embryo," nor the heavy laughter of ridicule, but a genial laugh of humane irony, viewing at once man and the visions of man.

Chapter IX

ROLES OF FOLLY IN ENGLISH MORALITIES

La vertu ne rompt son chemin ny son train, pour orage qu'il fasse.

—*Montaigne*

The educated and revolutionary society of the fifteenth century evolved the figure of Mother Folly, epitome of man's perennial weakness but also of his vitality and of his ability to criticize himself. Erasmus used her as the composite symbol of both these aspects of man and invested her with affectionate and life-giving tyranny over her subjects. But the separate activities of the fool in literature continued their existence, and actual jesters and mock fools still flourished. The fool continued to play a part in the didactic moralizings of the 1500's, to figure in dramatic rôles, to frequent in person the courts of kings and noblemen, to gambol in the streets in holiday processions, to provide story material for popular jests. The antithesis of the wise man and the fool continued to pass current as a measure of differences in human adequacy. But no fresh use of the composite idea of personified Folly was made after Erasmus, and outside of the drama the vogue of the fool as a literary figure of any symbolic quality at all was small. No more lists of follies appeared, or at least those that did were pale reflections of their predecessors. The sixteenth-century list, when the device was used, was one of plain knaves individualized as gamesters, drunkards, deceitful servants, without any particular reference to their essential weakness and ignorance. Other antitheses like that of the just and the unjust man joined that of the wise man and fool as popular terms expressing the poles of conduct. The amplest body of material presenting fools was the group of jest-books in which he figured quite simply as a clown whose limitations were accepted without thought. The fool practically disappeared as a symbol of man's conflicting capacities.

Against this general background, however, a distinction must be made between what happened in France and what happened in England. Both countries had shared the literature of didactic folly, and both had liberally supplied examples of court jesters and folk fools. But Folly in native English literature up to 1550 though sometimes a mirthmaker was none the less uniformly a symbol of condemnation and scorn. Later, in the plays of Shakespeare, the fool became an inspired interpreter of events, but the mystic glorification of unreason did not produce any notable pieces of English writing in terms of folly.

Joyous societies had not flourished in England.[1] The English dramatic impulse produced mystery plays, moralities, interludes of a farcical kind, but no such group of satirical pictures of society as the sotties. Comic characters lent relief to the tension of the cycles of Biblical plays, but no such use was made of the figure of the fool as we have seen in the longer French plays.[2] Interludes commenting on current events were given in schools, at court, or in towns in a manner suggestive of the sotties, but there is no indication that they used the dress or the name of fool to point their morals.[3] A record from Ipswich as late as 1568/9 informs us that there was "paid to Martyn the mynstrel for him and his companye for playing the Fooles in the Halle . . . x.s."[4] but it gives no sign that Martin and his fellows did anything but tumble and talk patter. In the morality of *Mankind* three characters enter with dancing and somersaulting, embarrass the sober preacher Mercy by their ribald anecdotes and devote themselves to the business of perverting Mankind. Their names are Nought, New-Gyse and Now-

a-days. They are assisted by a rascal called Mischief and by
one Titivillus who comes in "drest like a devil," bearing a net.
Between them they bring Mankind to swear assent to a series
of articles similar to the familiar list of follies, in which he
engages to break all the commandments, to sin according to
all the deadly sins, and totally to disregard the voice of the
preacher. We are told that the three Ns represent the world,
and that Titivillus "sygnyfyes the fend of helle," but although
the procedure in this play would be suitable to a sottie, no
specific use is made in it of the figure of the fool.[5] Yet fools
did appear in English plays, and a figure of abstract folly was
occasionally presented. He—for in English, Folly is masculine—
was in some cases notably merry and in some cases claimed to
rule mankind. But his ultimate fate was represented by the
position in which Queen Elizabeth saw him during her corona-
tion festivities, trodden under foot by Wisdom.[6] He never triumphed, and his merry appearance was excused as Barclay excused the gaiety of Latin satire: it existed,

nat . . . to the intent to exercyse wanton wordes or unrefrayned
lascyvyte, or to put . . . pleasour in suche dissolute langage: but
to ye intent to quenche vyces and to provoke the commons to
wysdome and vertue, and to be asshamed of theyr foly and excessyfe
lyvynge.[7]

Three English personifications of folly in morality plays before 1550 used it as a symbol of weakness and ignorance either
leading to sin or practically equal to sin itself. The first of
these is in the *Castel of Perseverance*, longest and loveliest of
the moralities. When Mankind, newly christened, betakes himself with his Bad Angel to serve the World, Stulticia and
Voluptas receive him and he is committed to their care to learn
his duties. Stulticia appears only during the first part of the
play. From his position in the story one understands him to
signify susceptibility-to-sin-through-weakness, as Voluptas is
perhaps a young Sensuality. Stulticia is spoken of as a "yonge

Foly." He promises to bind Mankind hopelessly to the service of the World:

> & I, Folye,
> schal hyen hym hye,
> tyl sum enmye
>   hym over-goo.
> In worldis wyt
> þat in folye syt,
> I þynkë ȝyt
>   his sowle to sloo.[8]

Or again, he prophesies Mankind's eventual worldly success and spiritual ruin:

> With ryche rentys I schal hym blynde,
>   Wyth þe werld tyl he be pytte;
> & þanne schal I, longe or his ende,
>   make þat caytyfe to be knytte
>   On þe werld whanne he is set sore
>
> Cum on, man! þou schalt not rewe,
> for þou wylt be to us trewe
> þou schalt be clad in clothis newe,
>   & be ryche evere-more.[9]

Like the codes of conduct for worldly success given in the sotties, these speeches indicate man's misconception in thinking the way to heaven is the same that leads to earthly prosperity. Covetousness is necessary for advancement in the world, and covetousness is a sin. Man may grow avaricious because he is only a fool, but as in *Proverbs,* his folly makes him a guilty sinner.[10] The sins themselves recite a list of the faults to which they lead man which coincides in many particulars with the lists of follies in the didactic poems. Pride advises Mankind to be boastful, to wear fashionable clothes, to scorn his father and mother; Wrath recommends that he make himself feared by being quick to revenge and always ready to spill blood; Envy promises him that revenge can best be accomplished by back-biting and the dissemination of false reports, while the sins of the flesh praise sweet spices, gay girls lolling in bed instead of attending Mass, and all the delights of "fleschly folye."[11]

This representation of Folly showed him as the quality which preëminently laid man open to sin; even Voluptas seemed to give priority in the antechamber of sin to Folly.[12] And other plays emphasized this same function of the symbol. Saint Paul in the play of his *Conversion* associated sin and folly closely,[13] and in the shorter morality of *Mundus et infans* Folly was quite simply described as all the sins together. Mankind in this play serves the World under names which change as he passes through the ages of man. At one point Conscience accosts him and converts him to a better life:

Manhood.	What, Conscience, should I leave all game and glee?
Conscience.	Nay Manhood, so mot I the,
	All mirth in measure is good for thee:
	But, sir, measure is in all thing.
Manhood.	Measure, Conscience? What thing may measure be?
Conscience.	Sir, keep you in charity,
	And from all evil company,
	For doubt of folly doing.
Manhood.	Folly! What thing callest thou folly?
Conscience.	Sir, it is pride, wrath, and envy,
	Sloth, covetise, and gluttony,
	Lechery the seventh is:
	These sins I call folly.[14]

Once warned to avoid Folly, Mankind of course immediately meets him, is seduced by him, earns from him the name of Shame, and follows him until at last reclaimed by Age, Conscience and Perseverance.

Folly, who here epitomized not only man's evil tendencies but his evil acts, was nevertheless a merry person, a wandering tinker who like the Folie in the *Sottie des gorriers* was at home in all parts of the world. He knew London and the law courts, the taverns, the private houses, the stews, the abbeys and the nunneries. His recital of his extensive acquaintance suggests the overlordship of folly in the world, but he himself did not claim to be a king and he was apparently not dressed as a fool. The character of Folly in Skelton's play of *Magnificence* was however represented as a fool. He claimed, too, to be all-powerful in the world, and he also symbolized some fusion of man's tendency to error with the actual errors which he commits.

Skelton's play was an allegory of the Ruler, not of simple Man, and the outcome of the conflict presented involved the safety of a kingdom rather than the salvation of a soul. In his conduct with regard to Felicity (Wealth), Magnificence the king may accept the advice of either of two groups of counsellors, Measure and Circumspection, or Fancy with his associates Courtly Abusion, Crafty Conveyance, Cloked Collusion, Counterfeit Countenance and Folly. The action of the play shows Measure dismissed by Magnificence upon the maligning reports of the four court vices, and Felicity committed to the care of Fansy Small-Brain while the King amuses himself with Folly. As a result, Adversity, Poverty and Despair take possession of the King, and he would allow Mischief to persuade him to kill himself if Good Hope, Redresse and Sad Circumspection did not intervene and restore him to the path leading to true prosperity.

Fancy and Folly are both fools—buffoons or jesters—as they make plain in their first meeting with each other, but they differ as sheer witlessness differs from wilful persistence in evil. Fancy is also a dwarf. When the court vices have left him alone upon the stage, he carries on clownery with the audience. On his wrist is perched an owl, in parody of the hawks sported by fine gentlemen. He examines her affectionately, then turns to the audience:

> Nowe let me se about
> In all this rowte

> Yf I can fynde out
> So semely a snowte.

He then describes his own nature and abilities:

> That was before I set behynde;
> Now to curteys, forthwith unkynde;
> Somtyme to sober, somtyme to sadde,
> Somtyme to mery, somtyme to madde;
> Somtyme I syt as I were solempe prowde;
> Somtyme I laughe over lowde. . . .
> With a pere my love you may wynne,
> And ye may lese it for a pynne. . . .
> Fyrst to tell you what were best,—
> Frantyke Fansy-Servyce I hyght;
> My wyttys be weke, my braynys are lyght;
> For it is I that other whyle
> Plucke down lede and theke with tyle;
> Nowe I wyll this, and nowe I wyll that;
> Make a wyndmyll of a mat;
> Nowe I wolde,—and I wyst what;
> Where is my cappe? I have lost my hat!
> And within an houre after
> Plucke down an house and set up a rafter.[15]

Fancy seems by his own description a natural fool. Folly's stupidity is, however, clearly assumed. The two, who are brothers, argue over their pets, Fancy's owl and Folly's cur dog. Folly pretends not to understand the abuse which Fancy levels at his dog, but when the subject changes he hears well enough and answers to the point. He explains why Fancy doesn't grow any more:

> By God, I can tell the; and I wyll:
> Thou art so feble-fantastycall,
> And so braynsyke therwithall,
> And thy wyt wanderynge here and there,
> That thou cannyst not growe out of thy boyes gere;
> And as for me, I take but one folysshe way,
> And therfore I growe more on one day
> Than thou can in yerys seven.[16]

When the other conspirators come in to arrange their deception of Magnificence, Folly reveals his malicious and surly shrewdness:

Crafty Conv.	What, Fansy! Let me se who is the tother.
Fansy.	By God, Syr, Foly, myne owne sworne brother.
Crafty Conv.	Cockys bonys! it is a farle freke;
	Can he play well at the hoddypeke?
Fansy.	Tell by thy trouth what sport can thou make.
Folly.	A, holde thy peas! I have the tothe ake.
Crafty Conv.	The tothe ake! lo, a torde ye have.
Folly.	Ye, thou haste the four quarters of a knave.
Crafty Conv.	Wotyst thou, I say, to whom thou spekys?
Fansy.	Nay, by Cockys harte, he ne reckys;
	For he wyll speke to Magnifycence thus.
Crafty Conv.	Cockys armys! a mete man for us.
Folly.	What? wolde ye have mo folys, and are so many?
Fansy.	Nay, offer hym a counter in stede of a peny.
Crafty Conv.	Why, thynkys thou he can no better skyll?
Folly.	In fayth, I can make you bothe folys, and I wyll.[17]

Folly then tricks Crafty Conveyance out of his coat by pretending to find a louse on it. His attitude is superior, sarcastic, indifferent to authority, while Fancy's is childish, fitful, and unstable. Folly is sure of his power over all classes of men:

> Nay, it is I that foles can make;
> For be he cayser or be he kynge,
> To felowshyp with Foly I can hym brynge.[18]

And he delivers a caustic description of the idle people whom he seduces to theft, bribery, lechery, tale-bearing and other of the misdemeanors which prove the folly of him who commits them. Finally when Magnificence has discharged his wise counsellors and is completely under the control of Fancy and his fellows, it is Folly who entertains him with the distorted patter-talk of a fool until Adversity appears and the ruler's real predicament is made plain.

In *Magnificence* Fancy and Folly between them represent

weakness and sin. Instability of purpose leads to evil-doing, and evil-doing itself hardens into a purpose of persistence in evil. "Insipiens" once erring becomes "stultus." Both are buffoons but ignoble in their clowning rather than interesting. Folly is even sinister, for one recognizes that he brings disaster. Still, these fools imitate the incoherent babble of the half-wit, and were probably dressed in motley and carried baubles[19], and one of them claims extensive power over mankind. The surface resemblance between these figures and those of Folle Bobance or Sottie is clear. But the English figure of Folly conveys a distinct threat to erring man, while the French Folie ridicules him, condemns him, yet betrays some philosophical acceptance of his existence. To condone folly was apparently un-English in the sixteenth century.

Not even in argument for the sake of argument was folly allowed a complete apology. John Heywood in his *Dialogue of Wit and Folly*, said to be imitated from a French original[20], followed a line of reasoning which ended by dismissing the fool as only a harmless beast and extolling the power of the reason. On the thesis that the wise experience more pain and enjoy less pleasure than the fools, James, one of the disputants, has concluded that "Better be sott Somer than sage Salamon!"[21] Fools are cared for in this world and are sure of bliss in the next, for "Where God gyvyth no dysernyng God takethe none acownte." But Jerome, entering, routs James and convinces John that the fool is innocent but despicable, and that while he may not be punished in the after life, he can never aspire to the degree of bliss which is the inheritance of the wise man.

Only once in the English moralities did a figure of Folly appear which accused human weakness yet jested light-heartedly at it. Sir David Lyndsay, who may have been familiar with the tradition of folly in France through his stay there on an embassy from the Scotch king[22], closed his long play of the *Thrie estatis* with a "sermon joyeux" by Folly. After the

Estates have met, after the abuses in government and in church have been discussed, and as the company is about to scatter, Folly enters, protesting that his sow has misbehaved and needs correction. Diligence refers him to the King:

> Folie: The King? quhat kynde of thing is that?
>   Is yon he, with the goldin hat?[23]

Anecdotes about Folie's wife are then bandied about, after which Folie reveals that he has in his basket Folie Hats to sell but does not intend to part with them until market day. After considerable ribald by-play, he is persuaded to speak to the company, hangs his hood on the pulpit and preaches. His text is the familiar one: Stultorum numerus infinitus. He describes his ancestry and his present relatives,

> Erles, Duiks, Kings & Empriours,
> With mony quekit conquerors,

whose death is as certain as their accumulation of earthly treasure is vain. He has Folie Hats for everyone, but does not go through the long list we might expect. He mentions only the "insatiabill merchant men," the men of four-score who marry lasses of fourteen, the "Spirituall Fuillis," and then delivers himself of the general dictum, "You ar all Fuillis," closing with a running survey of the times and a version of Merlin's prophesy in Latin doggerel. When he has finished, Diligence summons the whole audience to go to the tavern and the minstrels blow up a "brawl of France"—the play is over.

This was the only embodiment of folly in English dramatic literature of the first part of the century in which its power over mankind was accepted without too much protest. The most complete antithesis to it was the figure of Moros the fool in the Protestant morality, *The Longer Thou Livest the More Fool Thou Art*. The central figure of this play is again Man, here called Moros. His entire life is shown, from his doltish inability to understand the teachings of Discipline, Pietie and

Exercitation in youth, through his subservience to Idleness, Incontinence and Wrath, his promotion by Fortune and his choice of Ignorance, Impietie and Crueltie as his counsellors, his accusation by People and God's Judgment, and his final dismissal to the devil. The text is laden with scriptural comments upon fools, and the audience is not for a moment allowed to forget that to be a fool is practically to be a condemned sinner hastening to damnation. The unfortunate Moros is a half-wit who enters "counterfaiting a vaine gesture and a foolish countenance, synging the foote of many songes, as fooles were wont."[24] Discipline rebukes him:

> *Gaudet stultis Natura creandis*
> Nature hath a pleasure Fooles to create,
> *Ut malvis atque urticis et vilibus herbis,*
> As Mallowes, Nettles and weedes of that rate.
> *Hii sunt obtuso ingenio, crasso cerebro,*
> These are dull of wit and of a grosse braine,
> *Et nihili pendunt animi bono, depeci ludi,*
> And set at nought Vertue, geven to pastime vaine.[25]

This same laborious condemnation accompanies Moros throughout his adventures. Even the vices which destroy him seem to think little of him, and Discipline of course despairs of his improvement:

> The longer thou livest the more foole thou art,
> A foole in childehood, a foole in adolencie,
> In mans state thou wilt play a fooles parte,
> And a foole die with shame and infamie.
> Beate a foole in a morter, saith the wise man,
> And thou shalt not make him leave his folly.[26]

Small wonder that one sees this character sent to the devil with relief!

Moros represented the unconverted Catholic seen through Protestant eyes, not the whole race of men. He was presented as a real idiot, incapable of education and open to every form of evil influence. In him the figure of the fool became simply the vehicle of bitter and tedious invective. But other figures of fools occurred in English moralities which combined the humor of the jester with the function of objectifying error. Hardy-Dardy in *Godly Queen Hester* is a court fool, into whose mouth is put a condemnation of the worldly-wise in terms of the wisdom of folly.[27] Significantly too he attaches himself to Aman at the point in the play where Aman's evil deeds are seen to be leading him to destruction. In the school play of *Misogonus,* Cacurgus, an artificial fool, accompanies the hero through his misadventures as his shrewd evil genius.[28] But the greater number of personages in these plays who are indicated as perhaps wearing the fool's costume, who talk a patter resembling the conventional fool's talk, or who claim overlordship of the world belong to the group of characters known in the English drama as "vices."

The question of the relationship of the "vice" to fools, clowns, devils, badins, sots and villains in the plays of both France and England has produced many studies. The problem is particularly difficult to resolve since to answer it means finding a posthumous logic to fit a spontaneous practice. Cushman, whose work has been the point of departure in this field for thirty years, stated that "the devil, Vice, clown, fool and villain are parallel figures of quite independent origin and function."[29] The general names of all these types, like the name fool, have no clear-cut meaning in themselves; the most definite thing about them is the costume they suggest for their characters—the devil has horns and a tail, the fool a bauble and cockscomb, and so on. The title Vice, it is agreed, was first used as a label for a character in a play by the actors themselves, some time after 1560 when the vogue of the moral interlude was already passing.[30] Looking at the names of characters called Vice and something more definite—Iniquity, Ignorance, Sensual Appetite, Nichol Newfangle, Hypocrisy, for example—one sees that these personages represent characteristics of man which make for evil. Cushman concluded that the Vice was originally "an allegorical representation of human weaknesses and vices, in short the summation of the Deadly Sins."[31]

The actual rôles of these characters, on the other hand, and contemporary comment upon them, show that the Vice was chiefly notable as the merry-maker of the play.[32] Where Cushman traced the origin of the Vice from the devil of the mysteries on the ground that the devil too was a mirth-maker and that he was gradually translated into terms of specific errors which in turn were later fused for the purposes of playmaking into the single Vice, Chambers argues that the Vice came into the play through the avenue of the farce and is intimately related to the fool:

And in later plays, even if he has some other dramatic function he always adds to it that of a riotous buffoon. Frequently enough he has no other. It must be concluded then that, whatever the name may mean,—and irresponsible philology has made some amazing attempts at explanation—the character of the Vice is derived from that of the domestic fool or jester.[33]

Others have different views. Miss Busby, discussing the Vice as a source for the Elizabethan fool and so reversing the direction of inference, describes his function without examining his origin, simplifying the problem by disregarding any possible psychological meanings attached to the Vice as villain, and by explaining only pragmatically his comic function.[34]

These views minimize the habitual moral attitude which underlay the thought of the play-goers and the play-makers, and which governed their artistic taste. To look at the rôles of Folly as part of a general fashion of symbolizing man, not just as a dramatic figure, seems to cast some light on the relations of these names and rôles. If the devil of the mysteries was a merry-maker, he also represented the "sum of the opposition which the individual's best desires encounter in the world"—the *sum* of all such opposition, not its detail. If the Vice was a jester, he represented, too, the subjective impediments to the fulfilment of the individual's desire, and if the fool was a Vice, it was because he too, in the early part of the sixteenth century, still stood for a summation of the defects of man which lay him open to vice. Satan in the *Disobedient Child*, Iniquity in the *Nice Wanton*, and Folly in *Magnificence* are all three generalizations for the impediments to man's accomplishment of his end, yet one is a devil, one a "vice," and one a fool. On the other hand, Hypocrisy and Nichol Newfangle, in their names at least, are more specialized in their definition of the quality of evil at work in the play, and at the same time more occupied with pure buffoonery. They are more like plain villains and clowns than like symbols of vice. The rôle of Folly serves as introducer of Man to the perils of the World in the *Castle of Perseverance*, epitomizes sin in *Mundus et Infans*, is definitely presented as a jester with blended humorous and sinister qualities in *Magnificence*, and finally loses its general name and disappears among jesters, clowns and villains. During the years when the pattern of the drama was concerned with expressing in action an elaborate psychological formula—or action so abstracted as to have become practically psychological—it used abstractions as characters, which yet had to fulfil the eternal requirements of the stage-play, intrigue and comic relief. As men, rather than Man, became the subject of the drama, the abstractions assumed more qualities apiece, became more human, and at the same time naturally acquired more specialized vice-names. They began to live in more dimensions at once, at the same time that for the purposes of the play greater emphasis was placed upon one of their attributes. When the moral interlude passed into the humanized drama, the vice perhaps became the villain. He might still happen to be amusing, but his part as a rounded-out character in the intrigue was more important than his power to amuse. Some other rounded-out character was invented to supply the necessary balance. The sinful fool appeared in an early play as Stulticia who introduced Man to the main action in the plot of his life. He became Folly the Vice, epitome of erring conduct. But when humanity itself, rather than the goal to which it is hoped to be tending, became more consciously the preoccupation of playgoers, the abstraction of Folly decomposed into the realistic personages of the intriguer, the funny man, or the real witless one. The general name of Folly was reserved for the use of those who still desired to rebuke men sharply. The history of the rôle of Folly in English plays shows this sequence of events, as it shows too the absence in England of any group of plays using the concept of folly to indicate a light-hearted comment on general human error.

CHAPTER X

THE FOOL EXHAUSTED

A fool's bolt is soon shot.

The plain fact that a literary fashion prevails for a time and then loses its effectiveness is the natural explanation of the sterility of the concept of the fool after the early years of the sixteenth century. "Fool" was only one of the many names by which moralists could rebuke erring conduct. Its metaphorical potency probably wore out through much use, leaving the term savorless. The jester was not the only comedian. The fool in fact had no monopoly on any of the attributes which, attached to him separately in his rôles of "incircumspectus," "temerarius," "iocularis," or "purus," had been welded into the personification of Folly. The personification itself received its plastic reality from its use in the drama, and when the drama ceased to utilize such personifications, Folly lost its ready visibility. The life-span of any figure devised to stand for a complex abstraction is short in proportion as the abstraction is unstable. The race interprets itself to itself differently from generation to generation; it apparently accepted the fool as a symbol of itself for a short while, then dropped it, while it continued fitfully to name "fool" the various embodiments of error, simplicity or gaiety which it at the same time called by other names.

The device of compiling lists of offenders against society survived for a long time, and many of the types described in later lists are those which appeared in the lists of fools. But the lists

are built on new patterns. One, which was illustrated by wood-
cuts from the *Ship of Fools*, represented a ship-full of rascals,[1]
one described candidates for admission to a charity hospital
(founded by a king's jester!),[2] one told over the roll-call of
the fraternity of vagabonds.[3] Only two compositions of the
kind made use of the figure of the fool. Of these, one, *The xxv.
orders of Fooles*, contained a selection of familiar fools, chiefly
from among those presented in the *Ship of Fools*, which had
after all made about as full use of the device of listing erring
fools as was humanly possible.[4] The other was an adaptation of
the list-device to what were perhaps a series of clown-imper-
sonations. It was the work of Tarleton, the famous comedian
who could "undumpish" Queen Elizabeth at his pleasure,[5] and
it showed how the allegorical symbol was giving place to the
realistic "character," for each of Tarleton's fools, the Puritan,
the fool of state, the poet-fool and so on, was hit off in a neat
description of his immediate Elizabethan pecularities rather
than of his general failings.[6] In more complex forms of satire
than the list, too, the expanded descriptive "character" replaced
the compact phrase which dubbed a man "fool," as the
rounded-out figures of the new drama replaced the older allegorical symbol-figures. *Follies Anatomie* (1609), for instance,
revealed such familiar types as the glutton, the drunkard and
the whore, not masked as fools but in their own undisguised
lineaments.[7] The idea of mankind as a kingdom of fools had
been assimilated by the public mind, and a new form was demanded to give cogency to criticism's eternal review of society.

Comments on "follies" did appear in the works of John Heywood who, with Sir David Lyndsay, was the Briton of the
first part of the century most influenced by the specific French
tradition. Among his proverbs one finds occasional mention of
what makes a man a fool, and one short poem on *Certain
Follies*.[8] Toward the end of the century Nicholas Breton, an

antiquary in literary conceits, again used the figure of Folly in his *Flourish upon Fancie*. The old description of the vices of the fool here accompanied emphasis on that wantonness which had come to be his main attribute in so far as he had any.[9] According to Breton, Fancy teaches the art of love in her school, before the fire of Desire, to which coals are brought by Care. One of the tutors is Folly:

> Some other schollers now
>   are taught within her Schoole,
> By usshers that teach under her;
>   of which one is a foole
> By nature and by name,—
>   for Follie men him call.
> And he will teach his scholler soone
>   to proove a naturall.
> The second Frenzie is,
>   in teaching too as bad;
> For he will teach his schollers most
>   the way to make them mad.
>
> The ussher Follie first
>   he teacheth to be bould;
> Without advice to give no eare
>   to counsaile that is tould:
> To take delight in gauds,
>   and foolish trifling toyes;
> In things of value little worth
>   to set his chiefest joyes.
> To prate without regarde
>   of reason in his talke.
> To think blacke white & wrong for right,
>   and know not cheese from chalke.
> To love the things in deede
>   whiche moste he ought to hate;
> For trifling toyes with deerest frends
>   to fall at dire debate:
> To loove to play at dice,
>   to sware his blood & hart.
> To face it with a ruffians looke,
>   and set his hat athwart.

To haunt the taverns late,
　　by night to trace the streets,
And swap ech slut upon the lippes,
　　that in the darke he meetes. . . .
To feede too like a horse;
　　to drinke too like an oxe;
To show himselfe in ech respect
　　a very very coxe.[10]

But these appearances of Folly are due to the casual resourcefulness of their individual authors, casting about for a convenient form for their compositions and lighting upon old devices. They are not evidence of any vitality or charm generally felt to exist in the literary symbol of the fool.

The actual person of the half-wit or of the artificial domestic fool, easily "moralized," easily made amusing, was the basis of the most successful fool literature in the sixteenth century in England. The translation of Garzoni's *Hospital of Incurable Fools,* most of whom are raging sick of one or another of the vices,[11] *Jack of Dover, his quest of inquirie, or his privie search for the veriest foole in England,* in the course of which he met with characters more hare-brained than the Wise Men of Gotham and more mischievous than Scogan[12], and Robert Armin's *Nest of Ninnies* are examples of this use of the fool. In the plan of Armin's book are perpetuated three of the interpretations of folly which had given it its earlier efficacy, the fool as sinner, the fool as a privileged critic of society, and the fool as merry-maker. The World, "wanton sick as one surfetting on sinne," calls on the philosopher Sotto for help. Sotto shows her the folly of the time through the characters of six domestic fools; and when she turns away disgusted with the exhibition, he "knits a betill brow" and exclaims, "The old payment still."[13] In this form, and in the work of a member of that class notoriously conservative of effective devices, the actors, these three outworn approaches to the symbol of folly survived into Stuart times.

English sixteenth-century literature, aside from the drama which is another and a much longer story, made no striking use of the fool as a symbol. The increasing realism of his presentation as a jester in the drama fitted the tendency of the times toward the humanizing rather than the allegorizing of character—to the humanizing of it *in spite* of allegorizing. In the jest-books, moralized though his pranks often are, they are better suited to stimulate laughter than criticism of oneself or others. His casual recrudescences are wellings-up of old forms of writing and thinking. Even as a device in the stringing together of satiric lists of errors he was worn out. His two more creative embodiments received no further expression in writing; the sheer vitality of the fool found no lettered apologist after Erasmus, and the sublime folly of love, whether for god or man, was degraded to a giggly irritability at the idea of licentiousness. Folly as a lover became simply an attendant upon a doubtfully respectable Venus.[14]

In France, too, the popularity of the fool diminished. He did not, as in England, provide a name in which to narrate facetious stories, although he furnished occasional incidents for inclusion among such stories; one can find accounts of fools in the *Eutrapel* of Noël du Fail, in the tales of Bonaventure des Periers, in the anecdotes of Tabourot, or in the *Sérées* of Guillaume Bouchet. But they do not furnish the thread on which the collection is hung together. As Bourdigné's prologue to *Pierre Faifeu* implied—

> Laissez ester Caillette le folastre,
> Les quatre Filz Aymon vestuz de bleu.
> Gargantua qui a chepveulx de plastre:
> Voyez les faitz Maistre Pierre Faifeu—[15]

the old devices were worn out and newer, more realistic ones were desired; the clever varlet, rustic, or clown was superseding the fool-proper as a source of amusement.

With the suppression of the Joyous Societies, the figure of the
fool lost effectiveness as a symbol of high spirits and of the
liberty to criticize. The facetious *Monologue des nouveaulx sotz
de la joyeuse bande* carried on the tradition of calling together
the orders of fools,

> Sotz glorieux et sotz cornuz,
> Sotz grans, sotz petis et moyens,
> Sotz villageois, sotz citoyens,
> Sotz gras, sotz maigres, sotz refaitz,
> Demi-sotz et sotz tous parfaits,[16]

for a regal banquet. The fool appeared incidentally too in other
popular poems, expressing in one case his carefree gaiety, useless in the face of death:

> Pour mon souhait, qui nuyt et jour m'assotte,
> Je souhaite des choses nompareilles:
> Premierement, une belle marotte,
> Et chapperon garny de grans oreilles,
> Des sonnettes faisant bruyt à merveilles,
> Fy de soucy, de chagrin et de deul,
> Dancer de hait soubz buyssons et soubz treilles,
> Bon appetit pour vuider potz, bouteilles,
> Et, à la fin, pour tresor ung linceul.[17]

The more sober spirit which emphasized virtue, not irresponsibility, as man's greatest pleasure was reflected, though perhaps
satirically, even in this type of ephemeral literature:

> Vivent sotz, de noble voulloir,
> Prenantz en vertu leurs adresses
> Car ainsy comme on peult scavoir,
> Sottye en vertu est noblesse;
> Celui dont péché l'âme blesse,
> N'est digne d'estre sot nommé
> Mais, selon droict, fol estimé
> Lorsque vice en son cueur parsiste;
> Pour ce tiens en bon cueur fermé
> Que Sottye en vertu consiste.[18]

The incursions of that "rationalisme qui s'essayait à organiser la vie" made themselves felt, presaging the defeat of both "fol" and "sot" by the wise and just man.

In compiling their works of satirical didacticism French authors like Jean Bouchet and Symphorien Champier tried, as did their contemporaries in England, to vary the devices upon which their collections of examples were hung.[19] But the figure of the fool, perhaps because of its connection with the Joyous Societies, was useful enough still to be employed once in such a work. The *Triumphe de haulte folie* was sober instruction, while Tarleton's *Horseload of Fooles* was popular jest. Printed with the wood-cuts which had accompanied an earlier triumph of Dame Verole, the *Triumph of Folly* passed in review the heroes of antiquity whose vices brought them to ruin, listed the vices themselves—Abus, Fol Appetit, Sot Désir, Volupté, Outrecuidance, Detraction—and the fools themselves—the usurers, the jealous husbands, the wrathful ruffians, the indiscreet—in order that man might learn "par règle ou discipline . . . éviter le dangier advenir."[20] In this composition, which was issued from a Lyons press in 1550, the medieval conception of folly, a hang-over from the past, was combined with the paraphernalia of a "triumph" suitable to the taste of the most Italianate city of France.

In *La Morosophie de Guillaume de la Perriere, Tolosain*, printed in the same city in 1553, a more interesting didactic use was made of the idea of folly, combining this time, not a medieval device with the external trappings of the Renaissance, but fifteenth century mysticism, the wisdom of the fool (derived from the words of Plato), the folly of all earthly wisdom in the eyes of God, and proverbial shrewd teachings—all in an emblem book. La Perriere stated in his preface that his title signified "fole sagesse en Françoys," and that he knew some reader would say that the author was illustrating his own folly in publishing a book on vices; but if his critic would read Plato, he would find that

bien souvent l'on ha veu sortir d'une bouche estimée fole, mainte parolle sage: car celle espece de fureur, que les vulgaires & ydiotz appelent folie, symbolize bien souvent à vaticination.[21]

His title was not really a contradiction:

Je puys respondre, que aussi bien me peult estre permise telle contradition de tiltre, comme au doctz Nicolas Cusan Cardinal, qui à l'un de ses livres mit le tiltre de docte ignorance.[22]

He went on to explain the range of reference in his title, citing the prophets and apostles as witnesses that there is no "Prudence charnelle, ne Sagesse mondaine, qui ne soit folie envers Dieu," and calling upon the Stoics for proof that he who thinks himself a fool is very nearly a wise man. In the emblems which follow, the fool appeared a number of times with his bauble, cockscomb and bells[23] but the interest of the book lay not so much in them as in the author's interpretation of his title.

These two compositions used the overworked figure of the fool in ways which suggested how he might have been assimilated into the literature of the new generation, but in spite of the signs they gave, the fool as a didactic tool was doomed. The revival and popularization of Stoicism, and, among a more limited group, the revival of Epicureanism, tended to make him a supererogatory symbol for man. Used as Brant had used him, he represented against a background of Catholic humility and of scorn of man's nature, the summing up of human weakness. But to both Stoics and Epicureans nature, although variously defined, was good. The "natural man" was the high-minded man, the "moral aristocrat, self-justified by unbreakable stamina,"[24] or he was the perfectly adapted man who enjoyed all those pleasures which are not attended by disagreeable consequences.[25] Unlike the sombre Hebraic morality out of which medieval sententious literature drew much of its conviction about fools, these revived philosophies taught an optimism in regard to man's nature in which the fool as a symbol had no place. Neither did he survive in the literature of French or English Reformation controversy. Protestant controversial writings in France, like the works of Tindale and his followers in England, were not light artillery. Reformation satire, as Lenient says,

s'inspire de colère et de haine contre ce qu'elle appelle mensonge et superstition; elle est passionnée, impitoyable; or, la passion la rend souvent éloquent, rarement spirituel.[26]

Since the idea of the fool suggested something gayer in France than in England, it was by so much the more unsuitable to religious satire. A poem of the time, indeed, observed wistfully:

> Car selon l'humeur de cet âge,
> Chacun, pour cacher son malheur
> S'attache le ris au visage,
> Et les larmes dedans son coeur.[27]

But the fool was not the proper mouthpiece for this desperate laughter. Efforts made by the Conards of Rouen to carry on their wonted satiric games were suppressed by "le menu peuple ... condamnant telles folies et meschancetés"[28] and the suppositious advice given to a royal fool by a well-wisher probably represented the attitude of the Reformers toward other fools than jesters:

Thou dost well to have small love for the Reformers. Satan himself looks on them only with regret; and for good reason, seeing that if the Reformers could have their way, there would soon be an end of court fools and buffoons. Ah, poor Mathurine, and you poor fellows, Angoulevent, Mâitre Guillaume, and indeed all you other fools, as well without hoods as with, where would all your pensions be if the Reformers had the upper hand?[29]

The fool, however, lived on as a symbol of creative high spirits and of divine love in the work of two partisans of Reform. Bonaventure des Periers prefaced his *Nouvelles Recreations et joyeux devis* by the Epicurean motto, "Bene vivere et laetari"—"Bien vivre et se resjouir"[30]—but his introductory sonnet expressed the moralist's wistful need for laughter and invoked the grace of folly:

> Hommes pensifz, je ne vous donne à lire
> Ces miens devis si vous ne contraignez
> Le fier maintien de voz frons rechignez:
> Ici n'y ha seulement que pour rire.
>
> Laissez à part vostre chagrin, vostre ire
> Et vos discours de trop loing desseignez.
> Un autre fois vous serez enseignez.
> Je me suis bien contrainct pour les escrire.
>
> J'ay oublié mes tristes passions,
> J'ay intermis mes occupations.
> Donnons, donnons quelque lieu à folie,
>
> Que maugré nous ne nous vienne saisir,
> Et en un jour plein de melancholie
> Meslons au moins une heure de plaisir.[31]

He still cherished the idea of the world as a kingdom of fools— "laissons-les icy et allons chercher les sages; esclairez pres, je n'y voy goutte"—and the fool to him was still the symbol of error, laughter, and criticism blended. But, at the same time, the idea of "folie" could mean simply "wantonness," could denote it as explicitly as it does in the licentious versifications of Mellin de Saint-Gelais and Ronsard.[32]

Marguerite de Navarre used the figure of the fool as a symbol of spiritual ecstasy. While she condemned "obscure Ignorance" which keeps man from understanding his "devoir et service," her representation of the highest joy of life is the mad shep-

herdess who interrupts the reasoning of La Sage and La Mondaine and La Superstitieuse with her wild songs. The good-and-
prudent woman exclaims upon hearing her, "Ha! n'est ce pas
langage d'une folle?" and the singer replies,

> Amour, nulle saison,
> N'est amy de raison.

Her song resembles the outburst of Jacopone da Todi:

> Helas! telle joye j'ay receue
> D'avoir sens et honneur perdu
> Pour luy, que mon cueur s'est rendu
> Entre ses bras, en sa puissance,
> Pour penser en luy nuict et jour.

The Sage insists that

> L'amour de Dieu faict l'homme saige,
> Prudent, de bonne conscience,
> Estudiant en sapiance,
> Jour et nuict et matin et soir.

But the shepherdess sings on, telling how earthly wisdom and
prudence are variable things, but the love of God steadfast:

> Or t'esvertue,
> Amour, et tout soudain me tue.
> Puis, quant tu m'auras abatue,
>   Me feras vivre.
> Pour toy veulx estre folle et yvre
> Sans jamais en estre delivre,
>   Mais toy, Amour,
> S'il te plaict me faire ce tour,
> Que tu me brusle sans séjour,
>   Ton consummer
> Me donra ung estre d'aymer,
> Me rellevant pour m'assommer,
>   Et ta lumière,
> Qui en moy sera toulte entière,
> Comme toy (me) legiere.
> Tu l'as faict et je t'en mercie.

Voila l'estat de bergerie
Qui suivant d'Amour la banniere
D'autre chose ne se soucye.[33]

In spite of the doctrine of the power of man's reasoned self-
will, and in spite of the controversies attending the assertion
of that self-will in religious matters, gaiety still was needed to
accompany goodness, and love still obliterated the reason.
Marguerite de Navarre acknowledging the changing fashion of
the times, made her ecstatic lover a shepherdess, but still a fool.

CHAPTER XI

CONCLUSION

With Marguerite's ecstatic shepherdess the French and English phases of the story of the fool in late medieval literature may be closed. New masks and new names were needed to body forth the eternal facts of human capacity and incapacity; new merrymakers, new critics of society were at hand to express the tastes of a new generation. It is possible at this point to summarize and to conclude the episode.

The fashion of calling erring man a fool and of thinking of fools as sinners existed as a literary convention in the fifteenth century, at the same time as a fashion of keeping household fools and a fashion of simulating folly in which the fool stood for unreasoning high spirits and the liberty of the irresponsible to criticize the social order. These fashions gave rise to points of view toward "folly" itself which were all incorporated in the figure of Folly as Erasmus presented her—critic of the two-fold nature of man, weak in reason and achievement, strong in imagination and love. But with the growth of a convention of realistic literary expression, the figure of the fool lost its symbolic quality and appeared as the simple clown, dunce, merrymaker. The word itself, grown colorless, became a simple term of condemnation. Sixteenth century emphasis on man's strength, either through himself or through God's grace, diminished his sense of his own weakness as the source of sin; man-the-fool became almost invisible behind the heroic figure of Man-Conquering. The fool was the shame of "nature," the exception to the rule, and the less said about him the better:

A fool is the abortive of wit, where Nature had more power than reason, in bringing forth the fruit of imperfection; his actions are most in extremes, and the scope of his brain is but ignorance: only nature hath taught him to feed, and use to labour without knowledge: he is a kind of shadow of a better substance, or like the vision of a dream, that yields nothing awake: he is commonly known by one of two special names, derived from their qualities, as from wilful Will Fool, and Hodge from Hodge-podge; all meats are alike, all are one to a fool: his exercises are commonly divided into four parts, eating and drinking, sleeping and laughing: for these are his chief loves; a bauble, and a bell, coxcomb, and a pied coat: he was begotten in unhappiness, born to no goodness, lives but in beastliness, and dies but in forgetfulness. In sum, he is the shame of nature, the trouble of wit, the charge of charity, and the loss of liberality.[1]

While England and France had shared the idea of the fool as a symbol for erring man and the cult of the folk-fool as a symbol of fertility, French minds rather than English developed the convention of using him for a symbol of gaiety and a vehicle of gay satire, and the ideas of his gaiety and of the power of his unreason persisted longer in France than in England.

Erasmus, whose tradition was European rather than national, was responsible for the fusion of the diverse connotations of "fool" into the figure which both condemns and vindicates man's nature. But the fate of Erasmus' reputation in the generation which followed his is like the fate of his version of Folly. A very curious Italian satire, translated into English in 1566, tells how a traveler toward heaven, uncertain whether the real destiny of man was to reach the Pope's heaven or the heaven of the scriptures, encountered Erasmus midway between the two:

And being nowe passed the sphere of the Moone, as we came to that of Mercurie, we founde a number of soules tormented in sundry sorts, amongs which was one that was tyed betwene two Postes, with a corde made faste about his middle, so that he hong, and coulde touche no grounde: he had upon his head two great harts hornes, & betwene the hornes was fastened a li(n)ne(n) cloth, after the manner of a saile, and at his feete hong a great pursse full of crownes, and so went this ghost continually whirling about, for as any winde blew, it stroke in the sayle, that was betwene the hornes, and turned him with his feete upwarde, and as the winde ceased the contrepoise of the Pursse tourned him with his feete downe agayne, and so the pore wretch was stil whirled about, and one whyle was hys heade and another tyme his heeles turned up on high to heaven. . . . Myne Aungell tolde me that it was Erasmus of Roterodam. *Marforius:* Alas what is this thou tellest me? and why was he that was so learned, and so honest a man, in this miserable case? *Pasquin:* The harts hornes signifie his fearefulnesse, and the pursse his covetousnesse, who two things were so muche in him, that the one whyle the one, an other whyle the other, made him bowe, now this way, now that way, so that it coulde not be discerned whether he drewe neerest to Gods heaven, or to the Popes heaven, & therfore is he placed in the middes betwene them both.[2]

Fear and covetousness may have been among Erasmus' failings, but it was not they which really won him his position in Pasquin's vision. It was his "passion for moderation." Professor Thomson has commented on Erasmus' failure to take sides in the controversies of his day:

The duty of the scholar is to expound the true meaning, as he sees it, of the written word. Erasmus did that. If the meaning he found was neither that of Luther nor of the schoolmen, whose fault was it? People want him to take sides. But how can the scholar take sides?[3]

He had, continues Professor Thomson, a passion for moderation, and

whenever civilization breaks down into barbarism it is only by a passion for moderation that it can be rescued and restored.[4]

In spite of the exhilaration of the times, it must have looked to many in 1500 as if disciplined human nature were on some fronts breaking down into barbarism. To realize the extremes, and yet to project some expression which falls between them, taking account of both, is to be moderate. The popular figure of the fool in literature represented extremes of feeling toward man's nature; Erasmus expressed his confidence in that nature in a version of Folly which united both extremes of feeling.

We have no popular literary figure of the fool or folly to-day, but the interest of Erasmus' point of view is still evident. We do have our privileged jesters, conscious and unconscious, whose comments on events lighten the reading of the daily press. We have stage clowns doing now the same tricks that aroused the wrath of Augustine and that entertained the spectators of the day-long French mysteries. We have moralists who rebuke our failings, calling them by new names. We have apostles of the subconscious, and both reason and unreason, as "ways of life," have champions. But the poised vision of man given by Erasmus in his figure of Folly is as rare today as it was in the sixteenth century and lacks even an expressive symbol. After reading the *Encomium moriae,* one can only echo the words of Lady Emily in the "excellent comedy of the *Heiress":*

> "Dear Lady Emily," says Miss Allscrip. . . . "Dear Lady Emily, don't you dote upon folly?"
> "To ecstasy!" replied her ladyship, "I only despair of seeing it well kept up."

NOTES

CHAPTER I

[1] The limitation of the subject to the types of fool here presented, and to France and England, is arbitrary. The popularity of the fool as a literary figure was perhaps greatest in Germany, and certainly extended to Italy. Other types of fool were familiar; the rustic fool is a frequent actor in *novelle* and is connected with the *zanni* of the *commedia dell' arte*, as well as with the "innocent" fool of the Percival type. The foolish *Bauer* is a stock figure of German folk-comedy. Cf. C. H. Herford, *Studies in the Literary Relations of England and Germany in the Sixteenth Century*, Cambridge (England), 1886; J. A. Symonds, *The Renaissance in Italy*, Vols. IV and V, "Italian Literature," New York, 1888; W. Smith, *The Commedia dell'arte*, New York, 1912.

[2] Cf. Sir J. A. H. Murray (editor), *A New English Dictionary*, Vol. IV (F and G), Oxford, 1901, *s.v.* "fool" and "folly"; also E. Littré (editor), *Dictionnaire de la langue française*, Vol. II, Paris, 1874, *s.v.* "fol" and "folie."

[3] S. J. H. Herrtage (editor), *Catholicon Anglicum*, Early English Text Society publication, original series, Vol. LXXV, London, 1881, p. 137.

[4] *Bibliotheca Eliotae. Eliotes dictionarie, by Thomas Cooper the third tyme corrected, and with a great number of phrases enriched, as to him that conferreth the other aedition, it may easely appeare.* London, 1559, *s.v.* "stultus."

[5] R. Cotgrave, *A Dictionarie of the French & English Tongues*, London, 1611, *s.v.* "fol."

[6] *Catholicon Anglicum, loc. cit.*

[7] *Bibliotheca Eliotae, loc. cit.*

[8] *Catholicon Anglicum, loc. cit.*

[9] Carolus Dufresne Dominus Du Cange (editor), *Glossarium mediae et infimae Latinitatis*, 7 vols., Paris, 1840-1850, *s.v.* "stultus."

[10] I am again limiting the idea of the "innocent fool" to an ethical and practical rather than to a mystical and religious interpretation, because the two chief works which I mean to analyse, *The Ship of Fools* and the

Praise of Folly, are both ethical rather than mystical and make no use of the "pure fool" idea. For the folk-tale of the "Great Fool" cf. Alfred Nutt, *Studies on the Legend of the Holy Grail,* London, 1888, chap. VI, especially pp. 160-161.

Chapter II

[1] Thomas Wright and J. O. Halliwell-Phillips (editors), *Reliquiae antiquae,* 2 vols., London, 1841-43, I, 15:

Let your concern be more to learn yourself than to teach. . . .

Plenty of words is there where lacketh plenty of meaning. . . .

Like the inconstant moon the fool is constantly changing,

Like the sun the wise man remains ever true to himself.

Now hither now thither turns the unseeing mind of the fool,

The prudent mind advances firmly from step to step. . . .

Let him (the fool) admit his faults, blame them, and seek to amend them,

Nor think himself good in his heart, while his mouth proclaims him in error.

[2] A. A. Renouard, *Carmina ethica,* Paris, 1795, pp. 8-26 *passim,* and E. Margalits, *Florilegium proverbiorum universae Latinitatis,* Budapest, 1895, *passim:*

The wise man will control his own spirit, the fool will be the slave of his passions.

It is virtuous to flee from vice, and the beginning of wisdom is to be lacking in folly.

Blame is more painful to a wise man than a blow to a fool.

He cannot but be wise who knows himself for a fool.

It is indeed the nature of fools to perceive the faults of others and be unmindful of their own.

To be of use to others and to injure oneself is folly, not kindness.

Fools fear fortune, wise men endure it.

A fair promise flatters many a fool.

It is folly to be ill-humored toward him whose power is greater than one's own.

When fools do business, merchants make profits.

Not to give heed to one's own affairs and yet to advise others is foolish.

The fool recognizes the accomplished fact.

[3] *Florilegium,* pp. 486-88 *passim.*

[4] Carl Schroeder, *Der deutsche Facetus,* Berlin, 1911, p. 27:

These three things overthrow good judgment: the passion for possessions, much money, and foolish (wanton) love of women.

[5] *Ibid.,* p. 24:

There are three follies by which the fool declares himself: that he talks so much that no credence attaches to his word; that he menaces so much that his threats are not respected; that he bestows so much that he appears to beg.

[6] E. Du Méril, *Poésies inédites du moyen âge,* Paris, 1854, p. 198:

This tale warns the fool to keep silent, lest by talking he betray the secret which he might have kept by silence.

[7] Collections of English proverbs furnish few illustrations of the use of the fool, except in proverbs which seem to be adaptations from the French or to date from later than the sixteenth century. Cf. W. W. Skeat, *Early English Proverbs,* Oxford, 1910; W. Carew Hazlitt, *English Proverbs and Proverbial Phrases,* London, 1907; R. Dyboski (editor), *Songs, Carols, and other Miscellaneous Poems,* E.E.T.S. pub., extra series, Vol. CI, London, 1907 (issued 1908), proverbs and maxims pp. 128-35.

[8] F. Leroux de Lincy, *Le Livre des proverbes français,* 2 vols., Paris, 1859, II, 394:

Virgil said:

He who sees the good and chooses the bad makes himself wittingly a fool; and he should be held a fool who seeks his own harm.

[9] Paul Meyer, "Les manuscrits français de Cambridge," *Romania,* XXXII (1903), p. 40:

Here begin the proverbs of Mary Magdalene

Know, now, that the appearance often declares whether a man is foolish or well-balanced. A wild exterior often shows the folly that is hidden in the heart, and it can often be concealed, too, by a feigned appearance of doing the right thing. But open folly is much better than concealed villany. Too soon or too late he who hides his evil deeds is known as well as he who cries his aloud.(?) A foolish exterior makes the fool known and feared, while a fair appearance makes its owner loved as an honest man.

[10] Paul Meyer, "Fragments de manuscrits français," *Romania,* XXXV (1906), 34.

[11] Leroux de Lincy, *op. cit.,* II, 459 ff.

[12] Given in Wright and Halliwell-Phillips, *Reliquiae antiquae,* I, 236, and in Achille Jubinal, *Nouveau recueil de contes, dits et fabliaux,* 2 vols., Paris, 1839-42, II, 373.

[13] Described by Gaston Paris in "Compte rendu de: Les Enseignements

de Robert de Ho, dits Enseignements Trebor, by Mary Vance Young, Paris, 1901," *Romania*, XXXII (1903), 141-50.

[14] Paul Meyer, "Bribes de littérature anglo-normande," *Jahrbuch für romanische und englische Literatur*, VII (1866), 56-57.

[15] Max Otto Goldberg, *Die Catonischen Distichen während des mittelalters in der englischen und französischen literatur*, Leipzig, 1883, p. 5.

[16] *The Book called Cathon,* Here begynneth the prologue or prohemye of the book callid Cathon / which booke hath ben translated into Englysshe by Mayster Benet Burgh . . . London, 1483. (Copy in the New York Public Library.)

[17] Joseph Nève, *Catonis disticha*, Liège, 1926, p. 10.

[18] *Ibid.*, p. 6, note 3, quoted:

I judge that (this composition) is attributed to Cato because its maxims are worthy of the name of Cato himself.

[19] Goldberg, *op. cit.*, p. 62.

[20] Leroux de Lincy, *op. cit.*, II, 439-41:

Here beginneth Cato. As I was considering how many men err gravely in their conduct, I concluded that their mistaken opinion of how to live ought to be given assistance and counsel, especially to the end that they should live well and attain to honor.

Now, my beloved son, I will teach you by what rule you should fashion your moral habits. Therefore read now my instructions so that you may understand them; for to read without understanding is to be carelessly stupid.

And so: pray to God. Love your parents.

Preserve those things which have been given to you.

Dress appropriately when you go to the marketplace.

Extend loans willingly. (Give like for like.)

Make good men the companions of your comings and goings.

Have a care to whom you give.

Come not to council before you are called.

Feast moderately. Be clean. Sleep just enough. Give greetings cordially.

Love your wife. Yield place to your elders and superiors.

Respect your master and teacher.

Temper your wine.

Be suitably modest.

Read books and remember what you read.

Be a true guardian of your property.

Educate your children. Be diligent and frugal.

Be smooth of tongue.

Keep your oath.

Rule well your household.

Do not become lightly angry. Mock at no one.

Shun light women.

Be present at the court of judgment. Take your place in the camp of war.

Study the writings of sound authors. Give advice when it is asked for.

Do good to the good. Make virtue a practice.

Keep your own counsel. Be not spoken ill of.

Let the harmless top be your toy; flee the dice.

Keep your opinion of others to yourself.

Endure the workings of the law which you yourself have made.

Judge fairly. Tell no lies.

Be mindful of kindnesses received. Talk little when feasting. Endeavor to act justly. Fight for your country.

Do not covet the goods of another. Prevail upon your parents by patience not force.

Be not scornful of those beneath you. Do not place too much trust in your courage or your virtue.

Undertake nothing simply as a test of your powers. (?)

Give your love freely to your friends.

[21] Cf. W. Carew Hazlitt, *Remains of the Early Popular Poetry of England,* 4 vols., London, 1864-66, "How the Wise Man Taught his Son," I, 168-77, "How the Goode Wif Thaught hir Doughter," I, 177-92; and Paul Meyer, "Les manuscrits français de Cambridge," *Romania,* XXXII, 68-73, "Urbain le Courtois."

[22] Cf. note 14.

There are sixty follies that are common in the world, and of all evil things these are the chief:

that a man should neither love God nor believe in Him;

that a man should persist in deadly sin;

that a man should not wish to learn what is good;

that a man should have plenty and be unwilling to give;

that a man should give all and receive nothing;

that a man should promise much and give nothing;

that a man should talk when no one listens to him;

that a man should threaten when no one fears him;

that a man should swear so freely that no one believes him;

that a man should claim everything he sees;

that a man should tell his counsel to everyone;

that a man should put his own self to shame;

that a man having nothing, should still trade his all;

that a man should spend wildly what he wins (cf. editor's note);

that a man should separate himself from his friends;

that a man should postpone attending to his duties;

that a man should scorn his neighbors and relations;

that a man should believe everything he is told;

that a man should do harm to father or mother;

that a man should not cherish his wife;

that a man should frequent another's friends;

that a man should lyingly praise himself;

that a man should wrongly claim the property of another;

that a man should be so fruitlessly active that no result comes of it; (?)

that a man should not respect Holy Church;

that a man should break his plighted oath;

that a man should take pleasure in his evil deeds;

that a man should repent of his good deeds;

that a man should not want to do good;

that a man should not want to escape from prison;

that a man should do injury to an honest man;

that a man should find fault with what is good;

that a man should not do as much good as he can;

that a man should do his duty grudgingly;

that a man should seek out a foolish fight or argument;

that a man should judge the conscience of another;

that a man should hate peace and love war;

that a man should hate the lands of his own manor;

that a man should act too haughty and fierce;

that a man should say or do anything foul . . .

    (fourteen lines omitted)

that a man should willingly ally himself with what is false;

that a man should hearken to slander;

that a man should seek out at least ten light women (cf. editor's note);

this man shall die in poverty, but he who learns this lesson shall have God's blessing.

[23] J. Kail (editor), *Twenty-six Political and other Poems,* E.E.T.S. pub., original series, CXXIV (London, 1904), 69-72, "A Remembrance of 54 Folies."

[24] A. Jubinal, *op. cit.,* II, 65 ff.

[25] C. Herford, *op. cit.,* p. 323.

[26] Cf. A. R. Gordon, *The Poets of the Old Testament,* London, 1912, p. 266.

[27] *S. Aurelii Augustini Hipponensis episcopi De Scriptura sacra Speculum,*

in J.-P. Migne, *Patrologia Latina*, Paris, 1865, Vol. XXXIV, col. 912:
"for the teaching of pious and good habits." Cf. also G. F. Moore, *The
Literature of the Old Testament*, New York, 1913, p. 229:

The theme of the book is "wisdom," by which is meant primarily a
practical wisdom in the conduct of the individual life under the social,
political, and economic conditions of the time. The end is enlightened
self-interest. Experience shows that morality conduces to prosperity and
happiness, and immoral and unsocial actions to the opposite. To inculcate
this truth and to apply it is the aim of the wise, who make this knowledge the foundation of virtue and of well-being.

[28] Cf. A. R. Gordon, *op. cit.*, pp. 276-77 for analytical lists.

[29] *Proverbs*, I, 7, 32, 33; III, 35; V, 22-23; X, 14, 19, 23; XII, 15,
16, 23; XIII, 16, 20, etc., especially XIV, XVII, XVIII, XXII, *passim*.
The references given here are based on the Vulgate version, *Biblia sacra
Vulgatae Editionis Sixtiv. Pont. Max. jusso recognita et Clementis VIII
auctoritate edita*, Tornaci Nerviorum, 1881. "Stultus" is used generally
throughout the Vulgate in those proverbs where "fool" appears in translation. Cf. J. Forshall and Sir R. Madden (editors), *The Books of Job,
Proverbs, Ecclesiastes and the Song of Solomon according to the Wicliffite
version*, Oxford, 1881, for uses of the words "fole," "unwis," and "of
litle wit" in the translation.

[30] Proverbs, XIII, XIV, XXIV *passim*.

[31] *Here begynneth the Proverbes of Salomon. Wherunto is added dyvers
other Bookes of the Byble. Very good and profytable for every Christem
man for to knowe.* Prynted in the yeare of our Lorde 1540. B-5 recto.
(New York Public Library.)

[32] A. C. O'Neil, "Sin," *Catholic Encyclopedia*, New York, 1912, XIV,
11, col. 1.

[33] S. Frette and P. Maré (editors), *Doctoris Angelici Divi Thomae
Aquinatis Opera Omnia*, Vol. II, Paris, 1872, *Summa Theologica*, Prima
secundae: prologus: "an intellectual being, gifted with free will, and able
of his own power to act."

[34] *Ibid.*, Prima secundae, quaes. I, art. 1:

Hence those actions alone may properly be called human, of which man
is the master. . . . Moreover the objective of the will is an end and a
good. Hence all human actions are necessarily directed toward an end.

[35] *Ibid.*, Prima secundae, quaes. LXXI, art. 5.

[36] *Ibid.*, Prima secundae, quaes. VI, art. 8.

[37] *Ibid.*, Prima secundae, quaes. LXXVI, art. 2.

[38] *Ibid.*, Prima secundae, quaes. VI, art. 2.

[39] *Ibid.*, Prima secundae, quaes. VI, art. 8.

[40] Thomas Wright, *Early Mysteries and other Latin Poems of the Twelfth and Thirteenth Centuries*, London, 1838, p. 57.

[41] O'Neil, *op. cit.*, p. 4.

[42] *S. Aurelii Augustini Hipponensis episcopi annotationum in Job Liber Unus*, Migne, *Patrologia Latina*, XXXIV, col. 829:

By "fools" is to be understood "wicked men." And on the other hand the wisdom of man is goodness, as is shown in what follows.

[43] *Salonii Episcopi in ecclesiasten expositio mystica*, Migne, *Patrologia Latina*, LIII, col. 993.

[44] *Salonii Episcopi in parabolas Salomonis expositio mystica*, Migne, *Patrologia Latina*, LIII, col. 979:

Veranus. Tell me, I beg, in what way *wisdom shineth in the face of the prudent man*, as Solomon says, *but the eyes of fools are in the ends of the earth?*

Salonius. The prudent man shows plainly by the light of his face the sobriety of his feelings and the clarity of his understanding. Fools however are not able to raise the eyes of their minds to follow and imitate this sobriety, but with all their efforts cast about to see how they may attain their own end, that is, the satisfaction of carnal desires.

[45] Salonius on *Ecclesiastes*, Migne, *Patrologia Latina*, LIII, col. 997:

for he hates heavenly things, and thus cannot like the wise man raise his eyes to heaven, because he does not reflect on those things which concern God but on the passing interests of this world.

[46] *Ibid., loc. cit.*

However his remembrance in the future will not be the same, nor will they receive the same reward, for the wise man on the day of judgment will be raised up into the glory of the heavenly country, but the fool will be thrust down into the eternal torments of damnation.

[47] Cf. Hugo of Saint-Victor, *In Salomonis ecclesiasten homiliae XIX*, Migne, *Patrologia Latina*, CLXXV, col. 255, and I. C. Lecompte, *The Sources of the Anglo-French Commentary on the Proverbs of Solomon*, Collegeville, Pa., 1906, *passim*.

The difference between "stultus" and "insipiens" is pointed out in Saint Augustine's (attributed) *Speculum peccatoris*, Migne, *Patrologia Latina*, XL, col. 992. "Insipiens" simply does not realize that his true home is in heaven; "stultus" realizes it but takes no pains to get there.

[48] *A Short, yet sound Commentarie; written on that woorthie worke called; The Proverbes of Salomon: and now published for the profite of Gods people*, London, 1589, folio 11 recto. (New York Public Library)

[49] *Ibid.*, folio 31 verso.

[50] *Ibid.*, folio 49 verso.

[51] Cf. J. Trenel, *L'Ancien testament et la langue française du moyen âge,* Paris, 1904, p. 4, p. 21, etc. Also J. R. Lumby (editor), *Ratis Raving and other Moral and Religious Pieces,* E.E.T.S. pub., original series, vol. XLIII, London, 1870, for examples of the absorption of Biblical proverbs into popular didactic literature.

[52] F. J. Furnivall and A. W. Pollard (editors), *The Macro Plays,* E.E.T.S. pub., extra series, XCI (London, 1904), 108:

Mankind has now come to my hall, to live with me on these barren downs (?); therefore, whatever else happens, you must make him part owner in your folly, or else you are unjust to him. For when Mankind is naturally covetous, he is also proud, wrathful and envious; at other times he is gluttonous, slothful and lecherous. Thus every sin leads on to another and makes Mankind a fool.

[53] *Ibid.,* p. 11:

Be not rebellious toward God, I pray you, but be his servant. Be steadfast in your estate, see that you be not changeable. Do not lose through folly what is sought after with such effort.

[54] F. J. Furnivall (editor), *The Digby Plays,* E.E.T.S. pub., extra series, LXX (London, 1896), 47:

Pride, which is the beginning of all bitter misfortune, keeping Mankind from his true faith, feeds itself (in his nature) and multiplies, as Holy Scriptures plainly bears witness—Pride is the beginning of all sins,—and often brings about the destruction of both great and small. Of all vices and folly pride is the root.

CHAPTER III

[1] Charles Baudelaire, "De l'Essence du Rire," in *Morceaux choisis* (Y.-G. Le Dantec, editor), Paris, 1929, p. 72.

[2] Jerome Rigollot, *Monnaies inconnues des évêques des innocens, des fous, et de quelques autres associations singulières du même temps,* Paris, 1837, p. 73.

[3] Cf. *I Kings,* III, X, etc.

[4] Cf. Mary W. Smyth, *Biblical Quotations in Middle English Literature before 1350,* New York, 1911, p. lix.

[5] F. J. Furnivall (editor), *Solomon's Book of Wisdom,* E.E.T.S. pub., original series, LXIX (London, 1878), 82-83.

[6] J. R. Lumby (editor), *op. cit.,* p. 11:

King Solomon says in his book of the contemplation and detestation of this world, that all this world is but vanity of vanities, especially all the labor that man expends to gain riches and lands in this world, with much busy care, not knowing who shall enjoy those lands and goods after him, which is great vanity.

[7] *Ibid.*, p. 12.

[8] *Ibid.*, pp. 13-14:

Item, I said in my mind and thought, that I should abstain from vice and that I should set all my heart to know wisdom and to meditate upon all errors and follies, until I saw what was most helpful to man's son upon earth. . . .

Item, I beheld then that both the wise man and the fool die, and yield up the soul in the same fashion. Then thought I, if our death be alike, what profiteth it me to turn my heart and my endeavor all toward wisdom, any more than it profiteth him who sets his mind care and endeavor toward folly?

[9] *Ibid.*, p. 14:

(I) considered and found wisdom excels folly as much as the light of the sun outshines the darkness of the dark night.

[10] J. M. Kemble, *Salomon and Saturn,* Aelfric Society Publication, London, 1848, p. 12:

For what other than profane writing is it, when they tell how Marcolf strove with the proverbs of Solomon? (Those are compositions) in which the words are fair, yet without truth.

[11] *Ibid.*, p. 17 ff.

[12] *Ibid.*, p. 21.

[13] *Ibid.*, p. 16.

[14] *Ibid.*, pp. 73-83 *passim:*

He who gives large gifts can rise in the world's esteem, said Solomon; he who clings to poverty is proclaimed a fool, Marcol answered him.

He who would be wise will never talk too much, said Solomon; he who never says a word will never do much damage, Marcol answered him.

[15] Leroux de Lincy, *op. cit.*, I, x.

[16] Kemble, *op. cit.*, p. 77.

[17] M. Méon (editor), *Nouveau recueil de fabliaux et contes inédits, des poètes français des xiie, xiiie, xive, et xve siècles,* 2 vols., Paris, 1823, I, 418.

[18] Kemble, *op. cit.*, p. 32:

Solomon the all-wise king, and Marcolf, deformed and most vile in appearance, yet, as they tell, most eloquent.

[19] Ewald Flügel (editor), *Neuenglisches Lesebuch,* Halle a. S., 1895, p. 285.

[20] *Frondes Caducae.* Reprinted at the Auchinleck Press, by Alexander

Boswell. MDCCCXVI. Dialogi due Rerum Verborumque lepore, et copia insignes: quorum prior, continet colloquium inter Deum & Evam (ut ferunt) eiusque liberos, posterior Salomonis & Marcolphi iucundissimam decertationem proponit . . . Argentinae. A-4

[21] Flügel, *op. cit.*, p. 285.

[22] *Frondes Caducae,* C-1 and C-2. Marcolf is of course a rustic lout as his pedigree in one case declares, but since he refers to himself as "follus" and since he appeared in English as "Marcolf the more fool," I am including him in the narrative of fools and omitting other rustics like him.

[23] *Ibid.*, C-3.

[24] *Ibid.*, D-1:

Salomon. So help me God, the Lord appeared to me in Gabatha and filled me with wisdom. *Marcolf.* He is considered wise who believes himself to be a fool.

[25] Cf. J. A. K. Thomson, *Irony,* London, 1926, Chs. 1-3.

[26] Kemble, *op. cit.*, p. 34.

[27] Leroux de Lincy, *op. cit.*, I, 53.

[28] J. P. Collier, *Punch and Judy,* London, 1828, p. 44.

[29] Rigollot, *op. cit.*, p. 5:

Should there be a dance of all the fools that have been since the beginning of the world, Solomon as the most distinguished should bear the bauble.

[30] J. O. Halliwell-Phillips (editor), *The Poems of John Audelay,* Percy Society pub., London, 1844, p. 13:

I, Marcolf the more fool, man, in my mad way send to thee brother Solomon to say what I hear—how mild husbandmen's hearts rise up within them, for they would fain have those men who lead and teach them act with wisdom. Tell thy message gently to priest and to friar, for they are the lanterns of life lent to men to give them light; but it is not unknown that they have been captured by covetise, that their consciences are unclean, against reason and justice and the laws of their Lord. Command them never to dare to despise any one else, for their own cursed covetise has blown their own horn.

[31] *Ibid.*, p. 50:

That thing whose end is good is all good. Thus Solomon has indeed spoken the truth, as Marcolf the more fool warned him of it I believe. But if this picture be well drawn, the gowns (of the erring clergy) shall be ruined and shall turn into a source of torment and vexation to them.

[32] Gregory the Great, *Moralium libri, sive expositio in librum B. Job,* in Migne, *Patrologia Latina,* LXXV, col. 947:

The wisdom of this world is, to conceal the truth of one's heart by trickery, to veil one's meaning in words, to make those things which are false appear to be true, to present the truth as falsehood. This prudence is known and practised by our youth, it is taught to our children as a thing of great value, those who understand it look proudly down upon everyone else; those who are ignorant of it, oppressed and timid, wonder at their fellows, for by them this deceitful iniquity, called by a kinder name, is sought after, while this perversity of the mind is called 'urbanity' . . . But on the other hand the wisdom of the just is, to make no pretences for a show, to make plain one's meaning by one's words, to pursue those things which are true, to shun the false, to do good deeds gladly, to bear evil more willingly than to do it, to seek no revenge for injury, to consider it a gain to sustain scorn for the truth. But this simplicity of the just is laughed to scorn, for worldly wise men believe the virtue of purity to be foolish. Indeed all things that are done innocently seem to them undoubtedly foolish. . . . For what seems more foolish to the world than to show one's true thought in one's words, to make no use of clever fraud, not to pay back scorn with injury, to pray for those who slander one, to seek poverty, to give up one's possessions, not to resist him who seeks to rob one, to turn the other cheek to him who strikes?

[33] *Ibid., Patrologia Latina,* LXXVI, cols. 168-69; translated in "Library of the Fathers," Vol. XXI, Saint Gregory the Great, *Morals on the Book of Job,* Parts III and IV, Oxford, 1845, p. 489:

But it is to be borne in mind, that whilst against the life of the wise man the fool being uppermost enforces the terribleness of power, whilst he wearies him out with labors, rends him with insults, such a person surely by burning he purges from all the rust of bad habits. Thus the fool even in ruling is "servant to the wise," in that by bearing him down he advances him to a better state.

[34] *Ibid., Patrologia Latina,* LXXV, col. 970; translated in "Library of the Fathers," XXI, 24:

For when foolish men behold the doings of the wise, they all seem to them to be worthy of blame; who, forgetting their own emptiness and deficiency, pass judgment on the concerns of others the more eagerly, in proportion as they are more deeply ignorant of their own.

[35] *Ibid., Patrologia Latina,* LXXVI, cols. 161-62; translated in "Library of the Fathers," XXI, 480:

It is right for us to know that some within the pale of Holy Church are styled "fools," but yet "noble," whilst others are "fools" and "base." For they are called "fools," but cannot be "base," who contemning the wisdom of the flesh, desire foolishness that shall stand them in stead, and after the newness of the interior descent are exalted by the nobility of virtue, who set at nought the foolish wisdom of the world, and covet the wise foolishness of God. . . . But contrariwise they are "fools" and "base men," who while in following themselves, they flee from the wisdom Above, are lulled to sleep in their ignorance as in the vileness of an abject descent. For in proportion as they do not understand that for which they were made, in the same measure they lose the relationship of high birth vouchsafed them in the Likeness. So they are "fools and base men," whom the slavery of the soul witholds from the fellowship of the Eternal Inheritance.

[36] *Ibid., Patrologia Latina*, LXXV, col. 972; translated in "Library of the Fathers," XXI, 27:

All that are conformed to this present state of being by an earthly temper of mind, mean, by all that they do, to leave the remembrance of themselves to the world. Some in the toils of war, some in the towering walls of edifices, some in eloquent books of this world's lore, they are eagerly toiling and striving and building up for themselves a name of remembrance. But whereas life itself runs on to an end with speed, what is there in it that will stand stedfast, when even its very self by nature running rapidly speeds away. . . . And so the remembrance of fools is rightly compared to "ashes," in that it is placed there, where it is liable to be carried away by a breath of air.

[37] Thomas Wright (editor), *The Political Songs of England from the Reign of John to that of Edward II,* Camden Society, London, 1839, pp. 109-14, *passim:*

It is some satisfaction to note down the vices of the world; for nowadays I see many people living in error in the world, spurning what is good, loving what is bad, and very often willingly choosing the bad. . . . All that concerns profit is too much regarded; whoever seeks profits is considered sensibly cautious; he who more rigorously preserves his property is called wise, and he who gives more generously is called a fool.

[38] E. Du Méril, *Poésies populaires latines du moyen âge,* Paris, 1847, pp. 109-14, *passim:*

Oh life of this world, unhealthy, prating, insolent, unbridled thing, since you are so totally concerned with trifles why do you cry out upon me? . . . When I wanted to be generous, you said: Be sparing, for the wealth you are long in getting will slip away fast. . . . Therefore, oh useless life, acceptable only to fools, since you are completely mean I repudiate you with my whole heart.

[39] Wright, *Political Songs*, pp. 10-11, p. 14, 32, etc.

[40] Halliwell-Phillips, *Poems of John Audelay,* p. 12.

[41] John Doran, *History of Court Fools,* Boston, Mass., n.d., p. 65.

[42] C. Guerrieri Crocetti, *La Lirica Predantesca,* Florence, 1925, pp. 312-13; translated in E. Underhill, *Jacopone da Todi,* London & Toronto, 1919, pp. 283-85:

How it is the Highest Wisdom to be reputed mad for the love of Christ.

> Wisdom 'tis and Courtesy,
> Crazed for Jesus Christ to be.
>
> No such learning can be found
> In Paris, nor the world around;
> In this folly to abound
>   Is the best philosophy.
>
> Who by Christ is all possessed,
> Seems afflicted and distressed,
> Yet is Master of the best,
>   In science and theology.
>
> Who for Christ is all distraught,
> Gives his wits, men say, for naught;
>   —Those whom Love hath never taught,
>   Deem he erreth utterly.
>
> He who enters in this school,
> Learns a new and wondrous rule:—
>   "Who hath never been a fool,
>   Wisdom's scholar cannot be."
>
> He who enters on this dance,
> Enters Love's unwalled expanse;
>   —Those who mock and look askance,
>   Should do penance certainly.
>
> He that worldly praise achieves
> Jesus Christ his Saviour grieves,
> Who Himself, between two thieves,
>   On the Cross hung patiently.
>
> He that seeks for shame and pain,
> Shall his heart's desire attain:
> All Bologna's lore were vain,
>   To increase his mastery.

[43] L. Salembier, "Gerson," in *Catholic Encyclopedia,* 1913 edition, VI, 530-32.

[44] John K. Ingram (editor), *The Earliest English Translation of the First Three books of the De Imitatione Christi,* E.E.T.S. pub., extra series, LXIII (London, 1893), 283.

[45] G. Paris and U. Robert (editors), *Miracles de Nostre Dame,* 8 vols., Societé des anciens textes français publication, Paris, 1878, III, 8:

For so truly do I consider the joy of this world vain, and so repugnant is it to my heart, that I long to go my way naked, worn and poor, playing the fool, not thinking of earthly comforts, working, suffering, and chastening my flesh so that each day it is more humbled than the day before.

[46] *Ibid.,* p. 9:

My friend, if you truly desire to humble your heart in this way, you will act wisely rather than foolishly if you play the fool in the place where you were born, to the end that you may not be known and that sin may not deceive you. God, who will surely see you, will accept as wisdom the folly you feign to flee the wiles of false tempting earthly vanities. To feign to be fools and yet wise in God and in his holy word which is full of the light of good teaching—this is a practice which teaches many a heart to hide and conceal his penance in this world and to open his heart in prayer to God.

[47] P. Meyer, "Bribes de littérature anglo-normande," *Jahrbuch für romanische und englische Literatur,* VII, 285:

This life is evil when man at its end cries "Alas!" A fool indeed is he who remains in such a state of soul that he dare not die.

[48] A. Montaiglon, *L'Alphabet de la Mort de Hans Holbein,* Paris, 1856, A4-2:

Death counts him but a fool who lives a contented life in gluttony and lechery; for all earthly things are vain and temporary, and neither old man nor young man is truly secure. Hence it is good to abstain from the evil pleasures of this life, since at the end each man encounters death and can by no means buy himself out of hell, that place so cruel and hard. And good it is so to shape oneself while young that one can finally reach God. Unripened fruit is worth little.

[49] *Ibid.,* p. A5-8.

[50] *Ibid.,* unpaginated illustration.

[51] Cf. G. Paris, "La 'Dance Macabré' de Jean Le Fèvre," *Romania,* XXIV (1895), 129-32.

[52] Georges Kastner, *Les Danses des Morts,* Paris, 1852, p. 76.

[53] Montaiglon, *op. cit.,* unpaginated illustration.

[54] Francis Douce, *The Dance of Death,* London, 1833, p. 36.

[55] Kastner, *op. cit.*, p. 115.

[56] *The Dance of Death; painted by H. Holbein, and engraved by W. Hollar,* London, 1794 (?), p. A2-verso. (Library of Congress)

[57] *Ibid.*, p. C4-verso.

[58] *A Collection of seventy-nine Black-Letter Ballads and Broadsides, printed in the reign of Queen Elizabeth, between the years 1559 and 1597,* London, 1870, pp. 173-74.

[59] A. Goette, *Holbein's Totentanz und seine Vorbilder,* Strassburg, 1897, p. 81.

[60] Montaiglon, *op. cit.*, p. A3-1.

[61] Douce, *op. cit., passim.*

[62] Cf. Kastner, *op. cit.*, pp. 57-58 on the relation of the skeleton and fool symbols.

[63] Kastner, *op. cit.*, p. 5, note.

[64] W. J. Deane (editor), *The Book of Wisdom,* Oxford, 1881, pp. 47-48.

[65] *Carmina Clericorum* (supplement to the *Commersbuch*), Heilbronn, n.d., p. 5:

I am telling you the truth about the order of the Wanderers, whose way of life is noble and pleasant and whose spirits are more pleased by a juicy roast of meat than by a measure of barley.

[66] *Ibid.*, p. 64:

While it is the quality of the wise man to place the foundations of his life upon the solid rock, foolish I am comparable to the flowing river, always changing my course.

[67] Wright, *Political Poems,* p. 137.

[68] Thomas Wright (editor), *The Anglo-Latin Satirical Poets and Epigrammatists of the Twelfth Century,* 2 vols., London, 1872, I, 3-4.

[69] J. O. Halliwell-Phillips (editor), *Nugae poeticae,* London, 1844, p. 7.

[70] F. J. Furnivall (editor), *Jyl of Breyntfords Testament . . . and other short pieces,* London, 1871.

[71] F. J. Furnivall (editor), "The Ordre of Folys," in *A Booke of Precedence,* E.E.T.S. pub., extra series, VIII (London, 1869), 79-84. The verses given here may be paraphrased as follows:

The order of fools, begun many years ago, increases the number of its brothers by many newly professed members; Bacchus and Juno have broached a tun and brought their brains into a ferment, Marcolf is their founder, patron and president, and the number of this brotherhood is three score and three, each carefully registered and their privilege endorsed with the promise that they shall never prosper.

The chief of fools, as men may read in books, the one equipped to be a resident lecturer on folly, is he that neither loves nor fears God, that pays no heed to his church, that does not revere the saints, that scorns the poor, and that does not assist his father and mother; seal up his patent, for he shall never prosper.

(The order also includes the man) that sells a fat swan for a gosling, that grazes on barren turf, that throws off his cloak in a shower when he might flee out of the storm, and the eunuch that makes love; (each of them) is one of those that shall never prosper.

Confirm the establishment of this order, and give it some sufficiently stupid bishop, and grant them a general pardon, and a patent for the beginning of their dispensation permitting them to walk freely in every country with open wallet, their organization ratified by a bull which concludes with the sentence that none of all this order is in the least likely ever to prosper.

Chapter IV

[1] Stanley P. Davies, *Social Control of the Mentally Deficient,* New York, 1930, p. 16.

[2] Francis Douce, *Illustrations of Shakespeare and of Ancient Manners,* London, 1839, p. 499.

[3] Rigollot, *op. cit.,* p. cxlii.

[4] Doran, *op. cit.,* p. 118.

[5] Edmond Faral, *Les Jongleurs en France au moyen âge,* Paris, 1910, pp. 21-22.

[6] *Ibid.,* p. 46:

The fables of Arthur of Britain and the songs of Charlemagne are more beloved now in many a town than are the Holy Scriptures. The jongleur is listened to with more attention than Saint Paul or Saint Peter, and the fool nowadays is given a more willing ear than Saint Peter or Saint Paul.

[7] Doran, *op. cit.,* p. 158 ff.

[8] *Ibid.,* p. 176.

[9] Article "Fou," in *La Grande encyclopédie,* edited by Berthelot and others, 31 vols., Paris, 1886-1903.

[10] Rigollot, *op. cit.,* p. cxliii; also E. K. Chambers, *The Medieval Stage,* 2 vols., London, 1903, I, 386.

[11] J. O. Halliwell-Phillips, *Nugae poeticae,* pp. 44-46. A note, p. 71, suggests that Lobe was the fool of Henry VIII.

[12] Doran, *op. cit.,* p. 291.

[13] Halliwell, *Nugae poeticae,* p. 55.

[14] *Ibid.,* p. 57.

[15] J. Th. Welter, *Le Speculum Laicorum,* Paris, 1914, p. 11:

Of the love of the world and its deceptions. . . . They tell the story that once there was in the house of a certain rich man a fool named Philip, to whom his master one day gave a new shirt. When he put it on, Philip ran through the hall and other rooms of the house asking who he was, for Philip the fool did not know himself in his new shirt. So it is with the lovers of the world, who blinded by the treasures and honors of their age do not give heed to the frailty of the body or the salvation of the soul.

[16] *Ibid.,* p. 17:

Of avarice and its effects. . . . A certain fool having a new pair of shoes hid them in his bosom and when he walked in rough places and gave his foot a bad cut rejoiced none the less that his shoes were un-injured. Thus too the miser exposes himself to all injuries of body and soul, if only his possessions may be preserved intact.

[17] Doran, *op. cit.,* p. 158.

[18] *Ibid.,* p. 178 ff.

[19] Article "Tarleton," *Dictionary of National Biography,* L. Stephen and S. Lee (editors), London.

[20] Edmond Faral, *Mimes français du XIIIe siècle,* Paris, 1912, p. 59:

One plays the drunkard, another plays the fool, one sings, another touches his instrument, or one recites *La Riote,* another *La Jonglerie.*

[21] A. Montaiglon and J. Rothschild (editors), *Recueil de poésies fran-çaises du 15e et 16e siècles,* 13 vols., Paris, 1855-78, XI, 181:

If I have a fool's hood hung about my neck, I act the witty fellow who sails up to you full of small flatteries; you never saw such an agreeable chap.

[22] *Miracles de Nostre Dame,* III, 27-28:

Turelu, hey, turelu, I must go play at magic. I won't do it for all the charms of Saint Susanna's feast. I must go hunt up Dame Osanna who puts me to sleep at night with her spinning. And I must go sharpen my nails on the bill of a white cock. I like clear milk and whey (?) better than soft butter.

He seems to sport his folly prettily enough. Let's get some mud and earth and make him go down the street ahead of us while we throw it at him.

[23] A. Jubinal (editor), *Mystères inédits du quinzième siècle,* 2 vols., Paris, 1837, I, 215:

> Leave your laughter and your playing,
> Your jests and songs, your rounds and dances,
> God cares not for such slight fancies,
> Heavenly joys are bought by tears.

[24]L. Petit de Julleville, *Les Mystères,* 2 vols., Paris, 1880, II, 17.

[25] *Ibid.,* I, 267.

[26] A. Lecoy de la Marche (editor), *Le mystère de S. Bernard de Menthon,* Societé des anciens textes français pub., Paris, 1888, p. 83.

[27] Petit de Julleville, *Les Mystères,* I, 268 and II, 412.

[28] *Ibid.,* I, 240:

I want my face to be well illuminated with the best red color of Beaune. Believe me, in drinking I'm a graduate doctor and no greenhorn. By the way, good father, do you know why a donkey has such big ears? Because his mother forgot to tie a little bonnet on him to hold his head in! Isn't an ass a wise beast! My lord, yes. Many's the time he has comforted me with his sweet and doleful song.

[29] *Ibid.,* I, 235:

What, do you think it is suitable that Robin, or Jehannyn, or Jehannet of our village should be tricked out in strange feathers as if he were a gentleman? I shall have to see to this, now that I've got the idea. Do you think it is decent to wear those trailing robes? I order that those amiable youths who drag them in the mire shall have them cut off two thumbs lengths below the belt.

[30] Lecoy de la Marche, *op. cit.,* pp. 19-20.

[31] Petit de Julleville, *Les Mystères,* II, 603.

[32] Doran, *op. cit.,* p. 308.

[33] Rigollot, *op. cit.,* p. lxix.

[34] F. J. Furnivall (editor), "The Sage Fool's Testament," in *A Booke of Precedence,* pp. 77-78.

[35] E. K. Chambers, *op. cit.,* I, 99.

[36] *Ibid.,* II, 153, records plays from Bruges in 1449 and Besançon in 1453.

[37] Kastner, *op cit.,* p. 72:

City women, wives and maidens, flee from presumptuous pride. . . . But be not cruel to your suffering servants, for you may all dance the dance of Narcissus who died because of his vanity.

[38] General discussions of these games and plays may be found in Chambers, *Medieval Stage,* I, chs. 5-17, Reginald Tiddy, *The Mummers' Play,* Oxford, 1923, and Maximilian J. Rudwin, *The Origin of German Carnival Comedy,* New York, 1920.

[39] Chambers, *op cit.,* I, 193.

[40] P. Manning, "Some Oxfordshire Seasonal Festivals," in *Folk Lore,* VIII (1897), 309.

[41] Chambers, *op. cit.,* I, 223.

[42] J. M. Manly, *Specimens of the Pre-Shakespearean Drama,* I, Boston, (1897), 296-311.

[43] Charlotte S. Burne, "Guisers' Play, Songs and Rhymes from Staffordshire," in *Folk Lore Journal,* IV (1886), 355.

[44] Chambers, *op. cit.,* I, 195.

[45] John N. Gough (editor), *The Diary of Henry Machyn,* Camden Society, London, 1848, p. 137.

[46] Douce, *Illustrations of Shakespeare,* facing p. 576.

[47] Chambers, *op. cit.,* I, 95.

[48] Petit de Julleville, *Les Mystères,* I, 357-61.

[49] Cf. Faral, *Jongleurs en France,* ch. II and app. III, for texts illustrating the condemnation of the "mimi" by the church.

[50] Rudwin, *op. cit.,* p. 48.

[51] Du Cange, *Glossarium,* s.v. "Kalendae."

[52] Rigollot, *op. cit.,* p. 6:

That superstitious and scandalous rite which some people call the feast of fools, and which derives its beginning and origin from pagan rites and the idolatry of infidels.

[53] Chambers, *op. cit.,* I, 292, note 2:

They are fools, and pernicious fools; they are not to be borne with, they must be put out of the way.

(The celebration is one in which) a detestable mockery is made of the service of the Lord and of the sacraments, where things are impudently and execrably done which should be done only in taverns and brothels, or among Saracens and Jews. For these outrageous words could not be uttered by cooks in their kitchens without shame and indignity, yet they are allowed to go on in our holy churches.

[54] *Ibid.,* I, 276 ff. for the whole description of the Sens missal.

[55] *Ibid.,* I, 276 ff.

[56] *Ibid.,* I, 294. Cf. E. Du Méril, *Poésies populaires latines du moyen âge,* p. 58, note 1, for the "Pater Noster" of the Messe des fous.

[57] L. Paris, *Le Théâtre à Reims,* Reims, 1885, pp. 30-31. Cf. G. Coquillart, *Oeuvres,* Paris, 1723, p. 69 ff.

[58] Chambers, *op. cit.,* I, 307-308.

[59] W. Hone, *Ancient Mysteries Described,* London, 1823, p. 163.

Chapter V

[1] Jean Hankiss, "Essai sur la farce," in *Revue de philologie et de littérature,* 1st and 2nd fascicules, 1924:

That spirit of relaxation after serious work, mad relaxation, the abandonment of oneself to folly, to the charm of irresponsibility, to a state which offers the irresistible attraction of contrast and novelty.

[2] Petit de Julleville, *Les Comédiens en France au moyen âge,* Paris, 1885, p. 193.

[3] *Ibid.,* p. 194.

[4] *Ibid.,* p. 196:

We decree, allow and accord, for ourselves and our successors the lords of the above-named estates, that this festival shall be held perpetually, one day a year—the first of January—and that all gay fools clad in the habits of our Chapel shall hold their revels safely, without suffering any kind of outrage or scorn. And let no one, not even the wisest, contradict this order. But let the fools caper, gently, one or two days, as long as their money lasts. For it would be hard to continue longer, or to extend their expenses farther. For their finances shrink as their expenditures grow. Therefore we command our subjects not to interfere with them but to allow them to go peacefully about their pleasures.

[5] Petit de Julleville, *Comédiens,* p. 197. Cf. also Gazeau, *Les Bouffons,* Paris, 1882, p. 246.

[6] Juliette E. Padé, *La mère folle dijonnaise,* unprinted essay for the Master's degree, Columbia University, 1920:

> Wanton fool, frantic fool,
> Chimerical fool, fantastic fool,
> Jovial fool, gracious fool,
> Court-making fool, loving fool,
> Mocking fool, fool full of facetious stories,
> Blithe fool, maiden-kissing fool,
> Shrewd fool and scatter-brained fool,
> Thirsty fool and dry fool, (?)
> Fool with empty noddle,
> Fool who seeks a good time and a full meal,
> Fool who loves carefully chosen tid-bits,
> Green fool, crimson-tinted fool,
> Plain-chanting fool, musical fool,
> Fool who thumbs his nose at wise men,
> Laughing fool, gay fool, witty fool,

Beneficent fool, fair-speaking fool,
Hairbrained fool, peevish fool,
Canny fool and pantagruelian fool,
Light fool, giddy fool,
Fool in folly completely blind,
Fool by land and fool by water,
Fool in the air, fool all the world over,
Complete fool, fool seated, fool standing,
Fool here, fool there, fool everywhere.

[7] Claude Noirot, *L'Origine des masques, mommeries, bernez, etc.*, in C. Leber, *Collection des meilleurs dissertations . . . relatifs à l'histoire de France*, Vol. 9, Paris, 1838, gives an extended description of these Burgundian May ceremonies.

[8] Petit de Julleville, *Comédiens*, p. 210:

As ill-luck would have it, he's beaten his wife! And worse yet, in this country, in a strange dwelling, before observers, and in this season! To beat one's wife in the month of May—what an infamy!

[9] *Ibid.*, p. 218.

[10] *Ibid.*, p. 199.

[11] The relation between these two societies is discussed at length in Chambers, *op. cit.*, I, 375 ff., and in E. Lintilhac, *La Comédie: moyen âge et renaissance*, Paris, 1905 (?), pp. 40-42. Illustrations of the type of performance indulged in by the Bazoches may be found in Petit de Julleville, *Comédiens*, p. 134 and p. 139, and in L. Paris, *Le Théâtre à Reims*, p. 28.

[12] Petit de Julleville, *Comédiens*, p. 127.

[13] Chambers, *op. cit.*, I, 373:

Go to the Fêtes at Tournai, at Arras or at Lille, Amiens, Douai Cambrai, Valenciennes, Abbeville. There you will see ten thousand folk thicker than trees in the forest of Torfolz, who, in chambers and in cities, indoors and out, are servants of your duke, the prince of fools.

[14] G. Lhotte, *Le Théâtre à Douai avant la Révolution*, Douai, 1881, p. 10.

[15] E. E. Fournier, *Les Chansons de Gaultier Garguille*, Paris, 1858, p. xxxvii.

[16] Lintilhac, *op. cit.*, p. 37.

[17] Chambers, *op. cit.*, I, 377.

[18] Lintilhac, *op. cit.*, p. 37.

[19] Lhotte, *op. cit.*, p. 11.

[20] As the Feast of Fools is known to have been more widely celebrated

in France than in England, so too records of Joyous Societies are more plentiful from France than from England. Chambers notes only three such orders in England (*op. cit.*, I, 383, and II, 333). Cf. also J. A. Lester, *Connections between the Drama of France and Great Britain, particularly in the Elizabethan period,* Harvard University thesis (unpublished), 1900, p. 521.

[21] A. Montaiglon and J. Rothschild (editors), *Recueil de poésies françaises des xve et xvie siècles,* 13 vols., Paris, 1855-78, VII, 81:

Jest-loving Carefree Companions, you pass the time gaily. Would to God we were like you. You banish vexation. And, alas, you often make sport, in order to banish mourning. You give welcome and honest diversion to the poor impoverished world.

[22] Lintilhac, *op. cit.*, p. 40:

A gathering of good fellows known as the Carefree Companions were once to be found between two bridges, near the Palace. There were others also who loved sweet repose after labor, and in the goodness of their hearts were horrified to lodge in the abbey of Holy Penury.

[23] Charles Merz, *The Great American Band-Wagon,* New York, 1928, p. 113.

[24] Lintilhac, *op. cit.*, p. 40.

[25] Some of the Enfants sans Souci were professional comedians or producers, like Jehan du Pont-Alletz and Gringore, and some of the plays attributed to the Paris and Rouen societies are as trivial as vaudeville "turns." The plays which comment on affairs of public significance, however, show an accomplished dramatic manner, applied to subjects which purely professional entertainers might not have treated.

[26] Clément Marot, *Oeuvres complètes,* 2 vols., (A. Grenier, editor), Paris, n.d., pp. 337-38:

Who are the men whose hearts are so heavy, so full of envy and distress—and whose lesson of boredom we through the whole course of our lives refuse to listen to? They are much in error, for see how happily we spend our green and flowering years. To leap, to dance and sing—is that, oh mistaken Envious One, a way of life that wounds the world? Nenni, indeed, but true gentility and the Will to Gaiety that holds us in its nets. So do not blame our youth, for the truly noble heart seeks only innocent solace.

We are lively birds, sorrow does not pursue us, and we do not feel the shivers of chill care. But what is the good of a dull head? As much good as an ox drowsing under a bush! Gossips whose tongues sting worse than hedgehogs' pricks and who are more stay-at-homes than any old crow in a cage never have a good word for any one else and are always thinking up crafty tricks. But we dwell cheerfully with each other, thinking no evil, more at our ease than prelates. Then it is plainly foolish to speak ill of us, for the truly noble heart seeks only innocent solace.

To bear a good heart, a good body and a cheerful face, to drink in the morning and to flee from brawls and wrangling, to sing a little song to one's beloved at the gate in the evening, to cut a figure as a brave bad fellow, to wander all night without harming a soul, to go to bed— there is our whole baffling plan! Next day we begin all over again. In conclusion, what we seek is lightheartedness, and of it we never tire, and we maintain that it is part of true nobility, for the truly noble heart seeks only innocent solace.

[27] L. Paris, *op. cit.*, p. 63.

[28] Petit de Julleville, *Répertoire du Théâtre comique,* Paris, 1886, p. 325.

[29] Petit de Julleville, *Comédiens,* pp. 122-23.

[30] A. Wiedenhofen, *Beitrage zur Entwicklunsgeschichte der franzözischen Farce,* Munster, 1913, p. 80.

[31] Lintilhac, *op. cit.*, p. 25:

The court has forbidden and now forbids all clerks and servants, as well those of the Palace as those of the Châtelet of Paris, of whatever rank they may be, from playing farces, sotties, moralities, from this time forward, on pain of banishment from the kingdom and confiscation of all their property.

[32] Petit de Julleville, *Comédiens,* p. 102.

[33] Chambers, *op. cit.*, I, 376:

That no student should dress up in the fool's costume that year, either in the college or outside, unless playing in a farce or morality.

[34] Rigollot, *op. cit.*, p. lxxxiv.

[35] Lintilhac, *op. cit.*, p. 38:

Fasten a bell on the dirty forehead of a monk, attach a long ear on either side of his head-gear, and there you have one of the fools of the Bazoche, painted as vividly as possible.

[36] R. Van Bastelaer (editor), *Les Estampes de Pierre Bruegel, l'ancien,* Brussels, 1908, plate 95.

[37] *Ibid.*, plates 225 and 226. Cf. also Joseph Strutt, *Sports and Pastimes of the People of England,* London, 1910, *passim.*

[38] Emile Picot, *Recueil général des sotties,* 3 vols., Paris, 1902, 1904, 1912, Societé des anciens textes français pub., II, 124-25.

[39] Doran, *op. cit.*, pp. 161-62.

[40] Petit de Julleville, *Comédiens,* p. 148:

One's head is green, the other wears a hood of green and yellow, one plays with bells, the other mutters nonsense.

[41] Cf. Chambers, *op. cit.*, II, 333, and Gough, *Diary of Henry Machyn,* pp. 13-14, for other uses of green and yellow in merry-makings.

[42] Rigollot, *op. cit.*, p. lxvi:

(The unfortunate victim was roused about six o'clock in the morning and dressed in a costume) made with bands of serge, one half green in color, the other half yellow, and where there were bands of yellow there was green trimming, and on the green bands yellow trimming. Between the bands there was also tafeta, part yellow and part green, which was sewn between the bands and the trimmings. The breeches and stockings were sewn together, and one side was all of green serge, the other of yellow; and a hood as well, half yellow and half green, with ears.

[43] *Ibid.*, p. lxix.

[44] Cf. L. Gazeau, *Les Bouffons,* Paris, 1882, p. 246.

[45] Rabelais, Clouzot ed., *Gargantua et Pantagruel,* Paris, 1922, p. 454. Cf. also Douce, *Illustrations of Shakespeare,* p. 509, and plates.

[46] A. L. Mayhew (editor), *The Promptorium parvulorum,* E.E.T.S. pub., extra series, CII, London, 1908, s.v. "babulle."

[47] Petit de Julleville, *Comédiens,* p. 104.

[48] M. J. Quicherat (editor), *Les Vers de Maître Henri Baude,* Paris, 1856, p. 49:

> Most giddily, and blindly all,
> Man in his folly makes his way,
> Comes, goes, or weds, as best he may,
> And butts his head against a wall.

> Some exchange blows, some pull and haul,
> Some threaten, and soon after pray,
>   Most giddily.

> Some talk, some listen not at all,
> Unless some scandal comes their way,
> Some make their plans, then change the day,
> And slanders generally fall
>   Most giddily.

[49] *Ibid.*, pp. 84-86:

> . . . a son of ours, by magic moon-milk fed,
> Who, if he had a hood upon his head
> Adorned with ears, would show his wisdom truly—

> . . . .

Trusting devoutly in his ignorance,
In diligence divided, and in will,
Too prompt in wishing, without care or heed
Beyond the reason of his nature's need,
Laughing without discourse, in discourse still
Confused and eager, wanting without fill,
Content to sleep at any time of day,
Quitting all work, yet working without stay.

. . . .

To watch all night, or slumber on a board;
Waking to find your purse's scanty hoard
Vanished, and you in great humility—
And, to supply your bare necessity,
You shall go often stumbling, without light,
To dawdle in a tavern all the night.

[50] Lintilhac, *op. cit.*, pp. 27-28.

[51] *Ibid.*, p. 50.

Chapter VI

[1] E. Picot, *Recueil général des sotties:*

Les Trompeurs—Sottie nouvelle a cinq personnages, III, 5 ff.
Des gens nouveaulx—Farce nouvelle moralisée, I, 113 ff.
Du Monde qu'on faict paistre—Farce joyeuse, I, 11 ff.
De Tout le Monde—Moral, III, 25 ff.
Le Monde et les Abus—Sotise, II, 1 ff.

[2] Cf. Hankiss, *op. cit.*, for discussion of the "sot"; also Littré, *Dictionnaire,* s.v. "sot." In general the distinction between "fol" and "sot" is the distinction between the morally defective individual and the plain clown.

[3] Cf. Thomas Sibilet, *Art poétique françoys,* F. Gaiffe editor, Paris, 1910, p. 162; August Beneke, *Das Repertoir und die Quellen der franzözischen Farce,* Weimar, 1910, p. 13; L. Paris, *op. cit.*, pp. 65-66.

[4] Cf. above, p. 85.

[5] Lintilhac, *op. cit.*, p. 179: Son caractère principal, tout extérieur, est d'être jouée par des Sots.

[6] Picot, *op. cit.*, I, ix:

Sotties may be recognized first by their titles, then by the fact that their characters are designated as ninnies, fools, gallants, companions, pilgrims, hermits; they may finally be recognized by their dialogue in which we always find traces of the fatrasie.

[7] *Ibid.*, I, v:

The more foolish words and various and strange rimes they contain, the better they are.

[8] Cf. Leroux de Lincy, *op. cit.*, I, 173.

[9] Sibilet, *op. cit.*, pp. 167-68:

The substance of it is the vice of individuals, which is there the more freely rehearsed as the author's name is suppressed. Its greatest elegance lies in the greatest absurdity in the sequence of remarks, which is increased by the "rime platte" and the eight-syllable verse.

[10] Picot, *op. cit.*, I, vi-vii:

Hence, on account of their disjointed statements, such satirical enigmas are well named "coq-à-l'âne," and not satires, for a satire is something different; but they are, as it were, satire-ated, not on account of their form but on account of their reproving comments, in the manner of Latin satire—although this same disjointed style may be used in matters other than satirical, like the *Absurda* of Erasmus, the farce of *The Deaf Man and the Blind Man,* and the *Embassy of the Conards of Rouen.*

[11] Rabelais, Clouzot edition, p. 89.

[12] Lintilhac, *op. cit.*, p. 39:

Here's the man who leaps best of all! Up, and jump, the high jump, the standing jump, the half-whole, the supple jump, the tied, the untied. Up! I'm hot! I'm cold! Isn't he good at it?

[13] Picot, *op. cit.*, I, 66:

Third: Tell me now, how many ways are there to begin to get one's Latin up?

First: The sun which rises early in the morning will be hard put to it to do any good.

Second: Dung of cat and dung of dog are sufficiently alike to look at.

Third: It is grand to eat boar's meat—you hear me?—for a solid hour.

First: By Saint John, he who would bore *her* with a saddle— "That's another story," said the cow.

Second: He who beats up a sergeant (à mache—greedy, boastful?) will gain a hundred days' pardon.

[14] Cf. *Le Sermon de Bien Boyre*, in *Ancien théâtre français*, Viollet-le-Duc ed., 10 vols., Paris, 1854-57, II, 5-20; and *Farce joyeuse du gaudisseur et du sot,* ibid., II, 292-302.

[15] Picot, *op. cit.*, III, 125-26:

First Gallant: Well?

Second: Fountain!

First:	Yes, and river too! This is your familiar line of talk. You are gay.
Second:	I am gay, and even in my poverty I frolic well enough, managing to get past my melancholy periods.
First:	Melancholy is nothing but folly.
Second:	Never burden yourself with it. How goes it with you?
First:	As it comes.
Second:	And how comes it?
First:	As it goes.
Second:	No chap ever talked such nonsense as you. Will you always act like such a scamp? How goes it with you?
First:	As I see it.
Second:	But *how* are you getting along?
First:	As I can.

[16] *Ibid.*, III, 127-28:

What a pity it is about poor married folks! They are often positively hunted! I'm told it's a kind of living death.

[17] *Ibid.*, III, 146-47:

Second:	He is in the clutch of folly Who shuns a life of wedded bliss.
First:	No folly can be worse than this— To wait till one is summoned twice.
Second:	Surely 'tis a fool's device, Utterly to fail to marry.
Fool:	He his folly long must carry, Who binds a scourge upon his back.

Nothing is wasted away when you wash a donkey's head
—except the labor of washing.

[18] *Ibid.*, III, 65-66:

These have been sold for one or two hundred écus apiece. Fools of this sort are full of high spirits; they are like tame monkeys in the house. They have less sense than a gosling, but still they are the best kind of fool, and great lords are glad to have them and treasure them well.

[19] *Ibid.*, III, 69-70:

They discover such profundities in their own wits that if one believed their writings one would think them God's own first cousins.

[20] *Ibid.*, III, 70-71:

These fools, if I remember right, are those who according to report let themselves be burned on faith, saying, "Listen to my prating: I am the one in ten thousand who will die for the people."

. . . .

No Greeks, Hebrews nor Latins will ever make me believe that I should let myself be burned! Bren, bren, bren! Life is what matters.

[21] *Ibid.*, III, 73:

Every man who thinks himself wise should be held a fool.

[22] *Ibid.*, III, 60-62:

Clowns are not true fools, but they are neither fools nor wise men.

Clown:	You are all fools, aren't you?
5th Fool:	Yes truly.
Clown:	Ah, then it's this way: if you are fools all the time, you must, if I understand correctly, be fools either by nature or by habit. A fool shall never become a wise man; therefore you will never be wise.
3rd Fool:	Poor clown, anyway I can promise you *you'll* never have to meddle with wisdom.
Clown:	No truly, for you must recognize that a clown who thinks of nothing at all knows more about the honorable and the good than a fool learns in his whole life.
3rd Fool:	For that I'd like to give you a good cuffing.
Clown:	A clown . . . eating, drinking, dancing or laughing, is worth more than all the fools put together.

[23] *Ibid.*, I, 15-46, *Des galans et du monde.*

[24] *Ibid.*, I, 121:

Second:	Let us make wingless birds that fly,
	And horseless horsemen riding too:
	New men must shape the world anew.
Third:	Let us make lawyers generous men
	Who give, not take, and give again,
	For fear their pleas be thought untrue:
	New men must shape the world anew.
First:	Let us make cowardly recruits
	So bold each is the first to shoot
	When the assault is ordered through:
	New men must shape the world anew.

[25] *Ibid.*, II, 17-104, Sotise à huit personaiges . . . *le Monde et Abus.*

[26] *Ibid.*, III, 31:

First:	You are seeking Pastime, are you not?

Second: That is the case.

First: I, like you, am seeking him.

Second: Pastime? Alas, he is half dead with horror. . . . Avarice has had his claws on him for so long that he is quite shrunken.

First: Lack-of-Cash still has him in prison, and Poor Judgment has quite conquered him.

[27] *Ibid.*, III, 34:

I never saw Everyman in such a condition. Either he is quite out of his wits, or else this man approaching us is not he but some clown recently arrived. Why, he wears the garments of Nobility, Commerce, Labor and Clergy all at once.

[28] *Ibid.*, III, 43:

To make a long story short and come to the conclusion, gentlemen, Everyman today is quite mad, and greatly in error. It is he himself who brings us misfortune, for he is not content with the condition he finds himself in, and he thinks as well of himself as of Saint Paul. Therefore I tell you again, we consider Everyman a fool.

[29] Petit de Julleville, *Comédiens,* pp. 243-44.

[30] Picot, *Recueil général,* I, 241-42:

Where are you, my foolish band of fools? Come out, all of you, and appear in my presence. What's this? Can't you hear me calling you? Hurry; come hither speedily, all you crazy fools, mad over folly, (and *I* am mad at not seeing you here). Where are you, my foolish band of fools? Come out, all of you, and appear in my presence. One-eyed, hunchbacked, stunted and mad, all wanton fools, you must give heed to folly; fools of Lyon, Geneva and Milan, lusty fools, scatter-brained wits— where are you, all my foolish band of fools?

[31] *Ibid.*, I, 247-49 *passim:*

First Fool (gentleman): Fie upon work!

Second (merchant): Fie, fie on labor.

Third (farmer): Fie upon care.

First: Fie upon sorrow.

Second: Some men sow grain and oats and never eat a kernel of the harvest.

Third (farmer): Some eat too much.

First: Some die of hunger.

Second: Some men wear themselves out cultivating their vineyards but never wet their throats with a drop of their own wine.

Third Fool (farmer): It's worth a lot just to rest oneself.

First Fool (gentleman): It's pleasant to lead a gay life.

. . . .

Foolish Display: Gentle Fools, you must know that the greatest satisfaction is to lead a life of pleasure. And so you can easily see that Foolish Display is an important part of life.

[32] *Ibid.*, I, 266-68 *passim:*

There you shall live in beggary until the end of your days.

I introduce all new-comer fools to folly. I give them a good time as long as they have income and revenue, but when they have expended everything—income, cash and possessions—I think nothing at all of shutting them up in this cage of poverty. When men are great landowners, rich merchants or farmers, I welcome them, as long as they have anything, until finally I reduce them to penury and imprison them in this dark castle, all hungry, yearning and unhappy. The workman must be paid in proportion to his task, and fools must pay for their welcome.

[33] *Ibid.*, III, 18-19:

Everyman, here are the chief points of what you must do. First, if you wish to ride on horseback and be a man of large affairs, you must imitate the behaviour of the wise man and attentive listener, tell all the ill you know and keep quiet about the good, and become a past-master in lying, jesting, fibbing and tale-bearing, swearing loudly and at random. But if you are not also a good flatterer, your chances of success are not worth a pin. Speak always evil of a man—in his absence of course —and if he learns of it, say "I was joking"; but in his presence smooth him down constantly with flattery and fair words.

[34] *Ibid.*, I, 148:

Good heavens, I am a woman loved and cherished by many men!

[35] *Ibid.*, I, 150-51:

Folly . . . I was born in the heart of the Earthly Paradise.

Second: What you say can't be true. You can't be twenty-five years old.

Folly: I am over six thousand and five hundred years old. I am in fact the very person through whose wiles Adam ate the apple.

[36] *Ibid.*, I, 164:

He who would live in great prosperity must keep himself from speaking the truth, must make many promises and keep none of them. He should make his way by slanders, as time and opportunity offer.

He should bite most subtly, under cover of laughter. And there where he sees that rewards may be gained, he should cordially (for his own profit) offer hospitality and friendship—he who would live!

To cajole the great with your importunities, to be most affable to those in authority, to pay nothing out and to hold on to the other man's money—this is the course that makes evil men rise to high estate, in imminent danger of sudden beheading—who yet would live.

[37] *Ibid.,* I, 172:

I am the real Folly, amiable, mad folly, authentic author of folly. Worry no more about it, for greater than you, by your leave, have risen through my offices to prelacies and benefices and married into noble houses.

[38] *Ibid.,* I, 174:

And in conclusion (I am), full of deceit and trickery; that is the common fame I enjoy.

[39] H. Oskar Sommer (editor), *The Kalender of Shepherdes,* London, 1892, *passim.*

[40] Picot, *Recueil général,* I, 195-231, "Sottie nouvelle de l'astrologue"; II, 199-244, "Sottie nouvelle des croniqueurs." Cf. also Petit de Julleville, *Répertoire,* p. 357.

[41] *Ibid.,* II, 323-46, "Sottie du monde" (Geneva); III, 99-120, "La Mère de ville" (Rouen); III, 149-168, "De la reformeresse" (Rouen).

[42] *Ibid.,* II, facing p. 126:

Mad fools, harebrained fools, wise fools,
Fools of cities, castles and villages,
Double-dyed fools, silly fools, subtle fools,
Loving fools, captive fools, wild fools,
Old fools, young fools, fools of all ages,
Reasonable fools, perverse fools, skittish fools,
Your Prince with no interruption will play his play in the market on Shrove Tuesday.

[43] *Ibid.,* II, 144:

Greetings! God save you, he-fools and she-fools! Benedicite, what a crowd of them I see!

[44] *Ibid.,* II, 149:

What have I to do with war, and what does it matter to me whether a wise man or a fool sits in Saint Peter's chair? What is it me if the Church is in error, as long as there is peace on this earth. No good ever came of outrage. I am safe in my village. I breakfast and dine when I please.

[45] *Ibid.,* II, 192:

You tell me Dame Folly is dead? Good Lord, what a lie! I never saw her so well and so powerful as she is at present.

CHAPTER VII

[1] For a complete discussion of the interrelations of the German, Latin, French and English versions of the *Ship,* containing proof of Barclay's dependence upon the Latin and French translations, cf. Fr. A. Pompen, *The English Translations of the Ship of Fools,* London, 1928.

[2] Aquinas, *Summa Theologia,* ed. cit., Vol. III, Secunda secundae, Quaes. XLV.

[3] Sebastian Brant, *Das Narrenschiff,* F. Zarncke editor, Leipzig, 1854, pp. 183-84:

Many things which lie open under the sun have I seen and seen again, and I have found nothing stable in the world. All things I have recognized as vain, foolish, perishable, doomed soon to slip like waters into the earth. Nothing is firm, solid, durable. This brief hour snatches away whatever you may for a short time possess, whether it be many herds, much gold, broad acres, a wife, children—whatever man's foolish will desires. . . . I flee you (oh world), I leave you, and abandon you completely. And may the gods, and God himself help me, that I may rather prefer to worship you alone, Holy Father, and to follow you, gracious Christ.

[4] *Ibid.,* pp. 153-54.

[5] *Ibid.,* p. 121:

We see that the fools have all pulled at the oars without order and regularity, that they have taken no reefs in their sails, and that as a result they have been cast upon Scylla and the Syrtes, dragged down into the whirlpool of Charybdis, and all suffered shipwreck. From these, following the history of fools back to their beginning, I find that they all have perished in this way, because they disobeyed the law, forgot the proportion, abandoned the road which God and the fitting order of things ordained. All things which live in the heavens, on earth or in the water are obedient to their own order and law, and survive and flourish through it. If they desert it, if they cease to move according to law, they immediately rush down to destruction and perish. If the elements were sustained by a feeble law, they would dissolve and perish. Time itself, each hour, has its own certain order; there is a rule for birth, and a most definite rule for life; there is a time and a fitting rule for death. The power of this order is this: that all things may be governed by a certain law and measure, according to the edict of God, that the lesser should respect and obey the greater, and should willingly endure the commands he himself desires to know.

[6] *Ibid.,* pp. 131-53.

[7] F. Zarncke, "Zur Vorgeschichte des Narrenschiffes," *Serapeum*, XXIX (1868), 49-54.

[8] *Narrenschiff*, Zarncke ed., p. 118:

Look into this mirror observantly, whosoever desires to understand the life of man and his grievous end. For whoever sees the reflection of himself and his life in this book will not easily proclaim himself good. And if anyone, thinking himself wise, should imagine that he is not of our company, he may know that he is with us at every turn.

[9] *Stultifera Navis*. . . . The Ship of Fooles, wherein is shewed the folly of all States with divers other workes adioyned unto the same, very profitable and fruitfull for all men. Translated out of Latin into Englishe by Alexander Barclay. London. Printed by John Cawood, 1570. F-118-recto.

[10] *Ibid.*, F-26-verso, F-27-recto and verso.

[11] Lintilhac, *Le Théâtre sérieux en France au moyen âge*, Paris, 1904, quoted from Honorius d'Autun, p. 43, note.

[12] Zarncke, *Zur Vorgeschichte des Narrenschiffes*, pp. 49-50.

[13] *Ibid.*, pp. 53-54.

[14] Charles Estienne, *L'Art de faire les devises*, Paris, 1645, p. 21:

An Emblem is properly a gentle and moral Symbol, which consists in the picture and the words through which an author presents some sober reflection. . . . The principal purpose of the Emblem is to instruct, by appealing to our eyes with its images and by striking our minds with their meaning. Therefore they must be a little obscure, subtle, merry, and laden with meaning. And if the pictures are a little bit obvious or commonplace, the sense they convey must be well hidden; if they themselves are a little obscure, they must correspond more directly to the sense intended.

[15] Sebastian Brant, *Das Narrenschiff*. Faksimile der erstangabe von 1494 mit einem Anhang enthaltend die Holzschnitte der folgenden Originalausgaben und solche der Locherschen Ubersetzung und einem Nachwort von Franz Schulz. Strassburg, 1913, p. 34.

[16] *Ibid.*, p. 54.

[17] *Ibid.*, p. 46.

[18] Henry Green (editor), *Whitney's "Choice of Emblemes,"* a facsimile reprint of the edition printed in the house of Christopher Plantin, Leyden, 1586. London, 1866, pp. xiv-xv.

[19] Ludwig Volkman, *Bilderschriften der renaissance*, Leipzig, 1923, p. 46.

[20] Zarncke ed. *Narrenschiff*, pp. lxi-lxvii.

[21] *Ibid.*, pp. lxvii-lxxii.

[22] Rudwin, *op. cit.*, p. 3, p. 6, p. 10.

[23] *Ibid.*, p. 12.

[24] *Narrenschiff*, facsimile edition, facing title page.

[25] Zarncke ed. *Narrenschiff*, pp. lvi-lvii, quoted:

Sitting in your little boat, you go down the river of voluptuous indulgence to the bitter dead sea. . . . In the waters of pleasure we row the great boat of sinners.

Idle fools, who imagine no other end and no other bliss for themselves, they let themselves be satisfied with these earthly things. They are the ones who know no place and no port whither they will steer on this great sea of the world.

[26] Pompen, *op. cit.*, p. 309.

[27] Alexander Barclay, *The Ship of Fools*, T. H. Jamieson, editor, 2 vols., Edinburgh, 1874, I, 17.

[28] *Ibid.*, I, 17-18.

[29] *Ibid.*, I, 122.

[30] *Ibid.*, I, 85-87.

[31] *Ibid.*, I, 148 ff.

[32] *Ibid.*, I, 137 ff.

[33] *Ibid.*, I, 215, 265.

[34] *Ibid.*, I, 191.

[35] *Ibid.*, I, 268.

[36] *Ibid.*, II, 116.

[37] *Ibid.*, II, 174 ff.

[38] *Ibid.*, I, 225 ff.

[39] *Ibid.*, II, 235 ff.

[40] *Ibid.*, I, 156.

[41] *Ibid.*, I, 159.

[42] *Ibid.*, II, 57.

[43] *Ibid.*, II, 153.

[44] *Ibid.*, I, 271.

[45] *Ibid.*, II, 224.

[46] *Ibid.*, II, 188 ff. and 202.

[47] Aquinas, *Summa theologia*, ed. cit., Vol. II, Prima secundae, Quaes. LXXXIV, art. 1.

[48] Barclay, *Ship of Fools*, Jamieson ed., I, 92; I, 181; I, 252; II, 276, etc.

[49] *Ibid.*, II, 98.

[50] *Ibid.*, II, 313 ff.

[51] *Ibid.*, I, 45; I, 234; II, 147.

[52] *Ibid.*, I, 75; I, 88; II, 43.

[53] *Ibid.*, I, 129; I, 244, etc.

[54] *Ibid.*, I, 19; I, 142.

[55] *Ibid.*, I, 176-78 passim.

[56] *Ibid.*, I, 24; I, 192; II, 48; II, 80.

[57] *Ibid.*, II, 69; II, 53; II, 259.

[58] *Ibid.*, I, 43.

[59] *Ibid.*, I, 104-5.

[60] *Ibid.*, I, 36.

[61] *Ibid.*, II, 26.

Chapter VIII

[1] *The Praise of Folie. Moriae encomium a booke made in Latin by that great clerke Erasmus Roterodame. Englished by Sir Thomas Chaloner Knight.* Anno. M.D. XLIX. Reproduction of the 1549 edition, Janet E. Ashbee editor, Essex House Press, 1901, p. iv.

[2] Cf. A. Renaudet, *Préréforme et humanisme,* Paris, 1916, for an extended study of conditions in France from 1450 to 1500, and the same author's "Erasme; sa vie et son oeuvre jusqu'en 1517 d'après sa correspondance," *Revue historique,* CXI, and CXII, 1912 and 1913, CXI, 225-62, and CXII, 241-74, especially CXI, 238-46.

[3] A. Pompen, *op. cit.,* p. 7.

[4] For studies of the "sermon joyeux" cf. Emile Picot, "Les Monologues dramatiques," *Romania,* XV, XVI, XVII, 1886-1888.

[5] Renaudet, *Préréforme et humanisme,* p. 7 ff.

[6] Pierre de Nolhac, *Erasme en Italie,* Paris, 1888, p. 7.

[7] *Ibid.,* pp. 13-14.

[8] Arthur Richter, *Erasmus-Studien,* Dresden, 1891, appendix B, p. xxi.

[9] The contrast of Erasmus' attitude toward rhetoric with Brant's is interesting. Brant's delight in the rediscovery of classical literature centers round his pride that a German invention, the printing press, has made it accessible to the people. Cf. Zarncke ed. *Narrenschiff,* p. 192, Brant's poem to Van Olpe on the arrival of the Muses in the Rhineland.

[10] *The Praise of Folie,* Reproduction 1549 ed., p. 1.

[11] Zarncke ed. *Narrenschiff,* p. lxxvii, quoted from the introduction to the *Adages:*

And indeed who does not know that the most notable charm and richness of a declamation lies in metaphors, parables, paradigms, examples, similitudes, pictures and that kind of thing. For they both give elegance to the speech, and also make a great and delightful improvement when, once received by the public, they pass into common parlance. For most people are glad to hear what they recognize, more especially when some sanction of antiquity is added to it.

[12] *Moriae encomion* (in Greek letters), *sive Stultitiae laus Des. Erasmi Rot. Declamatio*. Basilae, M.DCC.LXXX, reproduces Holbein's designs.

[13] *The Praise of Folie*. Reproduction 1549 ed., p. ii.

[14] *Ibid.*, p. iii.

[15] *Ibid.*, p. iv.

[16] *Ibid.*, p. iv.

[17] *Ibid.*, p. 37.

[18] *Ibid.*, p. 33.

[19] *Ibid.*, p. 34.

[20] *Ibid.*, p. 47.

[21] *Ibid.*, p. 35.

[22] *Ibid.*, p. 35.

[23] *Ibid.*, p. 36.

[24] *Ibid.*, pp. 62-64.

[25] *Ibid.*, p. 62.

[26] *Ibid.*, p. 47.

[27] *Ibid.*, pp. 47-48.

[28] *Ibid.*, p. 3.

[29] *Ibid.*, pp. 50-51.

[30] *Ibid.*, pp. 53-54.

[31] *Ibid.*, pp. 56-60.

[32] *Ibid.*, p. 43.

[33] *Ibid.*, pp. 29-30.

[34] *Ibid.*, p. 17.

[35] *Ibid.*, p. 9.

[36] *Ibid.*, p. 21.

[37] *Ibid.*, pp. 11-12.

[38] *Ibid.*, pp. 39-40.

[39] *Ibid.*, p. 26.

[40] *Ibid.*, p. 39.

[41] *Ibid.*, p. 15.

[42] *Ibid.*, p. 45.

[43] *Ibid.*, p. 32.

[44] *Ibid.*, p. 5.

[45] *Ibid.*, p. 70.

[46] *Ibid.*, p. 79.

[47] *Ibid.*, p. 81.

[48] *Ibid.*, pp. 83-84.
[49] *Ibid.*, p. 86.
[50] *Ibid.*, p. 87.

CHAPTER IX

[1] Cf. above, ch. V, note 20.

[2] Standard editions of these plays published by the E.E.T.S.

[3] Chambers, *op. cit.*, II, 219.

[4] Louis B. Wright, *Vaudeville Elements in the English Drama from the origins until the close of the theatres in 1642,* unpublished thesis, University of North Carolina, 1924, p. 29.

[5] Furnivall and Pollard (editors), *The Macro Plays,* p. 33.

[6] A. Grosart (editor), *The Complete Works in verse and prose of Edmund Spenser,* 9 vols., London, 1882-1884, quoted, I, 11.

[7] Barclay, *Ship of Fools,* Jamieson ed., I, 7.

[8] Furnivall and Pollard, *The Macro Plays,* p. 96:

And I, Folly, shall hastily raise him up (in worldly affairs) until some enemy (a deadly sin?) conquers him. I shall eventually kill the soul of those who trust in the wit of the world.

[9] *Ibid.*, p. 94:

I shall blind him with the charms of a big income until he is completely fixed upon the world; then, long before his time, I shall in the middle of his worldly absorption, make the slave firmly bound (to sin).

Come on, man, you shall not be sorry. Be true to us, and you shall wear new clothes and be rich forevermore.

[10] *Ibid.*, p. 108.

[11] *Ibid.*, pp. 112-14.

[12] *Ibid.*, p. 92.

[13] Furnivall, editor, *The Digby Plays,* p. 47.

[14] W. Carew Hazlitt (editor), *Dodsley's Old English Plays,* 15 vols., London, 1874-76, I, 258.

[15] John Skelton, *Magnyfycence,* R. L. Ramsey, editor, E.E.T.S. pub., extra series, XCVIII (London, 1906), 32-33.

[16] *Ibid.*, p. 34.

[17] *Ibid.*, p. 37.

[18] *Ibid.*, p. 38.

[19] *Ibid.*, pp. xcviii-xcix.

[20] Robert W. Bolwell, *The Life and Works of John Heywood,* New York, 1921, p. 84.

[21] John Heywood, *A Dialogue of Wit and Folly,* Percy Society pub., London, 1846, p. 18.

[22] Lester, *op. cit.,* pp. 546-47.

[23] Sir David Lyndsay, *Works,* D. Laing (editor), 3 vols., Edinburgh, 1879, II, 1-222, "Ane Pleasant Satyre of the Thrie Estatis"; Folly's sermon, II, 206-21.

[24] A. Brandl (editor), *The Longer thou livest the more fool thou art,* in *Jahrbuch der Deutschen Shakespeare-Gesellschaft,* XXXVI (Berlin, 1900), 17.

[25] *Ibid.,* p. 19.

[26] *Ibid.,* p. 39.

[27] W. W. Greg (editor), *A new Enterlude of Godly Queene Hester,* London, 1904, pp. 26-28.

[28] A. Brandl, *Quellen des weltlichen dramas in England vor Shakespeare,* Strassburg, 1898, p. 419 ff.

[29] L. W. Cushman, *The Devil and the Vice in the English Dramatic Literature before Shakespeare,* Halle, 1900, p. vii.

[30] *Ibid.,* p. 68.

[31] *Ibid.,* p. 63.

[32] Cf. New English Dictionary, s.v. "Vice."

[33] Chambers, *op. cit.,* II, 203.

[34] Olive M. Busby, *Studies in the Development of the Fool in the Elizabethan Drama,* Oxford and London, 1923, p. 27.

CHAPTER X

[1] E. F. Rimbault (editor), *Cock Lorell's Bote,* Percy Society pub., London, 1843. Cf. also A. Rey, *Skelton's Satirical Poems in their relation to Lydgate's Order of Fools etc.,* Bern, 1899, p. 32.

[2] W. Carew Hazlitt (editor), *Remains of Early Popular Poetry,* IV, 17-72, "The Hyeway to the Spittal House." Cf. C. Nisard, *La Littérature de colportage,* 2 vols., Paris, 1854, I, 484 ff. for a French version of the *Spittal House.*

[3] E. Viles and F. J. Furnivall (editors), *Awdeley's Fraternity of Vacabondes,* E.E.T.S. pub., extra series, Vol. IX, London, 1869.

[4] "The xxv. orders of Fooles," in *Black-Letter Ballads and Broadsides,* pp. 88-93.

[5] J. O. Halliwell-Phillips (editor), *Tarlton's Jests and News out of Purgatory,* Shakespeare Society pub., London, 1844, p. xxvii.

[6] *Ibid.,* p. 20 ff.

[7] H. Hutton, *Follies Anatomie, or Satyres and Satyricall Epigrams,* Percy Society pub., London, 1842. E. F. Rimbault (editor).

[8] *The Proverbs and Epigrams of John Heywood (1562),* Spenser Society reprint, London, 1867, pp. 89, 90, etc.

[9] "Greene's Farewell to Folly," in A. Grosart (editor), *The Works of Robert Greene,* 15 vols., London, 1881-1886, IX; and "The Debate between Folly and Love," *ibid.,* IV.

[10] Nicholas Breton, *A Floorish upon Fancie,* in *Heliconia,* T. Park (editor), 3 vols., London, 1815, I, part 2, pp. 5-7, *passim.*

[11] T. Garzoni, *A Hospital of Incurable Fools,* London, 1600.

[12] *Jack of Dover, his quest of inquirie, or his privie search for the veriest foole in England,* Percy Society pub., London, 1842.

[13] R. Armin, *A Nest of Ninnies,* J. P. Collier (editor), Shakespeare Society pub., London, 1842.

[14] R. Wilson, *The Cobbler's Prophecy,* Malone Society reprint, London, 1914.

[15] Charles Bourdigné, *La Légende de Pierre Faifeu,* ed. D. Jouast, Bibliophile Jacob, Paris, 1880, p. 3 :

Let them all be now—wanton Caillette, the four sons of Aymon all dressed in blue, Gargantua with his plaster hair—and see the deeds of master Pierre Faifeu.

[16] A. Montaiglon (editor), *Recueil de poésies françaises,* I, 12 ff :

Proud fools and hornèd fools, big, little and middle-sized fools, village fools and town fools, fat fools, thin fools, made-over fools, half-fools and perfect, whole fools.

[17] *Ibid.,* I, 161. Cf. also *ibid.,* I, 309 :

For my wish, which maddens me night and day, I desire most marvelous things: first, a fine bauble, and a hood garnished with long ears, and bells that make a marvelous noise, (to be able to say) fie upon care, sorrow and mourning, to dance joyfully under thickets and arbors, a good appetite to empty pots and bottles, and at the end a shroud for all my treasure.

[18] *Ibid.,* III, 14 :

Long live the fools, whose desire is noble, and who exercise their skill in virtue—for as you know, foolishness in virtue is nobility. He whose soul is wounded with sin is not worthy to be called a fool-innocent, but rather a fool-sinful, because his heart persists in evil. So remember well that true Folly lies in virtue.

[19] Cf. A. Hamon, *Jean Bouchet: Un Grand Rhétoriqueur poitevin,* Paris, 1880, pp. 24-30.

[20] A. Montaiglon (editor), *Le triumphe de haulte folie,* Paris, 1880, p. III.

[21] *La Morosophie de Guillaume de la Perriere Tolosain,* Lyon, 1553, p. a-5 recto and verso:

one has often known many a wise word to come from a mouth reputed foolish; for that kind of madness which uneducated and stupid people call folly, really may mean prophetic inspiration.

[22] *Ibid.,* a-7 (but no pagination here):

I can answer that this contradiction in my title may as well be allowed to me as a similar one was to the learned Cardinal, Nicholas of Cusa, who gave one of his books the title of "learned ignorance."

[23] *Ibid.,* d-8 recto, g-1 recto, k-1 recto.

[24] R. M. Wenley, *Stoicism and its Influence,* Boston, Mass., 1924, p. 65.

[25] A. Lefranc (editor), *Oeuvres de François Rabelais,* Vols. I, II, III, Paris, 1912, 1913, 1922, III, iv. Cf. A. Tilley, *Studies in the French Renaissance,* Cambridge (England), 1922, the essay "Follow Nature," pp. 233-58 for a discussion of the attitudes of both Stoics and Epicureans and their sixteenth-century followers toward "nature."

[26] C. Lenient, *La Satire en France ou la littérature militante au XVIᵉ siècle,* Paris, 1886, p. 171:

(Reformation satire) is inspired by anger and hatred of those things which it calls lies and superstition; it is passionate, pitiless; and passion makes it often eloquent, seldom witty.

[27] *Ibid.,* p. 60:

For, according to the spirit of this age, each of us fastens a smile upon his face, and hides his tears in his heart.

[28] A. Floquet, *Histoire des Conards à Rouen,* Bibliothèque de l'école des Chartes, Paris, 1840, p. 118.

[29] Doran, *op. cit.,* p. 78.

[30] *Oeuvres françoises de Bonaventure Des Periers,* 2 vols., Paris, 1856, II, 8: Live well and enjoy yourself.

[31] *Ibid.,* II, 5:

Oh pensive men, I will not give you these tales of mine to read unless you can control the proud expression of your crabbèd foreheads: what is here is only a source of laughter.

Put away your sorrow and your anger and your too-premeditated talk. Some other time you may go on being learned. I have been at great trouble to write these things.

I have forgotten my sorrowful passions, I have stopped in the middle of my other occupations. Come, come, let us give a little time to folly—

that it come not upon us when we do not want it!—and even in a
melancholy day let us find time for an hour of pleasure.

[32] Cf. *Blasons,* Paris, 1809; H. J. Molinier, *Mellin de Saint-Gelays,*
Rodez, 1910; P. Ronsard, *Livret de Folastries,* Paris, 1920.

[33] A. Lefranc (editor), *Les dernières poésies de Marguerite de Navarre,*
Paris, 1896, pp. 97-118 *passim:*

> Love, at no season,
> Is the friend of reason.

Alas! such joy has come to me from having given up all honor and
all sense for him, that my heart has thrown itself into his arms, into his
power, to live and think in him day and night.

The love of God makes man wise, prudent, clean of conscience, studying wisdom diligently, day and night and morning and evening.

So, do your best, Love, and kill me all at once; then, when you
have completely overcome me, you will make me live. For you I would
gladly be mad, drunk, without ever recovering. But, Love, if you mean
to treat me so—to burn me without interruption—your consuming fire
will give me a life of pure love, lifting me up to strike me down again
with bliss, and your light which will shine wholly within me, will light
my life as you yourself do. This you have done, and I thank you.—This
is the condition of the true shepherdess, who follows the banner of
Love and takes no heed of anything else.

CHAPTER XI

[1] Nicholas Breton, *The Good and Bad,* in *Archaica,* 2 vols., Sir E.
Brydges (editor), London, 1815, I, 23-24.

[2] Coelius Secundus Curio, *Pasquine in a traunce,* London, 1566 (?),
F-74 verso, F-75 recto.

[3] J. A. K. Thomson, "Desiderius Erasmus," in *The Social and Political
Ideas of some Great Thinkers of the Renaissance and Reformation,* E. J.
Hearnshaw (editor), London, 1925, p. 152.

[4] *Ibid.,* p. 156.

INDEX

COLUMBIA UNIVERSITY PRESS
Columbia University
New York

——

foreign agent
OXFORD UNIVERSITY PRESS
Humphrey Milford
Amen House, London, E. C.

DATE DUE

ILL 11/17/94		
MAR 14 1998		
NOV 06 2009		